PRESTEL
Munich · London · New York

Feel and Think: A New Era of Tokyo Fashion

texts and curation: Yoko Takagi, Hiroshi Narumi, Mariko Nishitani, Motoaki Hori

Preface

The world of fashion has undergone a drastic change since the beginning of the 21st century. High fashion has moved from the catwalks of Paris, New York, and Milan, and has lost its once unequivocal, centripetal force. Instead, global street styles and fast fashion have begun to exercise considerable influence on our relationship with clothes. Equally, heightened awareness of environmental issues and sustainable ways of living are greatly affecting our wardrobe choices. In this rapidly changing context, we think it is time to reconsider the meaning of fashion.

We believe that clothes have the power to change the wearer's life. Japan has a rich history of fashion with a high level of creativity. However, in recent years, business and marketing logics have seemed to take precedence over the importance of creativity. Fast fashion is widely accepted by consumers. And yet, we consider that creativity in fashion design cannot be based on practicality and affordability. Rather, the creativity lies within the possibility of initiating a dialogue between the designer and the wearer and an emotional experience that fashion can deliver.

This exhibition is unprecedented in the way that the ten participating groups of designers, all based in Tokyo, attempt to answer the essential question: what is fashion? These designers stand apart from the conventional framework of the fashion industry, and they have developed their unique creativity by thinking, making, and selling their creations independently. While their careers and philosophies vary from one another, these Tokyo designers share a keen awareness of the contemporary issues of society, and they explore their own reality for the new era. We hope that this exhibition will give spectators an opportunity to experience fashion while rediscovering its diversity and its new charm.

Finally, we would like to give our sincerest thanks to all the participating designers and the individuals involved in realizing this exhibition.

Feel and Think: A New Era of Tokyo Fashion
The Organizers

Contents

Works by and Interviews with the Designers of 10 Brands

Thirty years of Japanese Fashion

Hiroshi Narumi

Creativity in fashion can be found in many aspects: the construction of garments, the manner of its presentation and in styling choices made by consumers. The ways creativity manifests itself changes greatly depending on generations and various social contexts. This essay will review the history of contemporary Japanese fashion over the last thirty years and chronicle its transformation.

Originality and the Fashion brands of the 1980s

The 1980s were a great turning point for Japanese fashion design. This era witnessed the "DC brand boom", in which many independent designers and domestic fashion brands flourished, and consumer demand for their products soared.[1] This "DC brand boom" was instigated by independent designers who were commonly called 'mansion makers.' This moniker was based on the fact that these designers often had their offices in a rented room in apartment buildings (referred to as "mansions" in Japanese) in Tokyo neighborhoods such as Harajuku, Aoyama, Omotesando or Roppongi. Ready-made clothes became widely available to Japanese consumers in the late 1960s and the 1970s, and these young independent designers found potential for a successful business in the bourgeoning fashion industry. This new generation of designers established their own fashion labels with a new perspective, in the midst of the growing Japanese economy and an emerging youth culture.

Expression of originality was the paramount goal for these young designers. In contrast, the previous generation of designers around the time of the end of World War II had a completely different perception of their work. For them, clothing was considered a foreign import, and rather than 'designers', they considered themselves 'dressmakers'. Their objective was to learn about this new cultural import and to distribute it all over Japan. The new generation of designers was not interested in primarily absorbing and following the Western cultural model, but in finding their own individuality. For them, fashion became a manifestation of their unique lifestyles. This shift in attitude toward fashion became the driving force that fueled the "DC design boom", and with the booming economy of the 1980s, the Japanese public welcomed the explosion of creativity in the fashion industry.

Japanese society historically has a conformist tendency. People had no wish to dress differently from one another and stand out from the crowd. However, the post-war Japan raised a new consciousness to nurture an individual's uniqueness, and people were hungry for clothing that was different and trendy.

In the hyper-consumer society of 1980s Japan, shopping was considered the most important means of self-realization. People could no longer associate themselves with the 'grand narrative' of life, like a remarkable success story or a tumultuous political revolution. Instead, people sought fulfillment in their lives through the 'small narrative', such as romance and entertainment. Jean-François Lyotard presented this shift in social narratives in his seminal essay, "The Postmodern Condition: A Report on Knowledge" (1979). The consumer-driven society of 1980s Japan was equivalent to the postmodern society described in Lyotard's essay, and his philosophy was widely disseminated and accepted by the Japanese. For a young Japanese person, his/her raison d'être depended on distinguishing him/herself from others by putting on a piece of clothing, a symbol of his/her uniqueness.[2] The "DC brand boom" offered consumers a wide choice of colors and designs, and it could not have arrived at a better time and place. (At this time, I will not go into an argument as to whether wearing a designer's label is equivalent to expressing one's unique sense of style.)

The year 1981 saw the inauguration of the Tokyo Collection, formerly known as TD6 during the 1970s.[3] The Tokyo Collection aimed at providing a world-class stage for Japanese designers by following the examples of the Paris Collection and the New York Fashion Week. By 1985, the Tokyo Fashion Designers Association had been established and the scale of the Tokyo Collection grew much larger. At one point, over a hundred designers participated, and Tokyo became known as the emerging fashion capital of the world.

Among the many Japanese designers to achieve fame during this era, Issey Miyake, Rei Kawakubo of Comme des Garçons, and Yohji Yamamoto were especially remarkable in their success. They participated in the Paris Collection and won international acclaim for their groundbreaking creations.

Unlike many Japanese designers who eagerly adopted Oriental motifs in their designs for an international audience, Kawakubo and Yamamoto stood behind their own aesthetics and presented their idiosyncratic styles on the runway. Their provocative works challenged the status quo of the Paris Collection and caused much controversy in the world of fashion. Eventually, international journalists came to appreciate Kawakubo and Yamamoto's

Hiroshi Narumi
Hiroshi Narumi, associate professor at Kyoto University of Art and design, received his M.A. in philosophy from the Graduate School of Osaka University. After working as an editor, he received his M.A. in sociology from Goldsmiths College, University of London, and now specializes in sociology and cultural studies. He is the author of *Cultural history of 20th-century fashion* (Kawade Shobo Shinsha, 2007), the editor of *The Cosplays Society – Subculture and the Body Culture* (Serica Shobo, 2009), *Mode and Body—the Present and the History of Fashion Culture* (Kadokawa Shoten, 2003), and the coauthor of *JAPAN FASHION NOW* (Yale University Press, 2010).

exceptional level of creativity and saw their works as equal, if not superior, to their European counterparts.

Japanese fashion design was about to reach a new level of international recognition, taking a step closer to the level of European and American role models.

Styles and Streets: The 1990s

During the 1990s, Japan experienced a series of devastating events. The economic bubble burst, and the Great Hanshin-Awaji earthquake and the Sarin gas attacks in the Tokyo subway followed. In the rest of the world, the Berlin Wall fell in 1989 and the collapse of the Soviet Union ended the Cold War, yet new regional conflicts and the Gulf War broke out, destabilizing the state of world politics. As a result, the festive and glamorous mood of the 'DC brands' no longer seemed appropriate for this new era. The charismatic 'DC brand boom' quickly faded into the past.

A new type of retailer took a leading role in the Japanese fashion of 1990s. These retailers were called "select shops", and clothing stores such as BEAMS and United Arrows specialized in a distinctive selection of apparel items and unique styling suggestions for their customers. These new retailers emphasized the basics that customers could wear every day, and they developed original in-store brands to be sold at their shops. Rather than the fantastical, designer-centric fashion of the 1980s, young people in Japan were seeking a new, more reality-based fashion. These "select shops" satisfied consumers' needs for stylish, yet more understated clothes, and soon new "select shops" opened all over Japan, exerting considerable influence over the fashion trend of this era.

On the other hand, a new generation of fashion designers adjusted to these developments by paying closer attention to the current trends, rather than focusing on their own idiosyncrasies. Designers such as Tsumori Chisato, Akira Onozuka, Atsuro Tayama, and Yoichi Nagasawa were among the "post DC brand boom" designers who built their business based on a consumer-oriented vision. Yoichi Nagasawa launched a secondary label called "no concept but good sense", introducing his designs to young people who already had their own lifestyles and choice wardrobes. It became imperative for this new generation of designers to find a balance between exerting creativity and being conscious of the fashion trends on the street.

In the 1990s fashion trends were transmitted from the street, rather than from the fashion designers and mass media. One of the most remarkable trends of this time was called *Kogyaru* (Little Girls in Japanese), which was started by high school girls. *Kogyaru* gave birth to a series of new fads, including bleached and dyed hair (*Chapatsu*), loose socks resembling leg warmers (*Ruuzu Sokkusu*), pagers (*Pokeberu*), cell phones (*Keitai*), and teenage escort services (*Enjo Kosai*). These high school girls invented an eclectic style, mixing high and low fashion. They would wear items from the Shibuya 109 shopping mall, cheap cosmetics from Matsukiyo (Matsumoto Kiyoshi) drugstores, and carry expensive Chanel handbags.[4]

The *Kogyaru* trend soon evolved into more extreme subcultures such as tanning and darkening of the skin tone (*Gan-Guro*), bleached hair and make-up resembling a monster (*Yamanba*), and private social clubs for girls (*Gyaru Saa*).

In addition to this female-oriented style, another powerful trend was transmitted from the streets of Harajuku and Omotesando in Tokyo. Inspired by the cultures of American hip hop, punk rock, skateboarders and graffiti artists, many independent newly-launched fashion labels became known as *Urahara* brands. Charismatic designers such as Hiroshi Fujiwara, Jun Takahashi, and NIGO not only established their fashion labels but also produced music as part of a band or as a DJ. These designers distanced themselves from the mainstream trends and focused on basic, casual aesthetics. They collaborated with sporting goods manufacturers and issued limited edition items that became collectible and highly sought after.[5]

However, Japanese fashion in the 1990s cannot be summed up without mentioning the soaring success of the Big Three: Issey Miyake, Rei Kawakubo of Comme des Garçons, and Yohji Yamamoto. Issey Miyake started his iconic series "Pleats Please" and "A-POC" during this time. Rei Kawakubo's provocative "bump dress" from her 1997 collection, "Body Meets Dress: Dress meets Body", shattered the status quo of the Paris Collection and generated a huge controversy in the world of high fashion. On the other hand, Yohji Yamamoto pushed his unique aesthetics to the highest level of sophistication. Yamamoto's collections from autumn 1994 (spring/summer 1995) and spring 1995 (autumn/winter 1996-97) won overwhelming applause from the audience at the Paris Sorbonne University. All of these designers exerted a huge influence over the following generation of designers by mentoring them and employing them at their companies. Many young designers developed their professional skills working under the Big Three and eventually established their own fashion labels.

The decline of the Tokyo collection became apparent when the Big Three stopped participating in this lackluster event and shifted their focus to the Paris Collection. It was a dark time for many domestic fashion designers.[6]

To make matters worse for these domestic designers, they had to face new competition from powerful international luxury brands such as Chanel, Prada and Gucci. Although a few independent designers were able to garner international success with their innovative, artistic creations[7], many domestic designers lost business in this competitive market and terminated their activities.

Reality and Subculture The 2000s

With the arrival of the new decade, the Japanese economy showed no sign of recovery: unemployment figures worsened and people felt a sense of malaise. The dominance of the United States of America came under threat with the 9/11 terrorist attacks, the war against Iraq and the economic collapse following the downfall of Lehman Brothers. The world became an uncharted global territory, marked by the powerful, bourgeoning economies of China, India and Russia.

The world of fashion also witnessed a new wave of globalization. Many international luxury brands, some under the ownership of the LVMH group, opened their flagship stores in major cities in Japan. Some of these flagship stores boasted eye-catching, unique architecture, built by well-known architects.[8] These luxury brands shifted their market from Europe to Asia while making their aesthetics more appealing to contemporary consumers. Acknowledging their huge Japanese clientele, Louis Vuitton collaborated with the Japanese artist Takashi Murakami and produced a covetable, original line of handbags.

At the same time, inexpensive "fast fashion" became widely available to Japanese consumers. Uniqlo's success was especially remarkable due to their innovation in pragmatic, high-tech materials such as heat-tech and synthetic fleece. Furthermore, international "fast fashion" brands, including H&M and Zara, opened new stores in Japan. Consumers were thrilled to find reasonably priced and trendy clothes they could incorporate into their wardrobes easily. This affordable clothing was termed "real clothes."[9]

The "fast fashion" business model reflected the age of globalization. In order to cut the risk as well as the cost of production, these fashion labels outsourced their product planning, raw material production and manufacturing process to cheap labor abroad. On the other hand, many apparel companies in Japan and local manufacturers and growers of raw materials went bankrupt and had to shut down their businesses.

The street remained the thriving scene for generating new and diverse subcultures. On the streets of Harajuku, young people were seen in Lolita, Goth, and Goth-Loli styles. Another influential trend was *Cosplay*, formerly confined to the neighborhood of Akihabara and comic book conventions. People dressed in outlandish *Cosplay* costumes to emulate their favorite characters from Japanese anime. Their styles soon became part of mainstream Japanese fashion. The high school "Gal" trend died down in the late 1990s and a new style called *Ah-ghe Jo* emerged, inspired by the ultra-feminine employees of hostess clubs.

The international media took notice of these Tokyo subcultures, which were deeply intertwined with anime (animation) and manga (comics), and coined the term 'Cool Japan'. In the eyes of European and American audiences, Japanese fashion became more about Japanese street fashion and subcultures, and less about avant-garde designers.

Under this socio-economic climate, the creativity of many Japanese designers came under severe scrutiny. The Tokyo Collection had lost the momentum of its heyday in the 1980s. In 2006, the Japanese Department of Commerce became the primary financial sponsor for the event, which was reorganized to become JFW (Japan Fashion Week, departing from Tokyo). It declared its goals for making Japanese designers known to the rest of Asia, Europe and America, as well as nurturing young Japanese talents. However, the results have been lackluster.[10] In contrast to the declining influence of JFW, a new fashion event for "Gal" fashion rose to prominence: the Tokyo Girls Collection has been widely supported by the Japanese public and even in China.

In the 2000s, young Japanese designers are facing the difficult challenges of operating a sound business while creating original clothing. Cheap, mass-produced clothes have taken over the market. For an independent fashion designer in Japan, opening stores all over the country or showing their works in Paris and Milan have became an unattainable dream. These young fashion designers have adjusted to this new reality and developed business strategies to suit their individual goals. For example, minä perhonen, mintdesigns and matohu are small companies, focusing on creating timeless designs and using their own original fabric and textiles.

On the other hand, other designers have attempted to challenge the conventional meaning of fashion and brought their designs into the realm of fine art. Design labels such as THEATRE PRODUCTS, Somarta, and ANREALAGE are examples of such artistic efforts.

This brief essay has chronicled the changing phases of Japanese fashion trends. It has outlined the evolution of designers' labels and their changing roles in society. Once regarded as the symbolic means of expressing originality, a designer's label has become just one of many stylistic options for consumers. Different generations and lifestyles have called for different stylistic choices. However, the essence of fashion has remained unchanged: fashion is made as a result of communication between creators and wearers. Today's world may not be the easiest place for showing unique and creative designs. Yet, fashion is not just about clothes and designs. It can manifest how individuals confront their own identities and society at large. As long as this remains true, people will never lose their spirit for finding new potential for expression in fashion.

Notes:

1 The origin of "DC design boom": D stands for 'designer's brand', and C stands for 'character's brand'. The former category sells the unique creativity of designers, while the latter category is more affordable and accessible to consumers.

2 Since the 1970s the demand for fashion brands had increased among Japanese consumers. Trends such as "New Tra" (New Traditional) and "Hamatora" (Yokohama-based New Traditional) were based on Japanese women's love of conservative designers' labels. In his novel, "Nantonaku Crystal" (1980), the writer Yasuo Tanaka illustrated a typical youth who indulged in consuming these designers' brands.

3 TD6 was founded in 1974 by the top six Japanese designers of this era: Takeo Kikuchi, Kansai Yamamoto, Mitsuhiro Matsuda, Isao Kaneko, Junko Koshino, and Yukiko Hanai. The major objective of TD6 was to hold their fashion shows simultaneously.

4 The shopping mall Shibuya 109 consisted of many retail shops by "Gal" designers' labels such as Alba Rosa and COCOLULU. It became the most important gathering spot for high school girls embodying "Kogyaru" and "Gal" styles. In many shopping districts all over cities in Japan, drugstores and discount shops such as Matsukiyo and Don Quixote multiplied, selling cheap cosmetics to these high school girls.

5 "Urahara" is the abbreviated word for "Ura Harajuku" (the back streets of Harajuku, off the main streets such as Meiji-dori and Omotesando). These stores carried hip and casual clothes for young, fashion-conscious male customers. Because their merchandise was limited-run, they attracted a long line of customers waiting for the stores to open and buying them in frenzy. The sold-out items were occasionally found at internet auctions and on the streets, with a significant markup in prices.

6 There are more than a few well-known designers who have worked under the Big Three. Tsumori Chisato, Akira Onozuka and Kosuke Tsumura (Final Home) were at Issey Miyake. Atsuro Tayama and Hiroshige Maki were at Y's /Yohji Yamamoto, and Junya Watanabe launched a label at Comme des Garçons. In addition, many international designers acknowledge the influences of Japanese fashion in their works. Among them are avant-garde designers from London and many from Antwerp, Belgium.

7 Some of the examples of these artistic designers are: Takao Yamashita of Beauty & Beast, 20471120, and Shinichiro Arakawa who held an impromptu fashion show on the streets of Shimokitazawa. 20471120 was especially interested in integrating fashion, art and popular culture.

8 In Omotesando, the list of luxury boutiques built by famous architects includes Prada (by Herzog & de Meuron), Louis Vuitton (by Jun Aoki) Tod's (by Toyo Ito), ONE Omotesando (by Kengo Kuma), and Dior (by SANAA). The relationship between fashion and architecture has become more and more intimate.

9 "Real Clothes" can be defined in many different ways. But in this essay, the phrase stands for the affordable, easy-to-wear, and trendy clothes that gained popularity in the mid-2000s.

10 In 2010, the Department of Commerce terminated its financial support for the Japan Fashion Week. Mercedes-Benz became its new sponsor starting from the spring/summer 2011 shows. Due to the Tohoku earthquake and tsunami disasters, the majority of the fall/winter 2011 shows were cancelled.

Contemporary Japanese Fashion and Local Traditions

Yoko Takagi

Today we live in an era in which information is shared simultaneously and globally all over the internet. In the world of fashion, globalization has had an effect on product planning, manufacturing, distribution and consumption of goods. At the same time, we are witnessing the gradual fading of distinctive regional aesthetics based on their local histories and heritages. In this exhibition, we have assembled ten Japanese fashion brands that have risen to prominence since the turn of the 21st century. While examining their historical and social contexts, the designers will present their works as distinctive creative forces expressing a future of fashion design. The installations and the accompanying exhibition catalogue present their various approaches towards fashion that are unique and specific to Japan today. This project offers an invaluable opportunity for reexamining contemporary Japanese fashion and its relationship to various local traditions.

Japanese people first started wearing Western-style clothing in the middle of the 19th century. It has been only thirty or forty years since they left their kimono culture behind and adopted Western-style clothing as their regular wardrobe. Japanese people have quickly integrated Western style fashion into their cultural repertoire and made it their own. Around 1980, many Japanese fashion designers started winning international acclaim for their creativity and innovations, and Tokyo became one of the major international capitols of fashion.

In this essay, I will focus on the creativity in fashion designs by Japanese designers who emerged after the post-modern era. I will examine how these designers are connected to their local traditions, while questioning whether their relationships to their local histories can be transformed into 'universal values' in our global society.

In order to find the answer to this question, we will have to understand the following three historical backgrounds that have shaped contemporary Japanese fashion designs. First, I will trace various stages of the transition from kimono to Western-style clothing that took place from the mid-19th century to the year 1980. Then, I will show examples of traditional Japanese fashion that were exported and adopted by European cultures in the late 19th century. Finally, I will show the iconoclastic works by Japanese fashion designers who questioned the pre-existing systems of the fashion industry and describe their influences on the Antwerp School.

Japanese people and Western-style clothing

Before the arrival of Western-style clothing, Japan's sophisticated kimono culture had known a long history. The *kosode* of the *Muromachi* era (1336-1573) formed the prototype of the kimono. When they are laid flat, all kimonos have a fixed form and the same two-dimensional construction for both sexes and all ages. The length and width of the robe are adjusted according to the size of the wearer. In terms of its construction, a kimono is typically made out of a bolt of *tanmono* (fabric especially made for kimono, woven to be approximately 36cm wide and 12m long) and it uses almost all of the fabric, therefore resulting in a minimum waste of the material. In wearing a kimono, a person wraps the robe around his/her body, folding and tucking the excess fabric to follow the contour of his/her body, and finally fastening it by using an *obi* (belt). Kimonos are primarily made out of silk, cotton and linen. Various surface decorations are applied by using the techniques of weaving, dyeing, and embroidering. Historically, these surface decorations have often expressed themes such as dramatic changes in seasons, as well as visual motifs based on classical poems and stories that reflected the wearer's literary connoisseurship. In the late Edo period (1603-1868), decorations on kimono reflected certain aesthetic sensibilities that were popular among common people, such as *iki* (chic) and *shibumi* (cool). People have come up with their own styles of wearing kimonos by layering and matching obis and accessories. The art of wearing a kimono is about following a relaxed set of rules and being playful and inventive in coordinating various elements. In a way, it is similar to the idea of mixing and matching tools and utensils in the tea ceremony or the artful presentation of kaiseki dishes in Japanese cuisine. Extravagant combinations would become trendy once they were recognized as 'iki'. In the past, *ukiyo-e* (woodblock prints) acted as the medium for disseminating the latest trends in kimono patterns, and smartest ways of dressing and tying an obi sash.

Japanese people started wearing Western-style clothing in 1854, when Japan opened its doors to international trade and Western cultural influence. The government of the Meiji era (1868-1912) adopted a national policy to 'Westernize' Japan and required its military personnel, government workers and school students to wear uniforms made in the manner of Western-style clothes. By transitioning from kimonos to Western dress for all of its official uniforms, Japan symbolically notified its citizens of the significant change in Japan's social system: the end

Yoko Takagi
Yoko Takagi, professor at Bunka Fashion Research Institute at Bunka Gakuen University, received her MA in history of fashion from Ochanomizu University and her PhD in archeology and art history from Free University of Brussels. She organized and supervised exhibitions as follows: Katagami - les pochoirs japonais et le japonisme (The Japan Foundation/Maison de la culture du Japon à Paris, 2006-2007), Thiara (Bunkamura etc., 2007), A Night at the Opera - The HRD Awards Collection 2007: Antwerp Diamond Jewellery and Evening Dresses (Bunka Gakuen Costume Museum, 2008), and 6+ Antwerp Fashion (Tokyo Opera City Art Gallery, 2009). She is now preparing for upcoming exhibition KATAGAMI Style - Paper Stencils and Japonisme (Mitsubishi Ichigokan Museum, The National Museum of Modern Art, Kyoto, Mie Prefectural Art Museum, 2012).

of the Tokugawa shogunate era and the beginning of Meiji oligarchy.

There was a slight time difference between men and women for adopting Western-style clothing in Japan. This symbolic shift was marked when the Imperial Court of Japan switched their official attire from Kuge Shozoku, the official imperial court attire that had been worn since the Heian period (794-1185), into Western-style clothing, starting at two different dates: for men, it was in the fifth year of the Meiji era (1872) and for women in the nineteenth year of Meiji era (1886). The Empress of Japan was one of the first women to wear dresses and set an example for other women in Japan.[1] It was the first Prime Minister of Japan, Court Minister Hirofumi Ito, who recommended that the women of the Imperial Court wear Western-style clothing as their official attire. In order to reform various unequal treaties imposed by the West, Japan needed to demonstrate to the West that their civilization had reached the mature "Western standard". By having ceremonies at the Imperial Court in Western-style clothing, Japan attempted to symbolically show Europeans and Americans that Japanese people were no longer 'uncivilized'. The Rokumeikan building in Tokyo, completed in 1883, hosted parties that required its guests to wear Western style clothing, and it perhaps helped prepare people for the upcoming change in Japan's fashion culture. For women in the Imperial Court, the court minister suggested that they should wear suits and dresses tailored in a European manner and made from domestic silk fabrics.

The next moment of Westernization for Japanese fashion arrived after World War I. Unscarred by the war, Tokyo welcomed a period of brisk economic growth and increasing demands for military and civilian goods. Kimono merchants from the Edo period had transformed into department stores that catered to the middle class. They started to carry luxury items imported from Europe and showed consumers the latest European trends at almost the same time as in Europe. On the streets of Tokyo, young men and women who emulated the latest European fashion were called "Mobo" (Modern Boy) and "Moga" (Modern Girl). At this point, many Japanese men started wearing suits to work and in public places, but a majority of them were still wearing kimonos at home.

After World War II, Japanese people started adopting Western dress in every aspect of their lives. For the Japanese people, Western-style clothing became a symbol of American culture to be admired. Housewives started sewing clothes at home while tailors and dressmakers opened their shops on main streets. By the 1960s, Japanese manufacturers of synthetic fibers and apparel-making industries were fully developed, and large volumes of mass-produced, ready-to-wear clothes became widely available to people in Japan. In the next twenty years, even though nobody forced them to do so, Japanese people abandoned their kimono culture completely and switched to Western-style clothing. Today, Japanese people no longer experience kimonos in the same manner their ancestors did. Before World War II, kimonos were considered relaxing, and people used to change into kimonos after they returned home from work. Western-style clothing, on the other hand, used to be regarded as form fitting and not as comfortable as kimonos. Today, people only wear kimonos for special occasions in a very formal manner, so they tend to find kimonos constrictive to their bodies and their movements.

Japonisme in Fashion: the Nineteenth Century and the 1980s

While Japanese people started adopting modern Western-style clothing, an opposite cultural phenomenon was taking place in the West. Europeans and Americans were discovering the beauty of traditional costume cultures from the East. Exotic items such as kimono textiles, swords, *netsuke*, *inro* (pillboxes), *kushi* (combs), and *kanzashi* (ornamental hairpins) fascinated European and American consumers. These imported goods influenced artists and designers so much that they became one of the important vehicles for giving birth to the Arts and Crafts movement and Art Nouveau.

Ukiyo-e prints from Japan stimulated the imaginations of artists such as Claude Monet and Vincent van Gogh, while the traditional Japanese bird-and-flower motifs provided a spark of aesthetic inspiration for woven textiles in Lyon, printed textiles in Mulhouse, and wallpaper patterns for Liberty of London. In Paris, Charles Frederick Worth, the haute-couture designer, adopted certain visual characteristics from kimonos in his designs for dresses, such as asymmetrical decorations and patterns on the *eba*, a single continuous pattern on the entirety of a garment. During the turn of the twentieth century, women's clothes in the West went through a major transition. By this time, Europeans and Americans became aware of the sophisticated uses of materials, decorations and constructions in Japanese kimonos. Dressmakers started adopting the flat construction of kimonos into their dressmaking techniques, while taking inspirations from various visual characteristics of the kimono, including oversized sleeves, floor-length hemline, and nuki-emon (slouchy neckline).[2]

The next wave of Japanese influence in Europe was brought by Issey Miyake, Yohji Yamamoto and Rei Kawakubo. They were the pioneering generation of creative Japanese fashion designers who left a significant impact on the aesthetics of international fashion design in the late 1980s. During this post-modern era, designers from Tokyo and Antwerp challenged the status quo of the fashion industry centered in Paris. Rei Kawakubo, Yohji Yamamoto and the energy of the city of Tokyo became instrumental in giving rise to the first generation of Belgian avant-garde designers, the "Antwerp Six" and Martin Margiela.[3]

In the early 1980s, a feminine and elegant style of clothing was still taught as the primary example of high fashion design at the Antwerp Royal Academy of Fine Arts. Around the same time, Rei Kawakubo and Yohji Yamamoto brought their cutting edge designs to Paris and shocked their audience by showing visual elements such as asymmetrical silhouettes, the color black as their dominant palette, oversized forms, and a calculated use of distressed fabrics and unfinished edges. The seven Antwerp-based designers had seen the runway shows by Kawakubo and Yamamoto in Paris and spent time analyzing and studying their garments by going to various boutiques that carried their products. These Belgian designers were also sent by the association of Belgian textile and ready-to-wear fashion to Osaka in 1984 and to Tokyo in 1985 and held fashion shows and exhibitions of their works in these cities. Also, 1985 was the year that the Tokyo Fashion Designers Council was inaugurated. These Belgian designers mentioned how they were struck by not only Japanese fashion, but also by the graphic expressiveness of retail store designs, various marketing tools and customer service manners in the Japanese apparel industry. In 1986, the following year, the "Antwerp Six" held their debut fashion shows in London.

Wearing the Spirit of Kimonos through Western-style Clothing

For the creation of their garments, the pioneering generation of Japanese fashion designers tended to incorporate many elements based on the kimono, such as its garment construction and manners of wearing, as well as the traditional textile and dyeing techniques for producing kimonos. Kenzo Takada was inspired by ordinary kimonos and traditional farmers' clothes of Japan and applied the ideas of their aesthetics and functions into his Parisian ready-to-wear clothes. Similarly, Issey Miyake created the work titled "Ichimai-no-Nuno" (A Piece of Cloth) in 1974, taking inspiration from the fact that a kimono becomes completely flat when folded away. The theme of this particular work by Miyake was 'the loose fit' of a garment and 'the gap' between the fabric and the human body. Kawakubo and Yamamoto also used a lot of sculptural forms created by sagging voluminous materials in their designs.

These designers also incorporated traditional kimono manufacturing methods into their own creations. For example, Comme des Garçons made a dress with an elaborately painted hemline that was done by a traditional silk painter of Yuzen-style kimonos (autumn/winter 1991-1992). Another example was a dress made out of the "katazome" stencil paper that was used for applying decorative patterns on traditional kimonos. To create this dress, a polyester/rayon paper was used instead of the traditional shibugami, which is a paper treated with astringent persimmon juice. (spring/summer 1992). Yohji Yamamoto also employed traditional decorating techniques such as *shibori* (tie-dye) in spring/summer 1995, and *yuzen-zome* (*Yuzen* style printed textiles) in spring/summer 2002. The first generation of Japanese fashion designers used these traditional Japanese 'local' elements in their work as their strategic means of subverting the standards of Western-style clothing. However, these designers were extremely careful about keeping the identities of their fashion brands separate from their personal 'biographical' identities. Even when they used traditional Japanese motifs in their works, they took these traditional motifs out of their original contexts and used them only as formal solutions to bring innovations into their creative fashion designs.

At this time, we will shift our attention to the contemporary Japanese designers featured in this exhibition. How are they connected to their Japanese historical past? These designers belong to the generation of Japanese people who have had little experience wearing kimonos. Hiroyuki Horihata, one of the two designers behind the brand matohu, noted that he felt like a foreigner because of people's curious gaze directed at him when he wore a kimono in the street for the first time. He also discovered that a kimono provided a physical sensation that was completely different from wearing Western-style clothes. These experiences helped him crystallize his brand's theme, "creating new styles of clothing based on common threads found in Japanese aesthetics".

However, matohu's other designer Makiko Sekiguchi is cautious about blatantly declaring the brand's theme to their Japanese audience. She is aware that some Japanese people dislike seeing a Japanese cultural identity in fashion. She notes the irony of the fact that an international audience is more receptive to the Japanese aesthetics in their brand, matohu. For an international audience, the Japanese aesthetic in matohu's work is considered simply as one of many diverse expressions in their design. However, many Japanese people find it difficult to associate Japanese local traditions with innovative designs because of the feeling they have toward the West. This inferiority complex is the legacy of western cultural oppression since the Meiji era.

Many of the designers featured in this exhibition have lived or traveled abroad, and they have had experiences of confronting their Japanese identities. They recognize the significance of the word "origin" in the word "original", and they feel comfortable facing Japanese traditions in their works.

Kawaii (cute) is one of the most important aspects of Japanese aesthetics that are featured in many of the exhibiting designers' works. The aesthetic of *kawaii* has been made familiar to an international audience through exported Japanese character goods and *cosplay* items. There is a surprising connection between *kawaii*, the popular fashion design vocabulary today, and Japanese traditional values that have been cultivated over a long course of history. In the Heian period (794-1185), the word *utsukushii* (beautiful) was used to indicate something cute. In the famous collection of essays from this period, "Makura-no-Soshi", an essay begins with the phrase, roughly translated as "I find beauty in a cartoon of a little child's face, drawn on the surface of a gourd". In this poem, the authoress found 'beauty' in, among other things, a sparrow chick, a young girl's innocent gesture of cocking her head to the side, dolls and toys, an infant wearing oversized clothes, and a chick taking wobbly steps. She created a list of things that are small, vulnerable and helpless, and found 'beauty' and positive values in those that are still in an immature and incomplete state. It was not until much later in Japanese history that the word "utsukushii" was used to indicate something 'perfect and magnificent'.

Among the brands in this exhibition, mintdesigns, THEATRE PRODUCTS, minä perhonen and matohu share a common feature in their designs of women's clothes: a loose silhouette and a relaxed fit. The designers of these brands express femininity by emphasizing the "*kawaii*" sensibility and de-emphasizing female sexuality. In contrast, the traditional European fashion design has aimed at visualizing a mature sense of 'elegance' by emphasizing the curves of a female body, especially the breasts and waist. The Japanese designers mentioned above are starting to win support and popularity among many women abroad for their expression of non-stereotypical femininity in their designs.

Furthermore, h.NAOTO's theatrical "Goth-loli-punk" fashion and SOMARTA's form-fitting yet asexual looks of her dresses and chunky sculptural shoes recall the distinctive silhouettes of anime characters. These anime characters embody perpetual childhood and youth, never growing up or becoming mature.

In addition, keisuke kanda pursues *kawaii* aesthetics in his designs by creating clothes loaded with decorative details that girls find irresistible: ribbons, lace, and polka-dots. Also, the designer behind writtenafterwards presented a collection based on his vision of a 'mature-girlie' fashion in his sixth fashion show. The traditional Japanese view on femininity is about seeking mystery in the immature state of being and not forcing women to come to full maturity. This sensibility is shared and celebrated among many of the participating designers.

It is important to note that these contemporary Japanese fashion designers have been re-examining the current system of the international fashion industry while acknowledging their local heritage and traditions. In the case of minä perhonen, the designer Akira Minagawa aims to create clothes that are timeless and durable, and he has avoided using distinctive design elements that are easily 'dated'. Instead, he invests his creativity into the designs and manufacturing of the original textiles and fabrics that are used for his clothes. The designer has set up an extensive repair service for his customers so that they can wear their clothes year after year and appreciate the beauty of 'patina' on them. Minagawa's use of a simple form in his design, varieties of textiles, as well as his approach to after-purchase care of his clothes, seem to come close to the culture of kimono that used to be a part of everyday life in Japan. Minagawa's work even reminds us of *wabi-sabi*, the traditional Japanese sensibility for appreciating the weathered, worn, and aged appearances of items such as old utensils and ancient architecture. Another fashion brand in this show that shares an affinity with the culture of kimonos is matohu. The designers of matohu have created a clothing item called "Nagagi", a robe with two distinct inner and outer layers. Like a kimono, a "Nagagi" robe has a 'fixed-form', and it is made out of varieties of textiles and can be worn by men and women. Besides issuing new designs for "Nagagi" robes each year, matohu presented ten collections of their work based on the theme of "Keicho-no-Bi" (the beauty of the Keicho era). By announcing the ten future themes of their next five years' worth of work all at once, matohu questioned the conventional semi-annual cycle of the fashion industry.

Akira Minagawa of minä perhonen and Kunihiko Morinaga of ANREALAGE have recognized the unique business structures of Japanese fabric manufacturers. In Japan, weaving, dyeing and surface treatments of fabrics take place in separate factories. Minagawa and Morinaga believe that this manufacturing environment allows Japanese fashion designers to closely collaborate with domestic textile manufacturers and create their customized designs more easily. In Keisuke Kanda's case, his products are primarily sewn by hand and distributed to his customers directly through traveling 'pre-order' sales events.

As we recently experienced the devastating earthquake, tsunami and the accidents at the Fukushima nuclear power plants, we realized that nature cannot be entirely controlled by humans. We also came to know that modern civilization does not necessarily bring happiness to human beings. Perhaps we have reached a point in time when we need to re-evaluate our relationships with indigenous traditions, production processes and techniques that have been cultivated in response to each local environment over a long period.
Fashion is a form of expression that uses three sensory experiences: visual appreciation for forms and colors, an aural sense for listening to rustling fabrics, and finally, a physical sense of fabrics rubbing against one's body. While we need to verbally describe and explain an artwork from different cultures, we do not need words to understand the sensory experiences that clothes give us. Fashion is the perfect medium for cultural exchange on a global level. In this exhibition, we present the examples of fashion designers who have adopted their own local aesthetics. A fashion design, based on a specific local aesthetic, possesses a universal quality that can bring awe and inspiration to the rest of the world, just as Japonisme left a significant impact on European cultures in the 19th century.

Notes:

1 June 23rd: A notice from the Court Minister on women's dress code, Notice number 897 (Meiji 19th year, June 23rd).

2 *Japonisme in Fashion*, The National Museum of Modern Art, Kyoto, 1994.

3 Walter Van Beirendonck said, "The course of fashion was abruptly changed by the two Japanese designers." Dries Van Noten reminisced that he had "encountered a completely different and unconventional approach to fashion through conceptual Japanese fashion design."
Takagi, Yoko. "Antwerp Fashion through Japanese Eyes", "6+ Antwerp Fashion" (exh.cat.)Tokyo Opera City Art Gallery, Antwerp, Ludion, 2009.
Takagi, Yoko. "Why does Antwerp Give Birth to Fashion? Fashion and Education, and Japan" "So-en" 2009, May Issue, pp.26-49.

Independence, Venturing out of the Paris Collections, Comme des Garçons, and the Structural Components of Tokyo Fashion

Mariko Nishitani

Fashion = Trend?

Tokyo's curiosity towards fashion seems to be stronger than any other major city in the industrialized nations. For the teens and people in their twenties in this capital of Japan, fashion is everywhere, as if it is in the air. But what is the fashion that attracts the attention of Tokyo's youth? The answer is not simple.

Up until thirty years ago, the definition of "fashion" was interchangeable with "trend," or "wearing trendy clothes and accessories". When someone was said to be "fashionable", items with the most recent trend adorned this individual. Fashion trends were transmitted out of Paris and Milan collections. The Japanese fashion industry interpreted these European cutting-edge styles to suit the domestic market. In addition, casual American style, called *amekaji*, also shaped the fashion trends in Japan. These trends were the indispensable factors for generating economic activity in the Japanese fashion industry.

In the 1970s, numerous Japanese labels were established. Influential designers like Issey Miyake, Yohji Yamamoto, and Comme des Garçons pioneered their way to Paris and New York with much critical acclaim. In these international contexts, the Japanese public came to realize the value of creativity in fashion. It was not until the 1980s that fashion in Japan became associated with cultural activities, becoming more than just a marketing gimmick for selling clothing and accessories.

The Changes in the Value Systems within the Japanese Fashion Industry

The List of Criteria for Selecting Designers for this Exhibition

- Comme des Garçons's challenge against the preconceived idea of 'beauty'
- Martin Margiela's protest against the pre-existing systems of the fashion industry
- The burst of the Japanese bubble economy in 1993
- The Great Hanshin-Awaji Earthquake of 1995
- The emergence of a unique Japanese street-style fashion with the element of 'cosplay' (wearing costumes and alternative identities)
- The influences of *anime* culture, starting from Neon Genesis Evangelion
- The rise of low-priced fast fashion such as Uniqlo, ZARA, H&M, Topshop, and Forever 21
- Western luxury brands opening new flagship stores in Japan
- The launch of the Tokyo Girls Collection with its direct mobile shopping feature
- The collapse of Lehman Brothers in 2008
- 3/11, the Tohoku earthquake and tsunami disaster in 2011

Since 1990, the series of key events listed above have shifted the fundamental values of fashion in Japan. For Japanese designers, it has become increasingly difficult to design clothing based on naive aspirations such as 'coming up with beautiful, cool design', and 'creating a new trend'. Creative-minded designers have had few resources and support from their government or non-profit organizations. These designers were forced to find resources for their artistic pursuits on their own.

In this exhibition titled "Feel and Think: A New Era of Tokyo Fashion", the curators highlighted many designers who took an independent stance for their creative endeavors.[1]

For selecting the participating brands, we considered that the following important criteria needed to be met:

- The brand should be financially independent. (It should not be a subsidiary of companies like Issey Miyake, Comme des Garçons, World and Onward). Designers should be involved in the entire process, ranging from design, production, management, sales, to public relations.[2]
- The concept of the brand should be clear, and its creation should be original.
- Preferably, the brand operates and directly manages a retail store.[3]
- The brand's activities should show its diverse interest in art, design, music, and other cultural aspects outside of fashion.[4]

The selection was based on the creativity of the work by these brands, rather than their financial success or the size of their organization. Another important point is the last-mentioned one. In Japan, the designers express their curiosity towards various aspects of contemporary culture, and its diverse influences are directly reflected in their design work. We think this is a remarkable and unique characteristic of Japanese fashion that needs to be recognized by the rest of the world.

A brief history of independent brands

Comme des Garçons, now one of the largest fashion companies in Japan, started out as an independent label in 1973. Back in the day, such a small-scale business was called a "mansion maker" rather than a brand. Many independent fashion designers used an apartment (apartment blocks are referred to as "mansions" in Japan) as their office. In the mid-1980s, a phenomenon called "DC brands boom" took place in Japan. After Comme des Garçon's successful foray in Paris, many Japanese designers followed in its footsteps and established their new brands with significant corporate back-up. The economy's bubble burst in the 1990s, after which Japan witnessed the emergence of new designers who were truly independent.

From 1994 to 1998, cities like Tokyo and Osaka gave rise to numerous independent fashion brands. The new designers shared a newly found consciousness against the status quo and the pre-existing framework of the industry. Consumers openly welcomed the unknown potentials of these fashion designers. Japanese youths were seen dressing themselves in idiosyncratic styles on the streets of Tokyo and Osaka. Each of the independent (or 'indies') brands exhibited their collections through various creative means, guerrilla style, or something akin to art installations. The designers were directly involved in every aspect of production, including the music selection. They vied for people's attention with well-laid concepts and elements of surprise. The major fashion brands from this era are 20471120, Beauty Beast, Shinichiro Arakawa, Gomme, Undercover, and Miharayasuhiro. In the 2000s, brands like Number (N)ine, Toga, Dress Camp, and N. Hoolywood carried on the legacy of the earlier group of independent designers. They flourished and introduced the unique atmosphere of Tokyo to Paris. From Paris, the new Japanese fashion became known to the rest of the world via its fans in Europe and Asia (Hong Kong, Taiwan, South Korea.)

In the 1990s many of the participating designers in this exhibition were still students. Naoto Hirooka, designer of h.NAOTO, states that he was very much influenced by Comme des Garçons and Undercover. Kunihiko Morinaga of ANREALAGE was also inspired by the freedom of expression at fashion shows by designers like Comme des Garçons, Maison Martin Margiela, 20471120, Shinichiro Arakawa, and Undercover. The menswear brand SASQUATCHfabrix mentioned that the label's origin lies in the street fashion style of the '90s.

Previous generations of Japanese designers established their own brands after studying fashion in technical colleges, working for established brands and building their professional experience. The new generation of designers chose to take unconventional paths. For them, the framework of Japanese fashion has completely changed since the DC brand boom of the 1980s and the 1990s. "Fashion" is no longer equivalent to a "trend" manufactured by a corporation. Instead, the new fashion is based on the subjective and personal values of individual designers and consumers.

Japanese designers' experiences of living abroad The shifting perception of the Paris collection and its absolute supremacy

In this exhibition, a considerable number of participating designers have experiences of studying fashion abroad. The list is as follows: mintdesigns (Parsons The New School of Design and Central Saint Martins), Theatre Products (their producer went to Central Saint

Mariko Nishitani
Mariko Nishitani received her B.A. in French literature from Tokyo Metropolitan University, and then entered Bunka Publishing Bureau. She worked for magazines such as So-en and High Fashion. She was a correspondent in Paris from 1980 to 1982 and saw debut collections by Yohji Yamamoto and Comme des Garçons. As an editor, she was involved with features of 20471120, Shinichiro Arakawa, Gomme etc. for So-en, and those of the Japanese in Paris, Berlin, Cultural activities by Hermès, Le Corbusier, Maison Martin Margiela, Comme des Garçons free editing for High Fashion. She is currently working as a chief editor of High Fashion online. She edited *Fashion started to talk* (2011).

Martins), and writtenafterwards (Central Saint Martins). matohu worked in London for a year at a local fashion brand after working in Japan for 5 years. In Akira Minagawa's case, his brand minä perhonen is the result of an inspiring trip to Finland. His label's name is in fact Finnish.

It is interesting that these designers went abroad, but not necessarily to Paris. Rather than a sense of "la mode" or dressmaking techniques, they acquired a set of new perspectives, freedom of expression, and powerful communication skills. Participating in the Paris Collection used to be the pinnacle of achievement for Japanese designers. Successful brands headed for the city of light, beginning with Kenzo Takada, Kansai Yamamoto, Hanae Mori, Yuki Torii, and Issey Miyake in the 1970s, Comme des Garçons and Yohji Yamamoto in the 1980s, and Zucca, Undercover, tsumori chisato, Toga, and sacai after the 1990s. This world capital of fashion had the highest level of creation, prestigious workshops, top journalists and buyers, as well as mature consumers with discerning eyes. Yet, Paris no longer held the same level of compelling force for Japanese designers after the 2000s.

I believe this change in attitude was brought about by many designers' experiences of studying abroad. By studying fashion in Western countries, they became self-aware of their Japanese heritage, rather than learning and emulating the European styles. For example, after returning to Japan, matohu got the idea to use Japanese aesthetics as the principal philosophy of the brand. On the other hand, mintdesigns, the graduates of Central Saint Martins, felt uncomfortable about participating in the Tokyo Collection. At first, they were convinced that they would never become mainstream in Japan. Yet, after 10 years, the duo won the prestigious Mainichi Fashion Award. "We can no longer call our label marginal," said the designers. Twice a year, they present new collections during Japan Fashion Week. However, their attitude toward fashion is not based on the tradition of the Paris Collection. Instead, their underlying philosophy is based on product design and its application to fashion.

Comme des Garçons as the rite of passage

For the participating designers in this exhibition, encountering Comme des Garçons was a significant rite of passage. Among the Big Three – Issey Miyake, Yohji Yamamoto, and Comme des Garçons — the latter has exerted a considerable influence on designers since the 2000s. When they first began dreaming of becoming fashion designers, Comme des Garçons was already in Paris, attracting international attention with its unique and powerful creations, such as the provocative 'bump' dresses from the 2007 spring and summer collection. The designers in this exhibition grew up with Comme des Garçons. It was like the air they breathed as they developed their own sensibilities. They unconsciously inherited the legacy of Comme des Garçons, including its punkish, destructive attitude. Comme des Garçons' influences manifest themselves in their formal designs by way of irregular shapes, asymmetry and showing the seams inside-out. Just like their mentor, fashion is a creative endeavor for this new generation of designers.

A new grammar of fashion is taking shape in Japan, the country that gave birth to Comme des Garçons. Looking at the exhibition plans, my heart is full of anticipation for this new challenge presented by Japanese fashion today.

Notes:

1 Akira Minagawa of minä perhonen already launched his business before 2000. He established his brand "minä " in 1995 and opened a directly managed store in 2000. He changed his name of the brand to "minä perhonen" in 2003. The following list shows the years in which the brands were established: ANREALAGE (2003), h.NAOTO (2000), keisuke kanda (2005), matohu (2005), mintdesigns (2001), SASQUATCHfabrix (2003), SOMARTA (2006), THEATRE PRODUCTS (2001), writtenafterwards (2007).

2 The only exception here is h.NAOTO, which is an affiliate brand of S-Inc. h.NAOTO was selected for this exhibition because of its leading role in spearheading the distinctive Gothic Lolita street style and the fact that it occasionally presents new works during Tokyo Fashion Week. The designer Naoto Hirooka came up with the concept "Gothic Lolita" (or Goth-Loli for short). His position is more significant and influential than that of a corporate in-house designer.

3 Those who do not yet run their directly-managed retail stores are (as of August 2011): Somarta, SASQUATCHfabrix, Keisuke Kanda, and writtenafterwards.

4 For this reason, we had to leave out many brands. For example, brands such as support surface, sacai, kolor, suzuki takayuki, and PHENOMENON have products that demonstrate high quality and originality in design, combined with successful business models. However, we did not see a unique cultural movement established by these brands.

Exhibiting Contemporary Fashion — A New Collaboration between Architecture and Fashion

Motoaki Hori

Two Exhibitions of Contemporary Fashion

In the fall of 2010, two exhibitions of contemporary Japanese fashion opened and attracted worldwide attention. One of them was titled "Japan Fashion Now" at the Museum of Fashion Institute of Technology in New York (MFIT).[1] The second show was titled "Future Beauty: 30 Years of Japanese Fashion", held at the Barbican Art Gallery in London.[2]
While both these exhibitions focused on Japanese fashion after the 1980s, the contents of these two exhibitions were completely different. The exhibition "Future Beauty" listed four characteristics of contemporary Japanese fashion and divided the exhibition space according to the following four categories: "In Praise of Shadows," "Flatness," "Tradition and Innovation" and "Cool Japan".[3] By contrast, "Japan Fashion Now," organized by Valerie Steele, director and chief curator of MFIT, captured Japanese fashion in a more extensive and ambitious manner. The exhibition included not only examples of high fashion by prominent designers, but also various street styles based on Japanese subcultures such as Gothic Lolita, Cosplay, and *Mori Girl*. The exhibition "Future Beauty" was an attempt to study various formal aspects of costume design from an art historian's standpoint. On the other hand, "Japan Fashion Now" showed a particular interest in fashion from a sociological point of view, focusing on the cultural significance of fashion. The difference between their perspectives on fashion was clearly reflected in the design of their exhibition space.

In "Future Beauty", the architect Sosuke Fujimoto designed the exhibition space following the standards of a fashion exhibition. Groups of mannequins stood on platforms while sheer fabric divided the space, adding a subtle, delicate touch to Fujimoto's spatial design. Although some parts of the exhibition had large film projections and wall decorations, he did away with excessive décor. Close attention was paid to take advantage of a clean, white space. In "Japan Fashion Now," the main exhibition room was covered with monochrome photos of Tokyo's vibrant quarters such as Ginza, Shibuya, and Shinjuku, and numerous mannequins were displayed like a crowd marching through a cityscape. In "Japan Fashion Now", the curator offered a broad overview of contemporary Japanese fashion, ranging from high fashion to popular street styles. Mannequins in *tokkofuku* of the *Bosozoku*, (the kamikaze jumpers worn by Japanese motorcycle gangs) and *Mori Girl* (Forest Girl) fashion were juxtaposed with mannequins in various Japanese high-end fashion labels such as Undercover, Sacai, and matohu.

These two exhibitions took contrasting approaches in their contents and overall venue configurations. However, it is interesting to note that both of these exhibitions used mannequins and platforms as the main props for their displays.

How to Exhibit Fashion?

Fashion exhibitions tend to follow the standard method of presentation, using mannequins on platforms. However, in 2009, the Museum of Contemporary Art in Tokyo presented an exhibition that questioned this standard form of displaying fashion. The exhibition was entitled "Luxury in Fashion Reconsidered" and it also contained a special exhibit called "Kazuyo Sejima Spatial Design for Comme des Garçons".[4] When the exhibition was first held at the National Museum of Modern Art in Kyoto, the museum chose to use mannequins on platforms or glass display cases along the walls of its exhibition space. In Tokyo, each mannequin was placed separately on a white podium. Museum visitors were able to see the costumes up close, even though white lines around each podium were drawn to keep them at a certain distance. The main purpose of this exhibition was to re-interpret the meaning of "luxury" in terms of 'intellectual fulfillment' as opposed to 'opulence'. The humble presence and scale of these white podiums were appropriate for the purpose of this exhibition. The exhibit "Kazuyo Sejima Spatial Design for Comme des Garçons" went even further by completely eschewing the use of podiums. This exhibition took place in the vast atrium of the museum, expanding from the second basement to the third floor. It showcased Comme des Garcon's work from the archives of the Kyoto Costume Institute. Each of the thirty pieces of clothing was individually suspended within a clear acrylic cylinder, as if it was floating in the air. This method of presentation had less-than-perfect results. For instance, there were distracting reflections on the acrylic surface. However, the exhibition was radical in a sense that it removed clothing from the context of the human body and treated these clothes by Comme des Garçons as objects by displaying them in such a spectacular manner.

One year later, the Museum of Contemporary Art in Tokyo held another exhibition that was groundbreaking in its innovative methods of displaying fashion. The exhibition was titled "Hussein

Motoaki Hori.
Motoaki Hori received his MA in art history from Waseda University. After working as a curator at the Museum of Modern Art, Kamakura & Hayama, he became chief curator of Tokyo Opera City Art Gallery in 2003. He organized such exhibitions as Toru Takemitsu — Vision in Time (2006), Mika Ninagawa: Earthly Flowers, Heavenly Colors (2008), and Takashi Honma New Documentary (2011). He is the cowriter of *Japanese Modern Art 11, Sculpture in the Modern Era* (Otsuki Shoten), *Japanese Art History of Comics No.3: Art from the Meiji Era to the Present* (Bijutsu Shuppan), *Art of the 20th Century in color version* (Bijutsu Shuppan), *Very New Art 2000: 100 artists in 2000* (Bijutsu Shuppan), and others.

Chalayan - From Fashion and Back".[5] While focusing on Chalayan's recurrent themes for his collections such as "genes", "identity", and "immigrants", the exhibition articulated the social context of the designer's work, instead of simply showing the formal and sculptural aspect of his clothing design. In this exhibition, mannequins struck different poses as though they were engaging in various activities: cleaning a window, painting a wall, or watering an olive tree. Each of Chalayan's collection was presented in a dynamic installation with a sense of narrative.

Each of these three exhibitions presented their own unique and ambitious solution to the problem of displaying contemporary fashion in the context of an art museum.

The Museum System and Fashion

Fashion was never a popular subject for art museums in Japan, but a change came in the late 1990s when more of these institutions started actively organizing fashion exhibitions. The reason for this change is complex and probably not always positive. This shift in an art museum's attitude toward fashion seems to correspond to the trend in contemporary art, which has expanded its field of expression into various subcultures, advertising, industrial design and fashion. Art museums similarly started expanding their field of interest to genres other than fine art, such as architecture, industrial design, manga and anime.

Yet, fashion remains the most challenging subject to exhibit in the context of a museum because fashion by nature is essentially incompatible with the modern art museum system of today.

As is often pointed out, a gallery within a museum is based on the system of a 'white cube'. Although some may disagree with this statement, the Museum of Modern Art (MoMA) is said to be the first institution to adopt this system when it opened in 1929. The neutral 'white cube', surrounded by white walls, has been instrumental in the establishment of modern art by asserting the autonomy of art object and its abstract presence. The concept of modern art removed picture frames from paintings and pedestals from sculptures. The transcendental space of a 'white cube' fostered the principles of modern art by isolating exhibited objects from their surrounding environment.[6] As argued by Alfred H. Barr, the founding director of the Museum of Modern Art, modern art became predominantly oriented towards abstraction[7], and figurative art such as portrait painting remained unreasonably underrated for more than fifty years. Considering this historical context, it becomes obvious to anyone that a 'white cube' space would be essentially incompatible with the idea of showing a fashion exhibition. While paintings and sculptures could be removed from the context of a human body and moved toward pure abstraction, fashion could never exist on its own without a human body. As a result, an exhibition of fashion in a modern art museum has introduced a method of display that was the opposite of removing picture frames from a painting. Museums brought mannequins, the conventional method of display in a retail shop environment, into a 'white cube'. They subsequently added pedestals (stages) to the display. By placing mannequins on pedestals (stages), museum exhibitions tended to solemnize fashion and emphasize its extraordinariness.

Experienceable Exhibition?

Even though it is not unprecedented, as shown by the earlier example of the exhibition "Kazuyo Sejima Spatial Design for Comme des Garçons", it is not easy to remove a platform and place a mannequin at the same eye level with the museum visitor. In doing so, a museum becomes indistinguishable from a retail shop. A retail shop and a fashion exhibition both display various clothing items by lining them up next to one another. Yet, in a museum exhibition, a visitor must always remain a spectator because touching the objects in an exhibition is generally forbidden, as written on the notice next to an object. In order to appreciate fashion, we need to be able to physically experience it by touching its texture and feeling it against our skin. Within a system (or space) called a museum, we become acutely aware that fashion merely becomes a subject of visual appreciation.

The exhibition "Feel and Think: A New Era of Tokyo Fashion" showcases a group of ten designers. For these designers, the 'reality' of living and working in Tokyo in the 2000s has been an important factor in shaping their creations. In this exhibition, we asked each of them to display their clothes in various stages of completion and express their brand's image and their individual outlook on the world by using their own unique installation. We commissioned Ryuji Nakayama to design the overall venue configuration. I will not go into details on the display methods planned by each participating designer. However, I am happy to share that Nakamura proposed an overall design for the exhibition space that will help us resolve the historical dilemma of showing a fashion exhibition in an art museum.

Tokyo Opera City Art Gallery's two galleries will have thirty pieces of two hundred meter-long iron beams installed in every direction. These beams will be painted white like the surrounding walls. Their sterile forms and structures might make these beams look like Minimal Art. Since these 40cm wide beams will be at the spectator's eye level, it will be impossible for him/her to survey the entire gallery space. While walking around the galleries, a museum visitor will need to bend down in order to walk past the iron beams. In this way, without relying solely on his/her visual perception, a spectator will be required to use his/her entire body in order to face the works by these designers and their installations.

These beams might be characterized as 'theatrical', to borrow the expression by which Modernist art critic Michael Fried condemned Minimal art.[8] On the other hand, this exhibition design might allow the participating designers to define their work in relation to Nakamura's structures and the adjacent works by other designers. By actively engaging with the installations, a spectator will complete the process of giving a new meaning to these designers' works. Nakamura mentioned that he imagined Tokyo's vernacular landscapes within each gallery compartment in random sizes. In this site-specific installation accentuated by countless beams, a spectator will discover many forms of fashion and its essence, freely defined by our participating designers.

Notes:

1 Designers participating in the exhibition "Japan Fashion Now" (from September 7th 2010 to January 8th, 2011) included Yohji Yamamoto, Rei Kawakubo, Issey Miyake, Kenzo Takada, Hanae Mori, Kansai Yamamoto, Junya Watanabe, Tao Kurihara, Jun Takahashi, Toshikazu Iwaya, Chitose Abe, Hiroyuki Horihata & Makiko Sekiguchi, Tamae Hirokawa, Arashi Yanagawa, Daisuke Obana, Koji Udo, Yasuhiro Mihara, Takeshi Osumi, Yosuke Aizawa, Takahiro Miyashita, Naoto Hirooka, and Hiroki Nakamura.

2 The exhibition "Future Beauty: 30 Years of Japanese Fashion" (held from October 15th, 2010, to February 6th, 2011) was primarily composed of the collections from the Kyoto Costume Institute (KCI). In London, the exhibition was curated by the chief director of KCI and Kate Bush of the Barbican Art Gallery. The exhibition traveled to Haus der Kunst in Munich, Germany, (from March 4 to June 19, 2011; exhibition catalogue Published by Prestel) curated by Chris Dercon, the former director of Haus der Kunst, and Akiko Fukai. Twenty-three designers participated in this exhibition: Issey Miyake, Rei Kawakubo, Yohji Yamamoto, Junya Watanabe, Jun Takahashi, Tao Kurihara, Chitose Abe, Akira Onozuka, Hiroaki Ohya, Hokuto Katsui & Nao Yagi, Fumito Ganryu, Mikio Sakabe, Kazuaki Takashima, Akira Naka, Tamae Hirokawa, Taro Horiuchi, Hiroyuki Horihata & Makiko Sekiguchi, Akira Minagawa, and Kunihiko Morinaga.

3 In the exhibition venue in London, the section titled "Designers" featured major works by participating designers, and its sub-section entitled "Next Generation" introduced new designers such as Chitose Abe, Mikio Sakabe, Kazuaki Takashima, Akira Naka, Tamae Hirokawa, Taro Horiuchi, Kunihiko Morinaga, as well as Hokuto Katsui & Nao Yagi.

4 The exhibition "Luxury in Fashion Reconsidered" and its special exhibit "Kazuyo Sejima Spatial Design for Comme des Garçons" were held at the Museum of Contemporary Art Tokyo from October 31st, 2009, to January 17th, 2011. Prior to its Tokyo edition, the exhibition was held at the National Museum of Modern Art, Kyoto, from April 11th to May 24th, 2009.

5 The exhibition "Hussein Chalayan - From Fashion and Back" was initially held at the Design Museum in London from January 22nd to May 17th, 2009, and it toured to the Museum of Contemporary Art Tokyo (from April 3 to June 20, 2010) with newly revised contents.

6 O'Doherty, Brian. *Inside the White Cube: The Ideology of the Gallery Space*, Expanded edition, University of California Press, 1999.

7 Grunenberg, Christoph. "The Politics of Presentation: The Museum of Modern Art, New York "(1994) in Barker, Emma (ed.), *Contemporary Culture of Display*, Yale University Press, 1999.

8 Fried, Michael. "Art and Objecthood," in: *Art and Objecthood: Essays and Reviews*, University of Chicago Press, 1998.

Thoughts on Venue Configuration

Ryuji Nakamura

The major theme of this exhibition was intriguing. My intention was not to give a dogmatic interpretation of Tokyo fashion today, but I rather wanted to search for different possibilities of interpreting it in an exhibition format. It was about everything in sight. This kind of open-endedness would make a great exhibition that conveys a sense of tension and freedom to both the exhibitors and the viewers. During our first meeting, the curators reported on various fashion exhibitions abroad. Also, Kenjiro Hosaka, the curator and research associate of the National Museum of Modern Art in Tokyo, reported on various architecture exhibitions. They spoke about the difficulty of displaying fashion and architecture within an art museum. They mentioned the awkwardness of displaying clothes on mannequins in fashion exhibitions. They also stated that it was impossible to exhibit actual architecture in the context of an exhibition.

With these issues in mind, I had to design an exhibition space for ten groups of fashion designers. Although the possibilities were endless, I came up with two questions to shape my decision on the overall design. First, I need to consider how to design the overall exhibition. Should it be based on the display of items or the architectural space of the venue? Depending on which one I choose, it will create a big difference in how I configure the exhibition space. The second question is how to distribute and divide the space for ten groups of designers. I had the option to leave the space open and undivided. This option would affect the way I organize the exhibition space as well.

I thought that these two questions would help me narrow down a display format from endless possibilities. The process of selection could never be objective but spontaneous. Just like buildings in a city, I thought about the placement of the items in response to the form of the site and the surrounding environment. In other words, the idea was for each exhibitor to have a territory and yet avoid closure, so each display could interact with the others. I decided that the premise of the exhibition was the space, and that the display was to respond to it in some way or another. If designing clothes is a response to the form of the body, the material and the movement, I was curious to find out how a response to a space manifests itself.

After suggesting ideas to divide the space with strings or hills to mark the area in a remarkable and coherent way, I finally came up with the idea of dividing up the space with beams. The room is divided into different shapes by beams held at eye level, and each designer group chooses his favorite corner. The beams, supported by the walls of the exhibition space, are wrapped in the same wallpaper as that of the exhibition space itself. Therefore the sense of unity is retained. Designers can choose a single large space or several small compartments. They do not have to hold firm to the idea of compartments and use the space by cutting across the beams. Or they can even choose to move around and not have a fixed space. With their view blocked by the beams at their eye level, visitors are invited to constantly change their line of sight. They are to move around the space by passing under the beams, sit on the floor or climb on the stairs. The beams will also make us aware of the height of the space as well as of blind spots such as near the ceiling and the floor. Every inch of the exhibition space can be employed by both exhibitors and visitors.

By designing the exhibition space in this manner, I am creating a context in which the conventional relationship between the items, the exhibition space and the spectators no longer holds validity. Each of the components is independent. The spectators can slip into the exhibition space and become a part of it. I think it will create a dynamic situation that goes beyond an exhibition of static objects. Each exhibitor will shape their space based on their perception of this unique space. It is something that cannot be repeated elsewhere. A spectator will experience a unique happening, and consequently, another spectator observing the scene nearby will experience something different. This is the sort of evocative situation I picture.

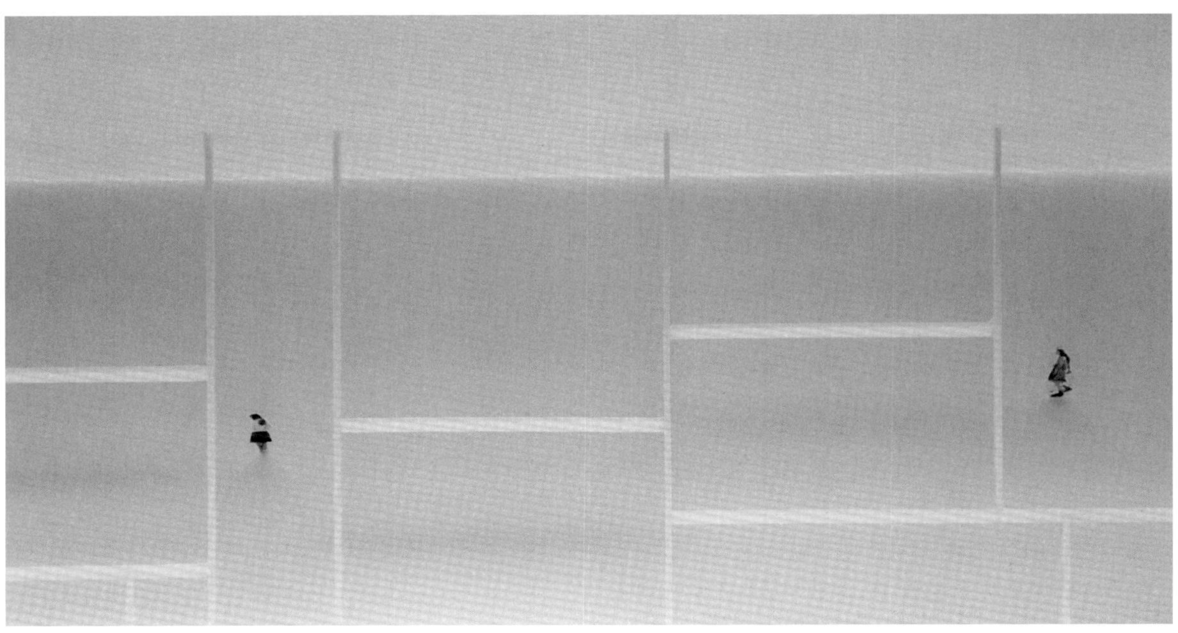

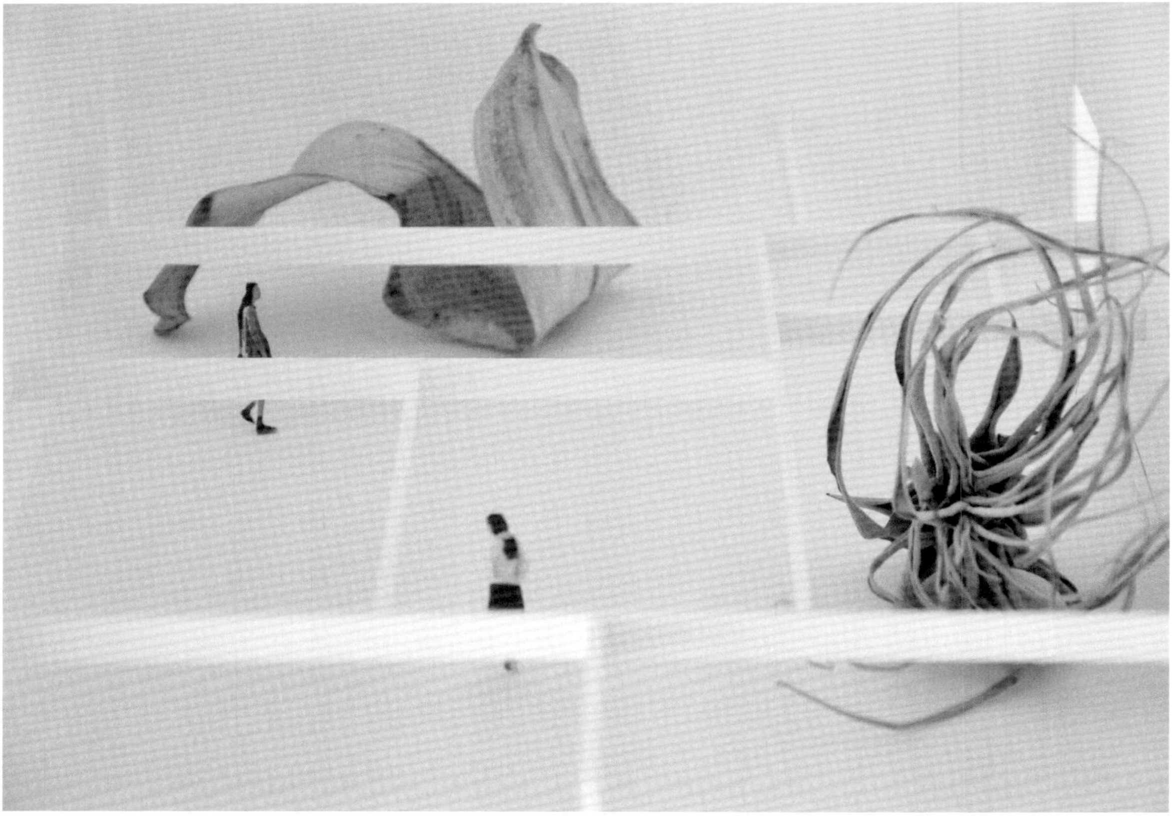

Ryuji Nakamura
Architect Ryuji Nakamura was born in Nagano in 1972. He completed the Master Course of Architecture at the Tokyo National University of Fine Arts and Music. After working at Jun Aoki & Associates, he founded Ryuji Nakamura & Associates in 2004. His main works include atmosphere (stage art work for Opera Le Grand Macabre at New National Theatre), cornfield (Where is Architecture? Seven installations by Japanese Architects at The National Museum of Modern Art, Tokyo), blank room (space design of DESIGNTIDE TOKYO 2010), ard pond (hotel LLOVE). He has won prizes such as Kumamoto Station West Gate Square Design Competition Award by Kumamoto Art Pclice Second Prize, Good Design Award, JDC Design Award Grand Award, and THE GREAT INDOORS AWARD in Netherlands.

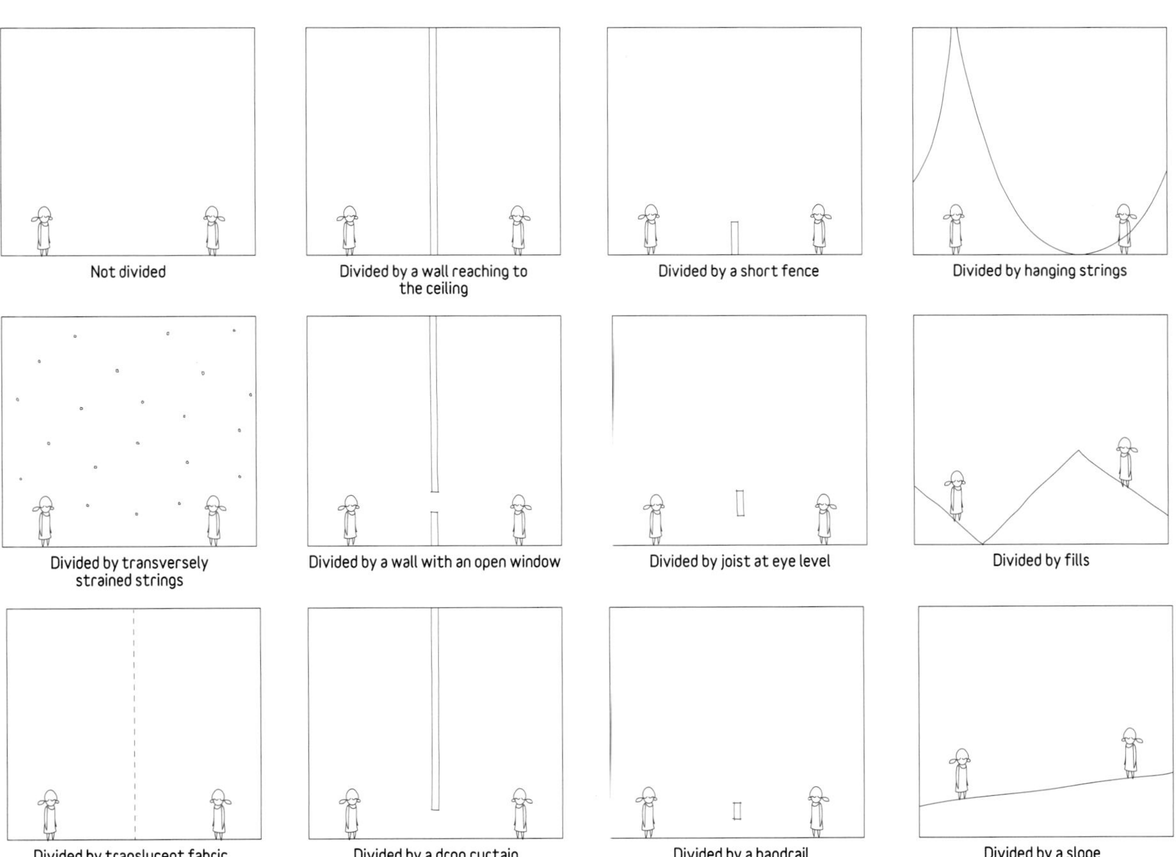

Study of the way to divide

How to move beyond the divided line is of the same importance in the sense of influencing the way to feel the space and the relationship with works as what is divided: is it done by moving through a usual opening, a hole like a crawl-in entrance to the tea room, or through an open window, or by pushing through strings or fabric, striding a fence or a handrail, ducking under the joist, or by going up and down on mountains or slopes... The choice of a method will define the distance from a way of appreciating so-called museum-esque "display."

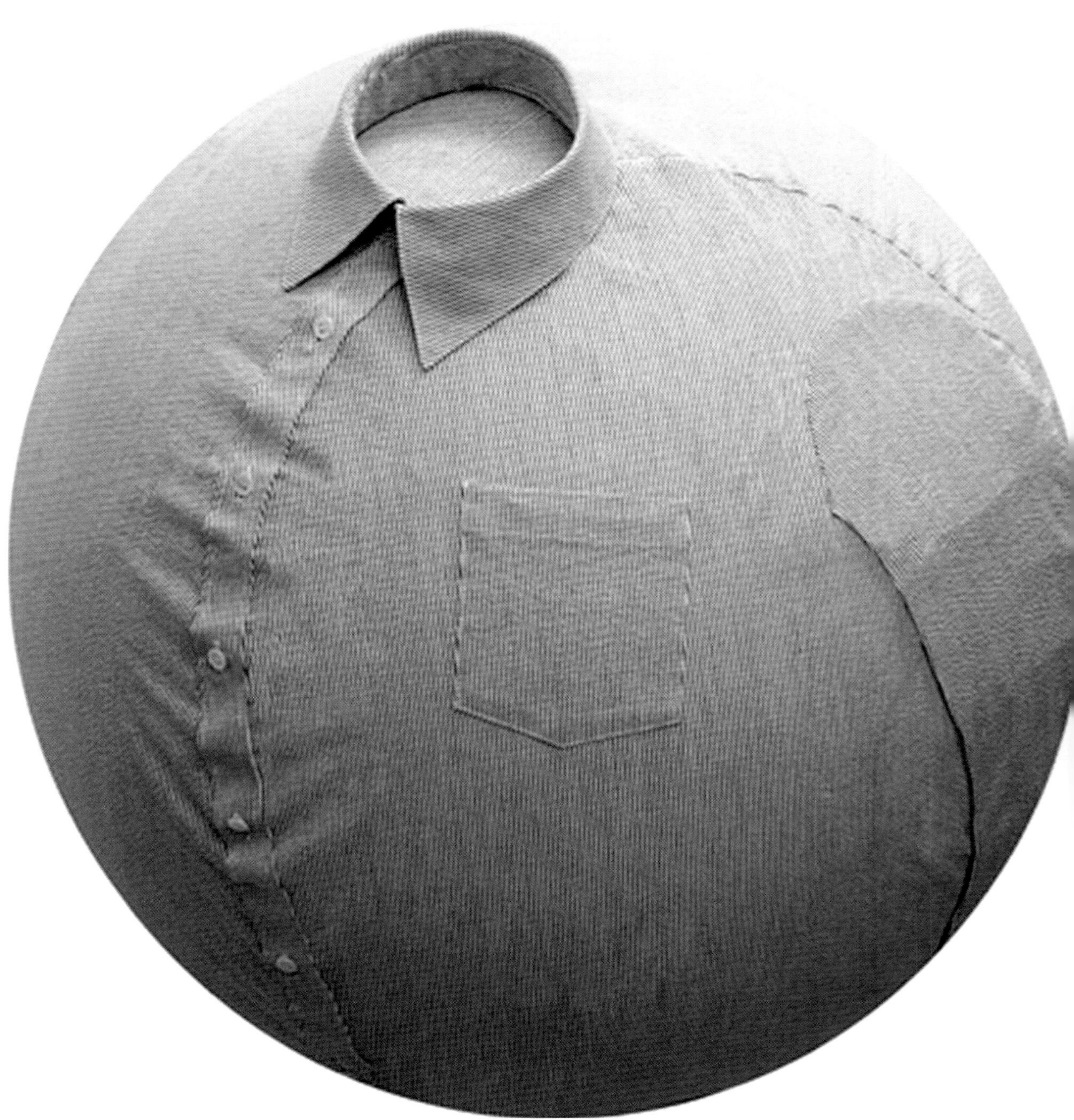

ANREALAGE

アンリアレイジ
森永邦彦

ANREALAGE
Kunihiko Morinaga

ANREALAGE

Kunihiko Morinaga

アンリアレイジ

森永邦彦

ANREALAGE / Kunihiko Morinaga

Clothes to Subvert the Visual Sense

Interviewed by Mariko Nishitani

The word Anrealage is derived from the words 'real', 'unreal' and 'age'. Since 2003, Kunihiko Morinaga has created clothing that embodies this paradoxical idea of living in a world that is both real and unreal. His early work explored the obsessive nature of craft. He started out customizing used clothes, covering their surfaces with minutely detailed patchworks. He once even painstakingly sewed ten thousand buttons onto a jacket (autumn/winter 2008-2009). Mies van der Rohe famously said, "God is in the detail". This idea had shaped Morinaga's policy for his creations until the autumn of 2008. His work arrived at a significant turning point when he exhibited his new body of works for the spring/summer collection that year. Titled "Circle Triangle Square", he produced garments that actually took the shapes of these geometric forms by putting them on special armatures. At the exhibition, these geometric garments were also shown on regular mannequins, by which he demonstrated their functionality as clothes people could wear every day. ANREALAGE presents clothes both as a sculptural objects and as a functional wardrobe. When Morinaga's attention shifted toward more conceptual work, his creations took a giant leap in evolution. He has continued creating his mind-twisting garments under such themes as "Bump and Dimple", "Silhouettes", "wideshortslimlong", "<the shape of air> " and "Low".

Finding a Conceptual Direction by Re-examining the Archetype

_ Could you articulate how you changed the direction of your work when you made "Circle, Triangle, Square" from the fall of 2008? Your work went from heavily craft-oriented to highly conceptual.

Morinaga: When I was making clothes that were heavily crafted, it was very important for me to spend a long time on making each and every one of them. But then, I came to realize that I could create something simple yet experimental that would have just as strong an impact on society. "Circle, Triangle, Square" was my attempt to create something simple and unprecedented. First, I came up with the extremely reductive idea that anything could become a piece of clothing as long as it had four openings: one for the head, two for the arms, and one for the torso. I realized that clothes do not have to fit the archetypal shape; they could be a circle, square, or triangle. I discarded the idea that the human form should be the basis of fashion design and started designing clothes without having a human body in mind. But then, I would eventually put these clothes back on the human body. My work has been about this contradiction between the process and the product.

_ Your "Circle Triangle Square" reminded me of the work by Erwin Wurm, the Austrian conceptual artist. When I first told you about him, you mentioned that you were not familiar with his work. This artist made a piece called "fat man", a photo of an actual man wearing what looks like the entire content of his closet around his body. He also took a rectangular form and put clothes on it. Wurm's work is about the act of wrapping and covering a form. On the other hand, ANREALAGE's work is about the process of making clothes without thinking about a human body first. Even if your clothes take the shape of a geometric form, in the end they still function as clothes we can wear. You calculated the measurements on these forms to be wearable.

Morinaga: I enjoyed Erwin Wurm's work. Thank you for telling me about it. In my case, it was important to come up with the right scale for these geometric forms so that they were easy to wear. It took a lot of trial and error to figure this out. I made a total of twenty-four clothing items in the shapes of circles, triangles and squares. Even though I only had these three basic forms to work with, the silhouettes of the clothes varied greatly depending on where I put the openings for head and limbs. This was the most interesting and challenging aspect of this collection. I made a cube form into a trench coat, and the shoulders were both on one of its sides. The buttons were bent at a straight angle at the corner of the cube. The size of the cube determined how long the coat would be, so even if I wanted to add more length to the coat, I couldn't.

The process to "wideshortslimlong"

_ Your next collection "Bump and Dimple" also features very unusual forms.

Morinaga: I was trying to come up with new shapes for clothing by imagining their profiles first. I have always wondered why a fashion drawing showed only the front and the back of the design. By paying attention to the view from the side, I could add a tremendous sense of depth to the garment. My designs were based on two principles: protrusion and indentation. Looking at them straight from the front, these clothes would look rather ordinary, but when you shift your gaze to the side, they would reveal an unexpected indentation or protrusion. I used a Styrofoam framework to create the forms to put the clothes on. The appearance of these clothes would be transformed in an unexpected manner when you put them on a human body. What used to be a big "bump" would become a drape. Another example is the polka dots border tee. I took some Styrofoam in the shape of a T-shirt and carved a big square indentation from top to bottom. Then, I covered this block with fabric. Due to the optical illusion, the front view of this form looked like a flattened black T-shirt with polka dots. When I lifted the shirt off the framework, the dots would transform into lines. I wanted to demonstrate the idea that a polka dot pattern could turn into a border pattern when you imagined adding a sense of depth to a flat pattern.

_ Then you moved onto your next collection, "Silhouette".

Morinaga: A lot of fashion brands often make their clothes based on their particular "silhouette". The word silhouette is typically meant to describe the contour and shape of clothing. In my case, I took the word "silhouette" out of the design context and returned it to its original meaning—the shadow, or the backlit image. For this collection, I presented a series of items on two-dimensional backlit panels in a dark room. These panels would show dark silhouettes of recognizable wardrobe items, such as a jacket or a sweater. But what looked like a jacket was actually a distorted T-shirt, and a sweater would turn out to be a pair of pants with the legs crossed. With this collection, I wanted to challenge the notion of categories in the fashion industry. A jacket is considered more valuable than a T-shirt. The "Silhouette" collection implied a potential for transcending categories and gaining a bigger perspective beyond categorization.

_ You subverted the viewer's expectation completely. The visual impact of this collection was very striking as well. And next, you created the highly acclaimed collection, "wideshortslimlong".

Morinaga: Historically, designers have used a well-proportioned form of the human body as a standard for measurement for designers. For this season, I was trying to come up with new ways of designing clothes by using distorted human forms as my starting point. The title of this collection, "wideshortslimlong", comes from the common terms to describe clothing styles. For example, a pair of wide pants, a short skirt, and so on. I wanted to illustrate the fact that these terms could also describe body types. In this collection, a standard mannequin was either elongated or widened/shortened, so they didn't look anything like standard human forms. I then made two versions of each apparel item: one to fit the 'elongated' mannequin, and the other to fit the 'widened/shortened' mannequin.

_ So the total 'volumes' of the fabrics were the same for both elongated and shortened versions of the apparel item?

Morinaga: Let's say that the standard mannequin is '100%'. For the elongated mannequin, the standard height was stretched by 150%, and the width was shrunk by 70%. So this elongated mannequin had a height of 276 centimeters. For the widened/shortened mannequin, the standard height was shrunk by 70%, and the width was stretched by 250%. The height of this mannequin came to about 100 centimeters. On a regular person, the seams at the shoulders of the

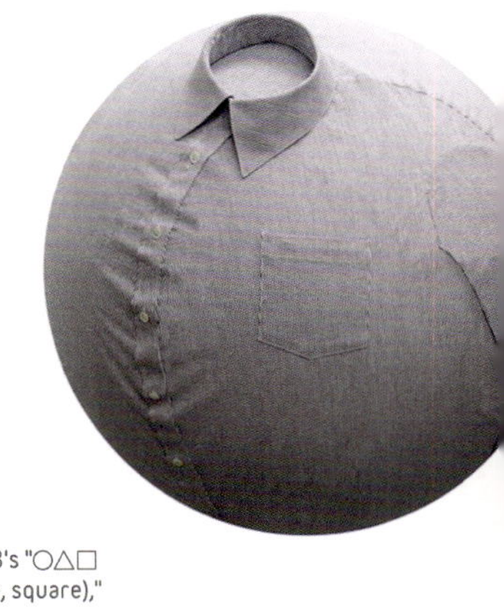

From A/W 2008's "○△□ (round, triangle, square)," in which a succession of clothed spheres, pyramids, and cubes was displayed alongside regular human forms, presenting all designs as real (see p.46). Morinaga used balls as a reference when designing the spherical clothes, which gave birth to the curved fastener. The shoulder part of the trench coat was fit around the corners of the cube, with buttons bent at a right angle around the edges.

From "凹凸 (irregularity)," Spring/Summer 2009. Morinaga designed clothes to fit an artistic object previously created from styrofoam. This fantastic idea came from reconsidering the usual way of presenting things on a flat plane and imagining ways to lend them unexpected depth.

wide mannequin would reach to their elbows. The decorative patterns and buttons were also stretched to fit the proportions of the distorted mannequins, so these details would look completely different when they were put on the standard human body.

_ On your 'elongated' version, the clothes looked impossibly slender. However, they were actually wearable, weren't they?

Morinaga: Yes they were. The clothes for the 'elongated' version were made with very stretchy materials. Even though these garments were long, people could still wear them by tucking and folding excess fabric with belts.

_ What motivated you to come up with the concept for this collection?

Morinaga: People have always told me, "There will be no new type of clothing unless the human body changes its shape." I don't agree with this idea. By dramatically changing the shape of a standard human body, I was able to come up with new designs. Changing the human form was a way for me to expand my design vocabulary.

What is clothing? About the "Bump" dress and spring/summer 2011

_ In October of 2010, you held a runway show and had models wearing your designs. It had been a long time since you presented your creations on models on the runway. Did you attempt to prove that it was possible for clothes to transform human bodies?

Morinaga: Yes, I did. For this collection, I made clothes that had air balloons inside them. Certain sections of a human body can sometimes swell up. We all know that pregnancy makes a woman's belly larger. For this collection, I thought about the human body as a "bag" that could be inflated in certain parts. By trapping air and other intangible matter inside, these clothes dramatically changed their shapes and forms. Once deflated, they became something ordinary that people could wear every day. At the runway show, one of the clothes had a balloon inside that was so gigantic that it looked otherworldly.

_ You presented the same garment in two different states; first, in the inflated state, and next, in the deflated state. It was like seeing two completely different garments. After the show, many interviewers brought up Comme des Garçons's famous "bump" dress in relation to your collection. Had you seen that 1997 show by Comme des Garçons?

Morinaga: I was still in junior high school at the time, but I clearly remember how thrilled I was when I first saw the collection.

_ Could you tell me more about your adolescence? Were you already interested in fashion at that time?

Morinaga: Yes, but I had no intention of becoming a designer. I loved fashion, though. Back then, the boutique NOWHERE had just opened in Harajuku, and that was where I discovered Undercover and the Tokyo-based

From A/W 2009's "wideshortslimlong." This epoch-making collection formed ANREALAGE's breakthrough. Morinaga's thought-provoking concept considered the length and width of clothes as a matter of relativity. Clothes were draped around specially-made forms, yet they were all designed to be wearable.

There is another face to ANREALAGE: that of elaborate craftsmanship and unparalleled commitment to detail. Shown here are the "Folded Jacket," presented at the S/S 2007-2008 collection, which sports 5000 buttons, and the "Full Metal Jacket" from A/W 2007-2008, which features 15,000 buttons. Morinaga still keeps a separate studio where he works on fine patchworks.

The Dick Bruna Huis in Utrecht, Holland, invited fifteen fashion designers from around the world to create party dresses for a 40cm tall Miffy, to mark the museum's fifth anniversary in 2011, the year of the hare. minä perhonen and ANREALAGE represented Japan. A Miffy made out of buttons by ANRE-ALAGE appeared on the cover of the pamphlet for the exhibition "miffy in fashion," which continued through December 2011.

designer Christopher Nemeth. I also learned about Comme des Garçons and their bump dress around that time.

_The period between 1996 and 1999 had so many designers doing conceptual and experimental works.

Morinaga: Yes, it was really amazing.

_I remember a highly experimental Martin Margiela show. It was not the usual runway show with models in pretty clothes. He had a slide presentation and a model in a white uniform explaining the concept behind each of the outfits. In Japan, Shinichiro Arakawa surprised the viewers by holding his fashion shows at a shopping arcade in Shimokitazawa and the Komaba student dormitories at the Tokyo University. Did you feel intrigued by these experimental fashion shows?

Morinaga: At first, I was just blown away. I couldn't believe that what they were making were actually clothes. Then, I began to accept their unconventional definition of what 'clothes' could be. I still find their works shocking. But I thought that their artistic clothes were too removed from our day-to-day lives. I couldn't imagine myself wearing one of their creations. I vaguely knew that one day I would find my own way to resolve this problem that conceptual fashion design presents.

_The "bump" dress by Comme des Garçons caused a sensation in the fashion industry. The dress had so much visual impact. This peculiar form kept reappearing in the later works by Comme des Garçons and it became one of their signature pieces, but as a piece of functional clothing it didn't work well. It made the person wearing it look weird. As a result, we didn't see many women wearing the "bump" dresses out on the street. You seemed to have noticed this problem of such an avant-garde design, and you have come up with an answer to solve this problem. ANREALAGE's "<The shape of air>" had the same powerful visual impact that the "bump" dress by Comme des Garçons had. Yet, once the air was removed from the balloons, your clothes became totally practical for everyday use. It was so refreshing for me to see that a piece of clothing could embody two dramatically different directions: on the one hand, it was a piece of conceptual sculpture, and on the other hand, it was a piece of comfortable clothing with a cool design.

Morinaga: I believe that first and foremost, I must make clothes that are practical. As a designer, I am interested in providing wearable clothing that people can wear every day. The older generation of designers might have been more interested in creating innovative forms and cutting-edge designs just for the sake of doing it. For today's generation of designers, the question is how to give your designs a certain artistic value while still making them suitable for ordinary people. I try not to forget that this is a business in the end, so I need to create clothes that not only provide a sense of awe and wonder, but also stay grounded in reality.

"LOW": 'The Process of Becoming'

_ The earthquake and tsunami disasters delayed your show "LOW" (autumn/winter 2011-2012). The title "LOW" was short for "low resolution" in a graphic design term. This is a new direction for your work, and this time there seems to be less concern about the 'body' and the 'form'.

Morinaga: Until the previous collection, 'the human body' had been the central theme of my work. I wanted to show that a 'human form' is not absolute. However, as the theme of 'the human body' kept recurring in my work, I realized that a body is never formless. It always has a shape and a form. At the end of last year, my interest shifted toward finding new ways of expressing the uncertainty of shapes. Previously, I expressed the idea of uncertainty of shapes by their absence. While I was playing on the computer, I stumbled upon the idea of "low resolution". I wanted to translate this idea of 'low resolution' into a clothing design. When something is in low resolution, it is in the state of becoming and coming into focus. My goal was to create a design that has yet to have a concrete shape and form. I also introduced the element of the 'viewing distance' in order to express this incomplete state of being.

_ You kept the shapes of the clothes ordinary, yet the patterns on them looked pixilated.
Depending on the viewing distance, the patterns would appear blurry or in sharp focus.
I remember a model wearing a mask with a large pixel pattern on it, so her face looked like it was blurred in Photoshop.

Morinaga: By using the visual motifs of pixels and mosaics, I wanted to show something incomplete, in the state of 'becoming'. Executing this idea was more difficult than I expected, though. Originally, I planned to have a video projection during the runway show to compare the low resolution on screen and on the model's clothes. However, due to an unforeseen circumstance, I couldn't use the video projection. It was too bad.

_ The Tohoku earthquake and tsunami disasters forced designers to change the logistics for their presentations. So your runway show was not to your satisfaction, but how about the production process? You mentioned that you challenged yourself with a new technology for making these clothes.

Morinaga: Yes, I did. I used laser cutters for trimming the fabrics and ultrasonic sewing machines for sewing them. I also introduced a new reinforcing technique, like seamless tape, commonly used on outdoor sporting gears.

_ In many ways, this collection was the step toward a new direction for you. I cannot wait to see your next project.

On Being Japanese

_ Have you felt conscious about your identity as a Japanese designer? I heard that ANREALAGE is very popular in Russia, Hong Kong and Germany.

Morinaga: I do not feel self-conscious about my Japanese identity because I have worked primarily in Japan. But when I go abroad, many people have pointed out how 'Japanese' my work is.

_ Do you wonder what makes your work 'Japanese' for the international audience?

Morinaga: I think it comes from the sense of freedom in selecting my themes and motifs. Unlike in many international cultures, Japan does not have a centralized religion and a single dominant ethnic heritage. For example, Christianity and Islam have determined people's cultural axis in their artworks. ANREALAGE is decidedly ambivalent about its core identity. Like a pendulum moving from left to right, ANREALAGE is always exploring different tastes in design. I wish I could locate the cultural axis of my work. In a way, I'm still searching for it.

_ You used to have a photo of Rei Kawakubo up in your studio.

Morinaga: Yes, it's still there.

_ It looked like your lucky charm. So you don't think of religion as the guiding principle for your work. Perhaps Comme des Garçons is the 'standard' against which you measure your work.

Morinaga: Do you mean that I worship Rei Kawakubo as God?

_ No, I did not mean it literally. Your conceptual designs seem to follow the footsteps of Comme des Garçons and its avant-garde spirit. In a way, you seem to be working within the conceptual framework built by Comme des Garçons.

Morinaga: Perhaps you're right. The iconoclastic legacy of Comme des Garçons is incredibly important. Rei Kawakubo cultivated the narrow but important path for designers who want to create innovative and experimental works. Without the pioneering designers like Comme des Garçons, I would not have found fashion so intriguing in the first place. I feel like I owe my career to Rei Kawakubo.

_ Contemporary Japanese design might be based more on the legacy of Comme des Garçons, rather than on traditional Japanese art. I wish that Japanese designers would become more self-aware of their Japanese heritage. It is the country that gave birth to the Big Three: Comme des Garçons, Yohji Yamamoto, and Issey Miyake. Japan has been a fertile breeding ground of creativity and an inspiring place, even for young designers abroad.

Morinaga: Yes it is. So what would be the next step for us? The problem is in figuring out where to go next with our heritage from the past.

A flat sketch for the "Pixel Trench," presented at Autumn/Winter 2011-2012's "LOW" collection. This laser-cut garment is assembled without the use of string, by means of a brand new technology. Shown below is a pair of shoes with heels composed of pixels.

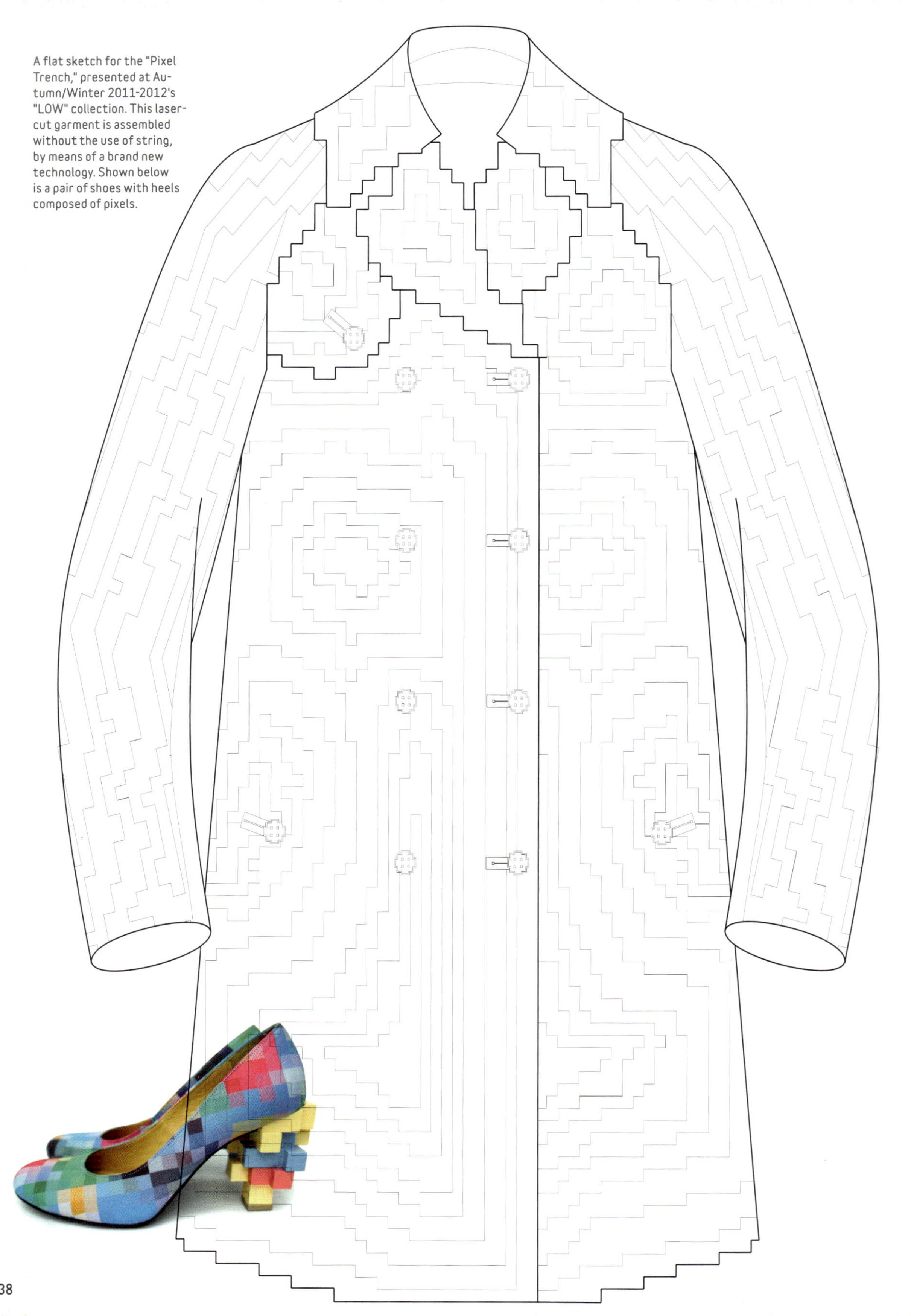

ANREALAGE's Autumn/Winter 2011 collection photographed by Berlin-based photographer Yosuke Demukai for his personal magazine, "pool." Especially striking is the contrast between the atmosphere of the traditional Japanese house and the futuristic clothes by ANREALAGE.

hair:Yoshiki Kirino (Mondo Artists) model:Rila (Image models)

2006 S/S Butter

2006-07 A/W Canon

Spring/Summer 2006: ***Butter***, Tokyo Tower. ANREALAGE's first fashion show was a joint venture with Keisuke Kanda, Morinaga's senior at Waseda University. Strongly influenced by Kanda, he started out by remaking second-hand clothes into his first collection.

Autumn/Winter 2006-2007: ***CANON***, Studio Bybros, Tokyo
These unisex alphabet clothes form an important precursor to Morinaga's later conceptual designs.
Spring/Summer 2007: "Pray", EBISU 303, Tokyo
Morinaga created his collection by focusing on dexterity, spending a lot of time and care on his hands and gestures, as if in prayer. The "flower field" jacket is a patchwork of waste pieces in a scraggly flower pattern, and the trench coat is pieced together from several hundred patches of lace. The "Clothes Scream" suit (left) was decorated entirely by hand with more than five thousand buttons and crystals.

Autumn Winter 2007-2008: ***Harukaharu – Over the Rainbow***, EBISU303, Tokyo
Under his motto "God is in the details," Morinaga presented a coordinated suit (right) covered with more than 15,000 gold buttons and bells, and a series of patchwork clothes made from several hundred different fabrics. He even designed custom buttons with soldiers and animals locked into them. The showstopper was a gathered dress made of sheeting, entitled "Unspoiled Scenery.".

Spring Summer 2008: ***No More***, EBISU303, Tokyo
Real time sounds formed the background music for this show. The Chanel-esque suit was a fake tweed made of discarded thread from countless buttons, while the seemingly white one-piece suit was actually made of a black fabric with numerous white threads sewn in. Morinaga here expressed the concept of "Zero" through a roundabout approach, adding something first and then subtracting.

Autumn/Winter 2008-2009: ***Inori***, 7th Floor, Shinmaru Building, Tokyo
Morinaga's installation consisted of a tiered platform in blue, in the motif of Japan's Doll Festival. Models dressed in his clothes walked down the platform one by one and remained seated there for an hour. The show featured a dress made of thirty layers of antique baby dresses, patterned after a twelve-layered ceremonial kimono, and a tweed suit colored by pressing flowers into vinyl chloride. The final piece of the show was a coat decorated with more than two hundred kinds of traditional Japanese beads. The result was a little girl's dream come true.

Autumn/Winter 2009: ***(round, triangle, square)***, Studio Sakeso, Tokyo
With this collection, ANREALAGE began to question the human body shape through its clothing designs. The exhibit featured twenty-four spheres, pyramids, and cubes, all enrobed, displayed alongside dressed human forms. The shapes were all the more eye-catching for very tactically corresponding to actual human body measurements.

Autumn/Winter 2009-2010: ***(irregularity)***, Lion Building, Tokyo
Morinaga added unexpected depth to solid bodies, then designed clothes to fit them. The interruption this creates in seemingly normal patterns proved very entertaining.

Spring/Summer 2010: ***Silhouette***, Gotanda Haiya, Tokyo
"Silhouette" is a word frequently used in fashion columns. The premise for this tricky exhibition was the idea that a silhouette can be a visual trap. This show can be considered an evolution of the "Alphabet" from Autumn/Winter 2006-2007.

Autumn/Winter 2010-2011: ***wideshortslimlong***, Aoyama Studio, Tokyo

Two custom forms were produced; one was 270cm tall, the other less than 100cm. Although one looks profoundly thin, and the other looks fat, the volume inside was the same,. This collection raised questions about sizes being merely a matter of relativity. Morinaga was particular about not only the patterns, but also accessories such as buttons, which were twisted in every direction.

Spring/Summer 2011, ***(The shape of air)***, Bellesalle Shibuya First, Tokyo
A return to the runway show format. The theme of "bloated body parts" gave us clothes made on the supposition that part of the human body wearing them was bloated like a balloon. They can be worn when the air is evacuated, after which the bloated parts become drapings of fabric, This creates a very amusing process in which strange, unrealistic forms revert to ordinary clothing shapes.

Autumn/Winter 2011-2012: ***LOW***, Laforet Museum, Roppongi, Tokyo
Presentation carried out in runway show form after the March 11 earthquake. Under the theme of "low resolution", Morinaga played video game music while showing clothes that looked like pixels when seen from up close, or like raised patterns when seen from a distance. Other items looked as if obscured by mosaic patterns. The experimental nature of the collection was typified by the patchworks created through the use of high technology and sewing without the use of string.

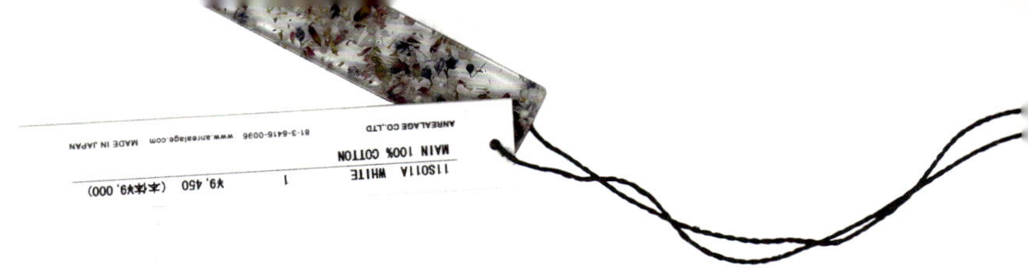

2011-12 A/W LOW

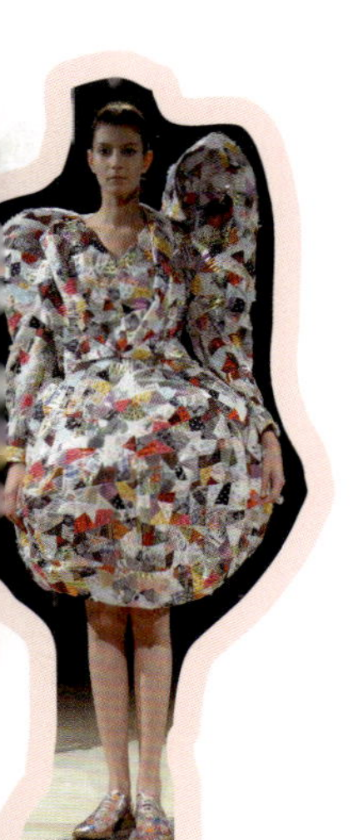

Designers' profiles:
ANREALAGE / Kunihiko Morinaga

Kunihiko Morinaga was born in 1980 in Tokyo. He studied sociology at Waseda University and went to Vantan Design Academy where he started remaking second-hand clothes while still a university student. The name of his brand ANREALAGE is derived from the combination A REAL—usual day, UN REAL—unusual day, and AGE—day. Under the motto "God is in the details", he has a meticulous approach to designing clothes, valuing the little things that go unnoticed in the rush of everyday life.

Brand history:

2003 ANREALAGE launched.

2005 Wins the Avant-Garde Grand Prix at Gen Art 2005 in New York.
Tokyo collection debut in S/S2006 at the main observatory of Tokyo Tower.

2008 S/S2009 collection under the theme "○△□" and in the form of an installation.
Consecutive collections are presented in the same manner, to display clothes not modeled after the human body.

2009 Exhibits his works at Souvenir from Tokyo at Tokyo's National Art Center and Östasiatiska Museet in Stockholm.

2010 Return to the runaway show format for S/S2011 collection under the theme " " *(The shape of air).*"
Participates in Future Beauty; 30 Years of Japanese Fashion at the Barbican in London and Haus der Kunst in Munich.

2011 Opening of a store in Harajuku, Tokyo.
Exhibits clothes specially designed for Miffy at 'miffy in fashion' at the Dick Bruna Huis in Utrecht.
Awarded the 29th Mainichi Fashion Grand Prix Newcomer's Prize.

photo:KUSHIDA(S-inc.)

h.NAOTO

廣岡直人
h.NAOTO

h.NAOTO
Naoto Hirooka

h.NAOTO, a self-confessed gothic Lolita brand, continues to advance against a background of Japanese pop culture, spanning animation, games and *visual-kei* music. The photo is from the 2010 Goth collection, which referenced romanticism and femininity in religious painting, where the brand previously emphasized destruction and rebelliousness.

h.NAOTO / Naoto Hirooka

Cool Japan Style

Interviewed by Hiroshi Narumi

h.NAOTO's rise to prominence coincided with the emergence of various Japanese subcultures. After its launch in the year 2000, the label caught the eyes of the *Visual-kei* musicians and their fans, and soon the brand's aesthetic became strongly associated with this particular genre of music. The brand invented a new style called "punk Gothic-Lolita." Since then, h.NAOTO has grown to encompass 30 different brands in response to the demands of its young clientele. Each of these 'sub-brands' caters to specific styles such as *goth*, *cosplay*, *otaku* and *anime*. This multi-faceted label has played a key role in Tokyo fashion of the 2000s.
The designer Naoto Hirooka remixes the styles of various subcultures and made them widely accessible to the Japanese fashion mainstream. h.NAOTO's decadently pop and kitsch universe illustrates the fantasies of many Japanese girls. This successful domestic brand has also gained popularity in Europe and Asia, thanks to the "Cool Japan" phenomenon, which was fueled by the export of manga, anime, and video games. h.NAOTO took its first step toward global expansion by opening a store in San Francisco in October 2011.

Launch of the brand

_ When you were in school, what kind of designers were you interested in?

Hirooka: I became interested in fashion during high school and decided to go to Bunka Fashion College. Although I knew hardly anything about fashion brands, I found 'Undercover' interesting. It was during 'the *urahara* boom'. Almost all of my friends were fans of 'Undercover'. This label represented an aspect of Tokyo's street culture that appealed to my masculine sensibility, and its collections were really interesting.
After I learned more about fashion, I became drawn to Comme des Garçons. - made trips to their shops often and saw photos and films that they produced. In the case of 'Undercover', I loved its use of details and the clever graphics on their sneakers, but Comme des Garçons presented an oeuvre I wished to study and emulate. It was amazing how they could come up with such inventive designs for each and every collection. In my third year, as I gained a deeper understanding of apparel design, I re-discovered Yohji Yamamoto. His clothes were simple yet sexy and idiosyncratic.
A simple shirt evoked a silhouette that was distinctively Yohji's.

_ How did h.NAOTO begin?

Hirooka: When I was still in school, there was a 'do-it-yourself' mentality among fashion students. Young students from the Mode Gakuen created their own fashion labels, rented a nightclub and held fashion shows every month. I wished to create my own label back then, but realistically speaking, I had to find a job to support myself. I ended up getting a job at my current employer, 'S-inc'.
In the beginning, I had an opportunity to talk with the president of the company. I got the sense that 'S-inc' was a relatively young company with a lot of potential and room for experimentation. When I joined the company in April of 2000, I started as a salesperson, after which I was transferred to the marketing department. My true passion was in making clothes. So, in my spare time, I customized clothes by other brands in the meeting room of my office. My day job was very demanding, so I did not have time to make complex alterations. What I did was mostly surface treatments. I bleached the fabric and splashed ink on top of the clothes. Then, someone from my department gave me a chance to present my ideas to our president. At the presentation, I showed him my customized creations. It was a store-bought wool jacket that I'd shrunk in a washing machine and decorated with stitches and paint. As a result of this,

the company agreed to launch the label h.NAOTO. We discussed that it was going to be based on punk aesthetics. All of this had transpired within eight months after I joined the company.

_ In the beginning, your label specialized in customizing clothes.

Hirooka: At first, I only made customized T-shirts. I applied paint splashes on new and used T-shirts from morning till night. The process had nothing to do with fashion design, but was more like action painting. My hands were always covered in ink. Basically, I stuck a bunch of T-shirts together with paint, pulled them apart the following day, put them in the washing machine and then sewed the label onto them. To my surprise, these T-shirts sold really well.
I wondered why they were so popular. As it turned out, it was the *visual-kei* musicians who started the hype for these T-shirts. They thought it was cool that the paint stains looked like blood, so they wore these T-shirts during their performances. At this point, I was not familiar with their music.
Then, their fans took notice of the T-shirts worn by their favorite bands. We started getting more and more *visual-kei* customers in our stores. We received so many orders for red T-shirts! At the time I thought my work was a natural extension of Martin Margiela and his philosophy of painted clothes. But in fact, I was just churning out clothes for the *visual-kei* musicians and their fans. Initially, I felt uncomfortable about this type of music, but I quickly got over my reservation and decided to be the best I could be and make what they wished to wear. I started printing skulls and spider motifs on top of the painted surfaces, and this style became another huge hit. Around that time, the second wave of the *visual-kei* boom arrived, with bands such as Luna Sea, L'arc en Ciel, Glay, and Pierrot leading the way. There had already been lots of fashion labels that catered to these *visual-kei* musicians,

From the h.NAOTO 03 collection in the second year since the brand's launch. With the designer's longstanding interest in punk culture, his initial collections carried a hint of romanticism (though not yet of the lolita variety) in the women's clothes, and of punk in the men's.

photo:KUSHIDA

The design on this page, Autumn/Winter 2006-2007, shows Hirooka's propensity for Gothic punk. This fantastical image consists of a dozing man in a studded black leather jacket covered with nails, which blankets his back in a wild and decorative Mohawk style. The style expresses h.NAOTO's philosophy that "clothes are for performing, not for dressing up."

but none of their styles went beyond the classic punk rock, gothic, or Lolita aesthetics. For example, in their version of punk rock outfits, the iconic Sex Pistols checkered motif and the gauze shirt typically remained unaltered. On the other hand, I experimented with combining goth and punk aesthetics, and I eventually mixed everything up. These visual-kei musicians were constantly looking out for something new and cool, and they found h.NAOTO really appealing.

_I always thought that you came from a *visual-kei* or gothic background, but you actually did not. This explains why you are so versatile in your stylistic expressions.

Hirooka: I was always interested in high fashion. While my commercial work catered to my *visual-kei* clients, I was able to integrate my personal interest in fashion into these commercial works. For example, I made items that had a goth feeling, but I would add some chains and other details that had more of a punk rock sensibility.
Originally, the goth style existed in the underground and revolved around the color black. However, the goth style at the time hadn't been associated with the distressed look until I started doing it in my work. By creating tattered, torn-up dresses with layered paint and silk-screen images, I basically came up with the 'Goth-Loli-Punk' style.
Around this time, the editor-in-chief of Kera magazine took notice of my work and he wrote a series of feature articles on my clothes. Kera had become a successful magazine during the visual-kei craze. Many other 'Gothic Lolita' magazines were launched around this time. Kera magazine gave me the opportunity to dress various *visual-kei* musicians. For the monthly photo shoots, I had to come up with many different styles for these musicians. My repertoire revolved around the goth, Lolita and punk-rock aesthetics.
It used to be the case that the *visual-kei* fans dressed the same way as their favorite bands when they went to their concerts. The more loyal the fans were, the more closely they tried to copy the musicians' looks. This *cosplay* became a legitimate aesthetic style as the popularity of the *visual-kei* musicians soared in the mainstream culture.
I do not belong to this exclusive world of cosplay. Instead, as a fashion designer, I adopted and converted their aesthetic into something palatable for mainstream consumers. My flexibility as a designer can be an advantage or a disadvantage, but for the last ten years, it has helped me expand my business in a positive way.

Growth in changing times

Hirooka: The reaction to my work was so immense that the company decided to multiply the number of brands. We created new distinctive brands that isolated the specific aesthetics like goth and Lolita. We had so many brands that I had to delegate the design work for the Lolita line to my young assistants. There was a time when we created too many spin-offs of h.NAOTO. We had Blood (goth), FRILL (Lolita), Anarchy (punk), Hn+DIE (menswear), h.jelly (Gal-kei), h.jelly&Honey (Lolita Punk), Roots (gothic-ethnic) and so on. A lot of these 'sub-brands' were derived from various collaborations with other designers. Today, we have a more stable vision for our business, and a lot of these 'sub-brands' were sorted out and reorganized.

_Instead of changing your principal label h.NAOTO, you created its offspring. you were reading the trends by observing what was happening on the street.

Hirooka: The president of S-inc makes the decisions for the brand. I am more like an actor who responds to the president's direction. My job is to supervise the designs and create marketing strategies for the new products.
Many of the designers for h.NAOTO's sub-brands are my former assistants. These designers are chosen based on their specific strengths, like an eye for detail and their skill at manipulating lace and frills. I give them opportunities to develop their skills and nurture their talents.

_You have multiplied your brands and showcased them for a limited time according to the needs of the times.

Hirooka: Basically, our business strategy is about showcasing our designers' talent. It is important for us to remain distinctive and eccentric. The market already offers so many options for consumers. Our main job is to offer something surprising. When I started the brand, the public had little knowledge of the *visual-kei* fashion. Mainstream fashion had no idea what *cosplay* was, and some were dismissive about it. But I came to specialize in this particular style because I saw the potential marketability of the *visual-kei*. As a result, the market for *visual-kei* fashion has expanded significantly. I think that the key to our future success is to keep our eyes open for things that are marginal and idiosyncratic.

_The *visual-kei* craze seems to have quieted down. How is your clientele changing?

Hirooka: Recently our customer base is shifting from *visual-kei* to *otaku*. It is hard to say who is *otaku*, because almost everyone is an otaku these days. Having said that, this shift in our clientele started when we began collaborating with the popular voice actors and actresses of anime programs. The fans of these voice actors became our new clients.
Goth-Loli, which was initially derived from the *visual-kei* craze, is now divided into two sub-groups: one of them caters to the fans of certain bands and the other is for anime fans and *otaku*. These days it's difficult to tell them apart from their appearances. In the past, *otaku* would typically be boys who indulged in their secret fantasy about animation characters, but now, there are more and more girls who unabashedly declare themselves *otaku*.
The Comic Market at Tokyo Big Sight attracts up to 500,000 visitors from all over the country, and there are many similar events in other countries too, such as the Japan Expo in France and the Anime Expo in the United States. People go to these events to feel free to share their love of certain fashion, anime, Super Dollfie and Blythe dolls. Today, Japanese girls in their twenties don't know much about luxury brands and high fashion. Instead, their attention is directed toward Goth-Loli styles and the street styles of Shibuya 109. When I talked to some students from Bunka Fashion College, they expressed their dream of designing clothes for the 'kyaba-kei' brands (a style resembling girls working at hostess clubs) sold in shopping malls like Lumine. They are not interested in foreign fashion labels at all. Niche fashion magazines also play a big role in shaping and influencing this trend. The number of 'Gal' and 'Goth-Loli' magazines has only increased in the last five to six years. I think that the *visual-kei* boom is on its way out. The height of the boom was around 2005. Today, there is no longer any

clear distinction among anime, *cosplay*, and *visual-kei* demographics. A young beautiful man with *visual-kei* makeup could be emulating an anime character, and many *visual-kei* bands are writing anime songs. The line between the two demographics is completely blurred.

Making clothes for the subcultures

_ The street styles, rather than your own aesthetic statement, have shaped your perspective throughout your career. What is your policy on making clothes?

Hirooka: First and foremost, my policy is providing what my customers are looking for. As a designer, my job is not about transmitting or imposing my vision on the consumer. Rather, I would like to form a bond with my customers and exchange inspirations with them.
I have no intention of making my own collections. I have participated in the Tokyo Collections but it was about being part of the event, not about showing my own collection. I brought my one-of-a-kind, unique samples that were never mass-produced.
For planning our products, we usually come up with a theme for the year and design new products based on this theme. We try to come up with the perfect balance between the classics, bestsellers and the new and experimental products. We have seasonal themes, but the core of our creation is the same every season. We change certain aspects of the details, like hand-written letters or dyes. Fundamentally, our style is punk rock. It is about coming up with different treatments of the same material every year. I was told that fashion was about creating something new every season. But look at Levi's: they consistently work with denim and they only change the forms and the rivets periodically. I believe we follow the same principle. If we changed our styles every season, our customers wouldn't be able to follow us. Punk is the integral part of our brand aesthetic. As long as we hold on to it, we will be able to come up with original ideas. We will change our designs based on the big picture in order to maintain and expand our brands.

_ How do you communicate with your clients?

Hirooka: We often organize special events, exhibitions and parties to build a strong relationship with our customers. These events become special occasions for our clients to dress up in our clothes. Advertising in fashion magazines has never been very effective for us. Instead, we make our own newspapers, organize events, and run a high quality website for our customers.
In fact, girls don't have a lot of places where they can wear h.NAOTO, except when they go to Harajuku or to concerts and special events. When girls from small towns outside of Tokyo come to our events, they change their clothes in the bathrooms of train stations and slip into their h.NAOTO outfits. They carry huge bags with extra sets of clothing, and they change their outfits to go to different concert events. They are so innocent and sincere, and that makes me happy. At my show during the Tokyo Fashion Week, my customers showed up in brand new wardrobes they'd bought just for this occasion.
Some of our customers buy our clothes, even though they will wear them only once. Some customers let their clothes sit in their closets. Some of them purchase huge amounts of clothes at our sales exhibitions. There are even collectors who rent an apartment just for storing their wardrobes. It's really incredible how many pieces of clothing they own. But my customers sincerely enjoy the experiences of dressing up. They told me that they work jobs just so that they can buy our clothes.

_ What do you keep in mind as a designer?

Hirooka: I always try to be different from my competitors. There are so many Goth-Loli labels in Japan these days. I would rather walk away from the Goth-Loli style if everyone were doing the same thing. I wouldn't collaborate with musicians if everyone else was doing it too. h.NAOTO shouldn't be lumped in with the rest of these fashion labels. I need to continue discovering new, unknown territories, otherwise these other designers will catch up with me soon.
In the beginning, it scared me to be the pioneer. I'm happy about the risks I've taken, because they have led h.NAOTO to gain a huge amount of recognition.
I don't rely on any marketing research. I let my inspiration guide my work. My inspiration comes from my desire to improve myself, as well as listening to positive responses from my clients.
h.NAOTO distinguishes itself from other Goth-Loli brands because it has a fashion designer representing the label. The designers of other Goth-Loli brands do not necessarily think of themselves as fashion designers with a capital F. For example, the designer for Baby, the Stars Shine Bright is a Lolita enthusiast in her private life. Similarly, the designer of alice auaa embodies the goth lifestyle and creates the goth-inspired designs as well. I, on the other hand, do not identify myself with either goth or Lolita. What motivates me is my desire to come up with new, creative fashion designs. My work has seen me crowned as the king of Goth-Loli, and I was able to secure a certain place in this Japanese subculture. However, I wouldn't want to stay in this realm of Japanese subculture forever. I will have to figure out how to move on.

Feedback from overseas

_ In 2010, h.NAOTO was extensively featured in the exhibition titled "Japan Fashion Now" at the The Museum at the Fashion Institute of Technology in New York. I hear that you are quite popular in the United States.

Hirooka: For the past couple of years, I have been participating in the Otakon in the U.S. and the Japan Expo in France. These conventions principally deal with anime and video games. I initially exhibited the characters representing some of our brands. But there was one occasion when I exhibited our fashion items. The response was huge. So we decided to sell more clothing at these events. In the last two years, we have been rigorously marketing our clothes in the United States. I was surprised at the level of h.NAOTO's international recognition. Our American fans tend to be more openly passionate about our brand. Similarly, the visual-kei musicians receive overwhelming responses when they play live at the Otakon. A lot of these musicians travel to the United States to perform live on the regular basis. The American fans of these visual-kei bands are quite familiar with h.NAOTO. We also collaborate with the manufacturers of dolls like Blythe and Super Dollfie, so people who like these dolls seem to be buying our clothes as well.
In the United States there seem to be two types of customers. Some people consider h.NAOTO to be a *cosplay* brand and they purchase our clothes to wear them as costumes. Some customers buy them as clothing they can wear everyday.

The collaboration with SUPER DOLFIE in 2006 gave h.NAOTO access to the world of dolls and made "Gothic Lolita" a household word. Shown here is the line called NAOTO SEVEN, which started in 2008; the pieces such as black jackets, platform shoes, lacing, chains, safety pins, and skull accessories represent Gothic Lolita and the Harajuku feel. These were exhibited at an event called the Dolls Party.

Detail from an artwork by h.NAOTO. This 300-piece collage, produced in 2008, forms a sequence of 300 letters that can be turned into 300 separate postcards. The full text is as follows:

h.NAOTOGOTHLOLIPUNK
ANIMEANIMALMONKEY
YELLOWJAPTOYOTATOK
YOKYOTOGEISHAKABUK
IGAYGUYFUCKYOUMOTH
ERFATHERBLOODREDWI
NEBREADEATFATPIGPIN
KWINKGALLARDWHITE
BLACKLUCKSHITASSKIS
SGASWEAPONPHILPOND
RUGKILLWARCOLORTER
RORBOMBBODYBONEDEA
THHELLHELPMEGODEGO
EROSSEXHOMEHATEHUN
GRYPOORANGRYPOWER
MONEYGAMEOVERSAVEL
OVEEARTHBIRTH

Many of our clients in the United States are art school students, goth fans, and eccentric older women who like to match our clothes with their cute backpacks.

_We can almost feel the global energy of Japanese subcultures.

Hirooka: In the United States, young people in their twenties associate Japan with Japanese cultural exports such as anime and video games. They have experienced the full effect of Japanese subcultures. Some of them even speak Japanese! People overseas really enjoy contemporary Japanese subcultures much more than I expected. It is exciting to figure out how we can develop our international market in such a promising global context.
Today, we need to focus on our global clientele from the United States and China. There is so much purchasing power in the customers outside of Japan. These days, it is not uncommon to see customers from Hong Kong and the rest of Asia travelling to Harajuku to buy our clothes. For them, flying to Tokyo to go shopping is an acceptable distance. When I hear Chinese being spoken in our Tokyo stores, I can't help but realize that Asia is a single market, undivided by international borders.
Yoshiki from X Japan and Sugizo from Luna Sea used to tell me that things have changed so much for them lately. Their international fans have embraced their music whole-heartedly, and they no longer feel the pressure to conform to the international standard in order to export their music abroad. In our brand's case, I used to think that we would have to adopt ourselves to the American and French markets. I never expected that our brand would become a global success by remaining true to who we are. I am so happy that we have kept working hard to experience such a positive change in the scene.

From h.NAOTO 2009., h.NAOTO has been participating in the Tokyo Collections since Spring/ Summer 2008. The theme for 2009 was "Crime and Punishment". Shown here is an image from Autumn/ Winter. The style incorporates military elements but the pastel blue wig gives it a look reminiscent of anime.

COLLECTIONS

2000. Hirooka launched his own brand a year after joining S-inc. The first h.NAOTO collection consisted exclusively of t-shirts; these were elaborate designs borrowing heavily from punk styles, with some ripped and others painted. These created a sensation thanks to the *visual kei* musicians that took notice of them. This is where h.NAOTO started in full swing.

2001. At first, h.NAOTO's designs were an action rather than a fashion. They were created by dyeing, degrading, and destroying ready-made clothes.

2002. Active collaborations with *visual kei* musicians. This period saw the first development of the concept of "Gothic Lolita Punk". The brand grows rapidly along with the boom in *visual kei* bands.

2003. Opening of two flagship stores in the backstreets of Harajuku: H and h.. The number of chain stores expanded and more subsidiary brands were added.

2004. Opening of the first flagship store in the Kansai area. Hirooka designs the tour costumes for singer Gackt. A further increase in sub-brands.

2005. Launch of the HANGRY & ANGRY brand. Hirooka opens the shop h.NAOTO hEAVEN in Harajuku, which became a space to show the world view of the brands spawned through his various concepts. His book "h.NAOTO Winter Collection" was published at the same time. Sub-brands continued to multiply prolifically, including "DARK RED RUM" with its decadent image, "CHANNEL H" with its cosplay theme, the Gothic mode of "NAOTO SEVEN", "Cupid H" targeted at children, etc.

2006. Gothic Lolita dominated the year thanks to the release of the film "NANA." h.NAOTO's collections became highly decorative at this point.

2007. Launch of a brand called Sixh., designed by IBI and MINT, as Gothic Lolita reaches its peak in popularity. Its central concept was the "Gothic Visual kei host." Hirooka developed a strategy that focused on a rising interest in men's fashion in Tokyo.

2008. First participation in the Tokyo Collections. Hirooka carried out his runway shows in two consecutive seasons, Spring/Summer and Autumn/Winter. The theme throughout the year was "Pelvis and Amniotic Fluid." His vision of world history as a tragedy of religion and war expressed a strong degree of nihilism, while the unique perspective "our skeletons are wisdom, the pelvis is a gender" equalled death to an end without flesh: "Violence and decadence after a final war. The birth and death of distorted animals affected by nuclear radiation. The birth of new life beyond the long dark ages. Towards the fountain of amniotic fluid... Gothic + Lolita + Punk + Anime + 'amniotic fluid'." Hirooka actively produced several artworks, including collages and films, in addition to clothes, and worked on turning Gothic Lolita into more than just a street fashion.

2009. The Spring/Summer 2009 collection, his third participation in the Tokyo Collections, took place under the theme of "Crime and Punishment", which it linked to seven deadly sins, including "the sin of narcissism and rape," "the sin of self-defense and counterattack," and "the sin of autosynnoia and love/hate." The collection demonstrated a sexier approach to punkishness, close to bondage fashion. Hirooka started the project h.ism to pursue "a collaboration for new creation beyond fashion and music" and supported the debuts of the bands GaGaalinG, HANGRY & ANGRY-f and MarBell. HANGRY & ANGRY-f is a *visual kei* group consisting of two women, Hitomi Yoshizawa and Rika Ishikawa, which evolved from a kitten character created in 2004.

2010. Opening of the flagship store h.NAOTO+ in Harajuku. Hirooka organized a fashion show during X-JAPAN's reunion concert, and launched the brand "N.Y" as a collaboration with X-JAPAN member YOSHIKI. Fellow band member SUGIZO took part in the h.ism project. Hirooka's new collection saw clothes in extreme styles named after torture devices. In the same period, he took his first steps overseas and became the only Japanese to participate in the "JAPAN FASHION NOW" exhibit at The Museum at FIT in New York, where he presented a fashion show and took part in a symposium. HANGRY & ANGRY-f also performed at the event.

2011. Opening of a shop in San Francisco. Hirooka presented his collection under the theme of "MONSTER," expressing femininity through the act of not wearing but removing clothes. Furthermore, the 8 SWEET LOLITA PARTY was set up in conjunction with his Lolita line FRILL: a series of monthly events hosted by Misako Aoki, renowned Lolita model and Japan's official "Cute Ambassador."

h.NAOTO

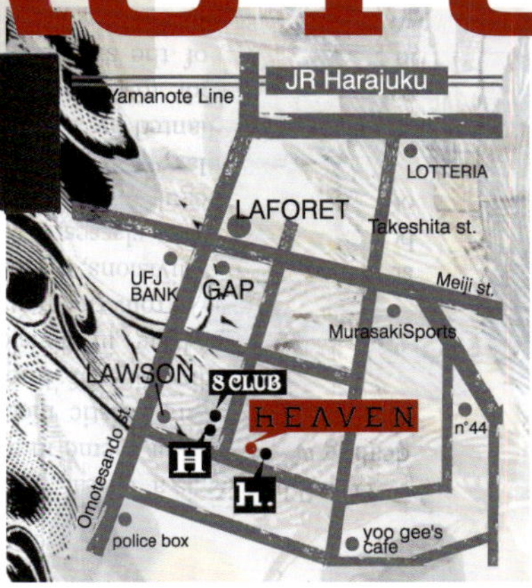

Designer's profile:
h. NAOTO / Naoto Hirooka

Naoto Hirooka was born in Hyogo in 1977. After graduating from Bunka Fashion College, he joined S-inc. in 1999. His brand h.NAOTO made its debut in the Spring/Summer of 2000. Identifying with the idea of "extreme punk," he expanded his unique views about fashion by assimilating Japanese subcultures such as gothic-lolita and *visual-kei*. He gained countless fans thanks to his high popularity among artists and musicians at home and abroad. He works and designs as a creative director by crossing the boundaries between music, film, cartoons, animation, game, dolls, pro-wrestling, art, etc.

Brand history:
2000 h.NAOTO launched by S-inc.
2005 Starts h.NAOTO hEAVEN to pursue a mix of fashion and art.
Co-designs stage costumes with Gackt for his show.
2006 Co-designs figures with Super Dollfie.
2008 Tokyo Collection debut.
NAOTO SEVEN line launched.
2009 Starts h. ism project to pursue a mix of fashion and music.
2010 N.Y,, a collaboration line with Yoshiki of X JAPAN, released in Japan and overseas.
Participated in the Japan Fashion Now exhibition at The Museum at FIT.
2011 Opening of the first overseas store in San Francisco.

keisuke kanda

art direction:Masaya Muto(NO DESIGN) photo:Seiji Ishigaki(BLOCKBUSTER)

ケイスケカンダ
神田恵介

keisuke kanda
Keisuke Kanda

keisuke kanda

Keisuke Kanda

神田恵介

ケイスケカンダ

"The flag of the Rising Sun with a collection of the girls' autographs written by myself "(produced by Keisuke Kanda, 2011)
(The idea of this work was drived by a custom during the war to inscribe words on the flag of the Rising Sun)

keisuke kanda / keisuke kanda

Back to the Source of 'Sweetness'

Interviewed by Mariko Nishitani

In 2005, Keisuke Kanda established his eponymous label with an eye on business. His brand was initially called Candyrock, which he started during college. His unique business operation sets his label apart from his contemporaries. Although Keisuke Kanda is mainly mass-produced today, the designer continues making customized and hand-sewn items. He tours around Japan to take pre-orders for his custom clothes at Happyokai (presentations). Today, the number of his clients exceeds one thousand. Last year, Kanda shared an anecdote about his first love during a public lecture he gave about his design philosophy. The designer confessed that, at the very beginning of his career, he fell hopelessly in love with a girl, so he made a dress for her. But the young designer did not feel courageous enough to give her the dress and tell her how he felt about her. Kanda explained that his unfulfilled love drove him to pursue a career in fashion and motivated him to be creative. How could an unpopular boy win a girl's heart? In Kanda's case, he sought to answer this question by making clothes bejeweled with pretty details that many girls find attractive, such as ribbons, lace and polka dots. Keisuke Kanda slowly emerged into the Japanese fashion scene with this bittersweet story in the background. Instead of using various conventional PR tools, the designer prefers having direct communications with his clients and uses word-of-mouth marketing. This primitive business strategy seems to give the designer an unmitigated power to challenge and dismantle the pre-existing system of the fashion industry. Since he does not expose himself to the media often, this interview will be an invaluable resource for those who wish to learn about keisuke kanda in depth.

Encounter with Fashion

_ You've often said that you gravitated toward fashion because you were not popular with girls. Is that really true?

Kanda: Generally speaking, when you are in an inferior position, you tend to look upwards and have all sorts of fantasies. You would say to yourself, "I wish I could live like that, if only I were rich." If you were unpopular, you would have a fantasy about going on a specific kind of date with a pretty girl. But people's fantasies are not directed the other way around. If you were already popular with girls, you would never fantasize about the life of an unpopular guy. People's aspirations and fantasies will never be about heading down from the top.

_ So when you were in school, were you trying to become popular by being stylish?

Kanda: I wasn't stylish at all. My mother bought all of my clothes until I was in high school. I was dorky and completely indifferent about fashion. I had an inferiority complex. I thought that stylish people were annoying. Perhaps all of these pent-up feelings have become a source of energy for me.

_ How did such a gloomy young man suddenly wake up to fashion?

Kanda: I started attending a university where students came from diverse backgrounds. My world suddenly became bigger after I left my insular high school community. In college, I became good friends with someone who was into fashion for the first time in my life. He enjoyed fashion as much as he enjoyed my favorite manga, literature and music. I was shocked to see how savvy he was about the whole thing. Thanks to his inspiration, I started feeling more and more familiar with fashion. Before I knew it, I fell in love with fashion. I was a brainy kid back then. At first, I liked talking about fashion theories using difficult vocabulary. I was enthralled by Roland Barthes' writing "The Fashion System". I was even the type of person who liked to transcribe Kiyokazu Washida's writings about fashion into a notebook. I loved his book "Chiguhagu na karada" (An Ill-assorted Body). I thought that I understood fashion intellectually.

But I gradually discovered the pure joy of fashion. I started dressing up in my favorite designers' clothes and tried to get in touch with the designer's world-view. First, I tried to understand fashion intellectually, and gradually, I allowed myself to enjoy fashion for all it's worth. Usually, people go through these phases the other way around (laughs). I was in heaven when I came into contact with the world of Comme des Garçons, Maison Martin Margiela, Undercover, Christopher Nemeth, 20471120[1], and so on. I was fascinated to hear that Shinichiro Arakawa[2] held impromptu fashion shows at a shopping arcade in Shimokitazawa and the Komaba student dormitories at Tokyo University. I saw an article about 'burnt' clothes by Takayuki Suzuki[3] in an issue of So-en magazine, and I found it really moving. At this point, fashion had become more about a sense of exaltation and passion rather than intellectual ideas. In 1998, I started making clothes on my own. At the time, I had a crush on a girl, and I wanted to give her a dress that I'd made for her. In the end, I didn't have the courage to give it to her.
I continued making more clothes even though my secret love for her remained unrequited. In my third year in college, I held a fashion show of the clothes that I had made and accumulated up until that point.

_ That was your first show. The following year in 1999, when you were in your fourth year at the university, you did a solo fashion show on a moving train.[4] At the time, your label was still called Candyrock[5] and not Keisuke Kanda.

Kanda: I held a show but I had no idea how to put a price on my clothes and sell them. I didn't even think about doing a presentation. I just wanted people to come and see my work.

The decision to become a professional designer — The launch of keisuke kanda

Kanda: In 2005, when I did my first keisuke kanda show at the Tokyo Tower with Kunihiko Morinaga (designer of the fashion label ANREALAGE), I made up my mind to become a professional designer and pursue my career in fashion.

_ Morinaga was your junior at the preparatory school and the university you both attended.

Kanda: He was three years my junior, but he started his career as a fashion designer before I did. I was still hesitant about pursuing fashion design as a business. I was still going after my ideals. After I graduated from the university, I started attending evening courses at Bunka Fashion College. I was a student until I was twenty-six years old. At that time, I was doing shows, making books and presenting both of them as my collections, but these activities were still at an amateur level. Morinaga told me, "Keisuke, your clothes should be known to the world." He woke me up. That was the only time he gave me advice. His words pushed me to do a fashion show with him. He dragged me onto the stage. We decided that we might as well go big and do a fashion show at Tokyo Tower.

_ What kind of collection did you present at that time?

Kanda: The collection was pretty much similar to the clothes I make today: customized vintage cardigans, T-shirts with Rising Sun graphics, hand-sewn jeans, etc. After our fashion show at Tokyo Tower, Morinaga and I shared another venue to present our individual collections. Unfortunately, all of the retail shop buyers were there for Morinaga's ANREALAGE. I hardly sold anything (laughs).

Illustration for the "Quilt" collection, Autumn/Winter 2008-2009

Displays for the "Dress-up T-shirts Exhibit" at specialty store Lamp harajuku, Tokyo. Birdcages displayed an assortment of collars, sleeves, and pockets. May, 2011. Photo by Lamp harajuku

_ Comme des Garçons also used a Rising Sun motif in 2006. It has been a taboo for Japanese designers who wish to assimilate themselves into the world of Parisian fashion.

Kanda: In my case, I do not have that kind of concern toward the West. I started engaging myself with fashion because I wanted to make a dress for the girl I liked. Perhaps my involvement in fashion is quite different from the way other designers engage with fashion. People have told me that I need to be more aware of the history of fashion in the West and to create my work based on my understanding of these historical contexts. But I don't really understand what they're talking about.

_ You created a graphic image of a Rising Sun treading over the Statue of Liberty. Was it an expression of your own personal anti-American feeling?

Kanda: It was not really a political message. It was more like a rebellious feeling a teenage son would have against his father. I have no resentment against the United States. It was just a childish expression of rebellion, like what little boys do. I wanted to capture this kind of 'anti-establishment' spirit in a graphic image on my T-shirts.

A unique system based on hand sewing

_ When did you start developing your hand-sewing techniques?

Kanda: It started out as a rather pathetic story. Actually, I wanted to create T-shirts on my own, but all I had was a sewing machine that could only make stitches in a straight line. It was impossible to sew T-shirts with it. So I began sewing T-shirts by hand, and the result came out fine. In the beginning, it was out of necessity that everything was hand sewn. Later on, hand-sewn stitches started giving certain meanings to my designs.

_ Recently, hand sewing has become an important trend in fashion.

Kanda: Certainly. Hand sewing has been used as a decorative accent, like adding spice, but for me, hand sewing is an essential part of my work. What I wanted to do was to sew the foundation of clothing by hand. In my case, hand sewing is like a pot of soup stock for a chef, rather than a spice. It may not be evident, but perhaps people can slowly come to understand the meaning of hand sewing. On the other hand, I don't mind if people do not get it. After all, I'm not doing it to enchant an audience. I would rather not make it into a strategy for my work. I started sewing by hand because

I had to. It was a desperate choice. I can't answer the question whether hand sewing equals 'fashion' or not. Making something by hand allows me to have better control over my work. In this way, I convey my spirit into my creation.

_ Today, you have even established your own hand-sewing production system.

Kanda: Around 2007, I was no longer able to meet the demands for my clothes on my own. My business started to take off and I couldn't let sewing monopolize my time any more. I started receiving a huge volume of orders, which was beyond my capacity. It was great, but I did not want to outsource my production to standard sewing factories. It would have changed the whole meaning of my work. I figured that I would have to create a new production system from scratch if none of the pre-existing systems for mass production allowed me to create the kinds of clothes I wished to make.

_ In your case, you had a direct relationship with your customers by meeting them face-to-face at your shows. You probably did not want to let them down by switching to mass-production at sewing factories.

Kanda: It didn't even occur to me to change my work.

All girls cherish the 'kawaii' (super cute) feelings

_ I find your clothes 'kawaii.' Where does this sensibility in your work come from?

Kanda: To this day, I still do not know what 'kawaii' stands for. For me, *kawaii* is something mysterious. One thing that I know for sure is that I love girls, and *kawaii* is a feeling that all girls tend to cherish. I want to please a bunch of girls and hopefully in return, they will turn toward me. This is basically the reason why I challenge myself to create *kawaii* clothes. Keisuke Kanda is based on a sequence of trial and error. Perhaps my constant perseverance in search of the essence of 'kawaii' has allowed me to find my own expression for it. I am constantly searching for this intangible quality. If I had gotten an answer to what kawaii signifies, I would probably be further away from its essence. *Kawaii* is truly elusive. Perhaps I'd better not chase after it. When I create women's clothes, I often ask girls for their opinions: "Look, I don't really understand what I'm making. Do you find these *kawaii*?" Actually, I am not interested in expressing my own aesthetics at all. All I'm doing is seeking approval from girls.

Proposals for a new type of a tribal robe

_ Since your last season, you have created and presented special wardrobes for a fictitious tribe called "Uragoi-zoku" (Tribe of secret love). Could you tell me about these?

Kanda: When I was still approaching fashion from an intellectual perspective, I was very much intrigued by ethnic costumes and did a lot of research on

art direction:Shohei Oyagi(HioN COMPANY)

The invitations for each season's "presentation" are always unique. On the left is the "summer gift towel" invite for the Spring/Summer 2011 show, which featured clothes made from towels. On the right is the "ribbon medicine" invitation for Autumn/Winter 2011-2012, consisting of mediecine envelopes filled with ribbons.

illustration:Momoko Kimura

初恋てろりすと

心恋族

Rather than using photography, Keisuke Kanda communicates his image of "kawaii" through these delicate and atmospheric drawings, which appeal to girls. Momoko Kimura on the left and Kana Shoji on the right are iconic figures. On the left is "Hatsukoi Terrorist" displayed at the "Neo Cos" exhibition held at WALL, Laforet Harajuku, in Autumn 2010, and the collection of Uragoizoku from Spring/Summer 2011. On the right is the look book for Spring/Summer 2011. Clockwise from top left: Work pants made by hand / Quilt and air raid hood with embroidered ribbons / White bear / Duffel down coat made from towels / Children's wear ccmbines into a skirt / Parka with floral design / Oversized salopette of ribbon quilt / Satin stadium jumper with flower garden quilt.

illustration:Kana Shoji

production:MUD SNAIL

"Plastic Model Ribbon Warrior for Girls", accessory kits of ribbons launched in 2009 that became a big hit. The kit is shown above. Below, the image design for Spring/Summer 2009. On the right is the image visual of the season. Photo: Masashi Asada.

them. In recent years, I've noticed the trend in "tribal fashion" on the streets of Tokyo. They tend to look so banal, like a poor imitation of a certain fashion brand. I thought that their looks were a disgrace to authentic tribal costumes. It may be presumptuous of me to say so, but I wanted to give my own response to this shameful situation. My attempt was not to create something based on actual ethnic costume design, but to take them in a completely different direction. I came up with an image of a tribal costume that had faint and ambivalent qualities, as opposed to the strong and distinctive qualities seen in real tribal costumes. I took a hint from the ancient Japanese concept of uragoi, which means 'to love someone secretly in one's heart', and I started constructing an image and my world-view around this concept.

_ This has nothing to do directly with your concept, but I remember *Karasu-zoku* (the Crow Tribe), which was all the rage in 1980s Japan – this tribe of fashionable men and women who wore black clothes by fashion labels like Comme des Garçons.
Kanda: Actually, I was thinking about

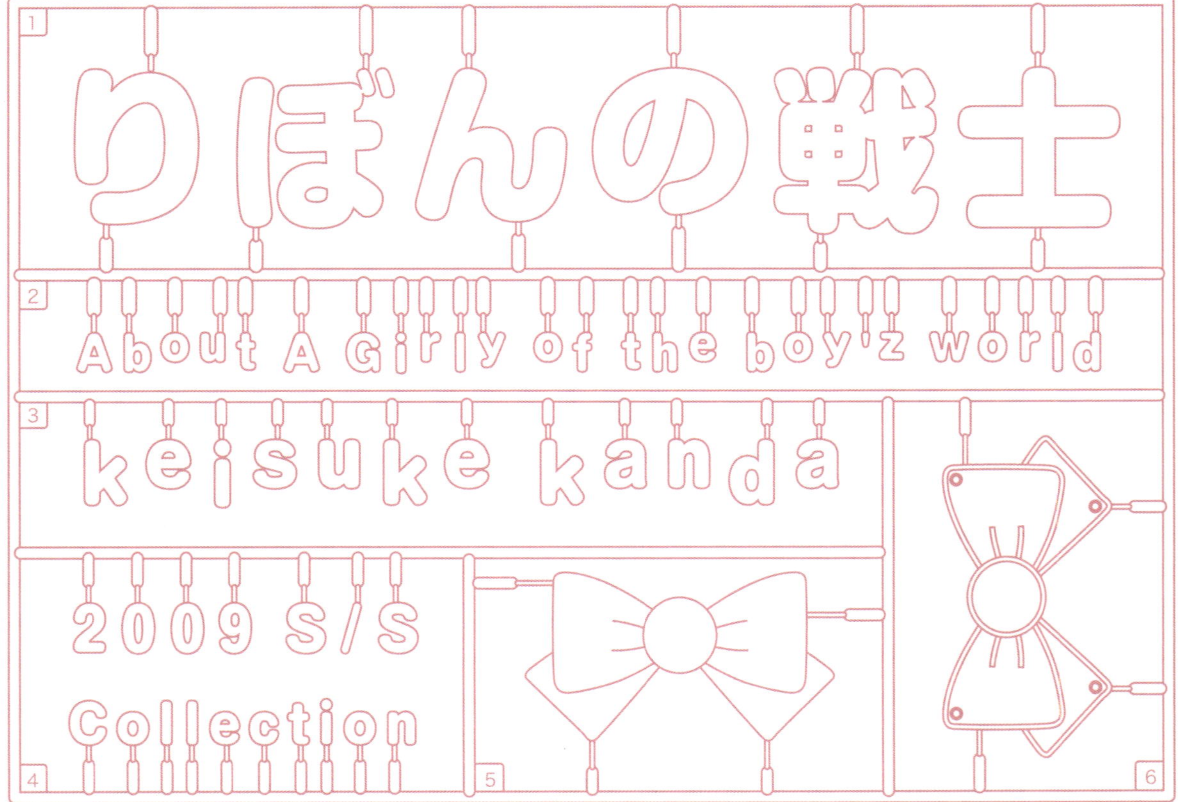

art direction:Shohei Oyagi(HioN COMPANY)

photo:Masashi Asada

The "Handsewn cardigan" is one of keisuke kanda's representative creations. It was made by piecing together worn-out, everyday cardigans. Colors include white, beige, blue, brown, and black, but the line-up changes each season.

photo:Tohru Yuasa(B.P.B.)

Karasu-zoku when I came up with my idea for the *Uragoi-zoku*.

_ Do you think that people are actually forming a tribe around your concept of *Uragoi-zoku*?

Kanda: Yes, I do. It is not as obvious as *Karasu-zoku*, but I think it's slowly taking shape. I stick to the word "zoku," (tribe) because I have the aspiration to turn *Uragoi-zoku* into a fashion/cultural phenomenon like the *Karasu-zoku* or *Takenoko-zoku* in the past.[6] Those phenomena were exclusively reserved for youths and were incomprehensible to older generations. We are not having fun unless we're making grown-ups wonder, "Why are these youngsters dressed like that?"

Collaboration with the photographer Masashi Asada

_ You are collaborating with the up-and-coming photographer, Masashi Asada. What is your intention with this collaborative project?

Kanda: We've known each other since the early days of our careers and we always wanted to do something together. He's been to many of my presentations and bought a lot of clothes from me. I have always been a big fan of his photography as well.

_ Did you make the suit that Mr. Asada wore at the ceremony of the Kimura Ihei Award in 2009?

Kanda: Yes, I did. When I saw Masashi early this year, he proposed to make something like yearbook photos together. Masashi has been taking photos of various families all over Japan, following the style of his award-winning photography book called "Asada-ke" (The Asada Family). We took inspiration from this particular project by Masashi and decided to travel all over Japan to take photos of high school kids. These high school students would be wearing one-of-a-kind school uniforms that I specially designed for them. I was convinced that this would be an exciting project for us. In my past collections, I have made a lot of clothes inspired by school uniforms such as sailor suits, *gakuran* (Japanese boys' school uniforms inspired by Prussian army uniforms), cardigans, jersey track suits and so on. I had seen Masashi's work in progress before he finished his book "Asada-ke", and I already knew he would be a big deal in the future. His work is really powerful.

_ Japan gave rise to a number of internationally acclaimed art photographers such as Daido Moriyama, Nobuyoshi Araki, Takashi Homma, and Rinko Kawauchi. But we have not seen many Japanese fashion photographers on the world-class level. I have always found this situation frustrating. I was thrilled to hear about the two of you collaborating on a photography project. I am sure that your project will be a break-through for Japanese fashion photography.

Kanda: Thank you for your compliment. In this project, we are basically interested in making serious fashion photography. It would be nice to have many fashion magazines feature more photos like ours in the future.

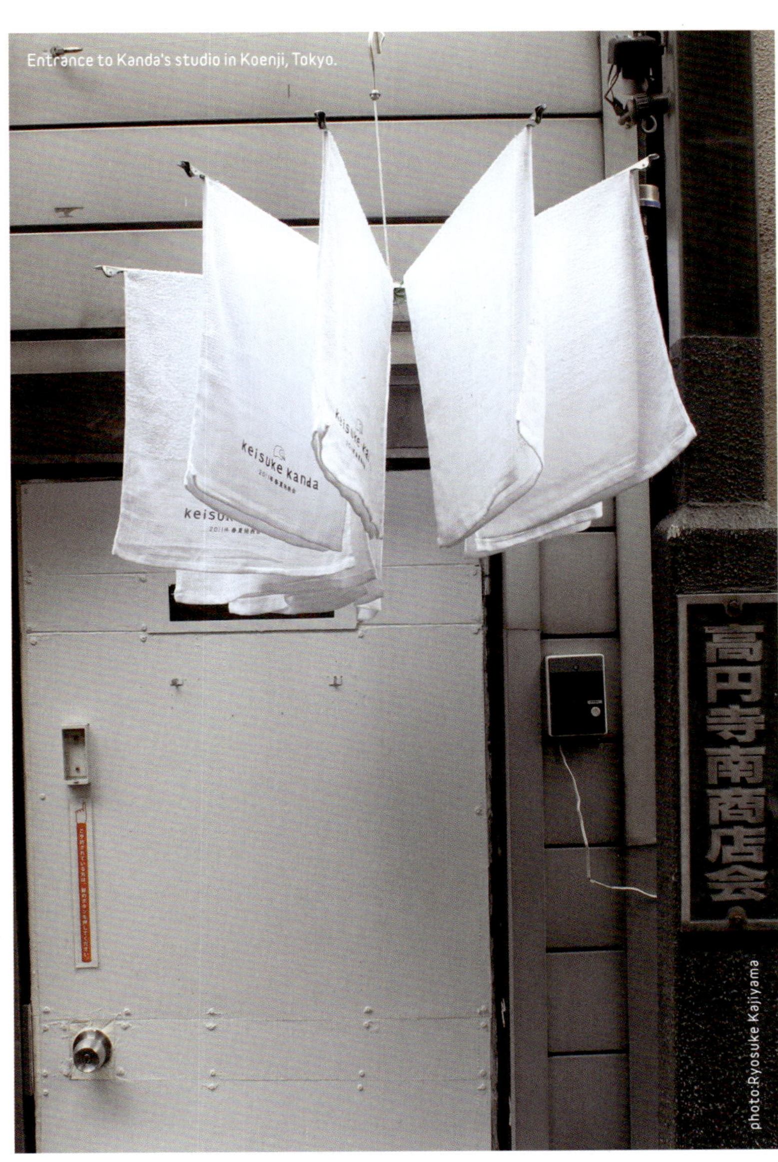

Entrance to Kanda's studio in Koenji, Tokyo.

photo:Ryosuke Kajiyama

illustration:Momoko Kimura

Notes:

1 20471120 is a fashion label established by Masahiro Nakagawa and Lica in 1992 in Osaka, Japan. The label, originally called Tra Venti, was renamed 20471120 in 1995 after the designers moved from Osaka to Tokyo in 1994. The label took the Japanese fashion scene by storm with its use of impressive forms inspired by the Japanese anime "Neon Genesis Evangelion," their invention of an original mascot named Hyoma and their spectacular fashion show which used a helicopter as a prop.

2 Shinichiro Arakawa started his eponymous label in Paris after graduating from the Parisian fashion college, Studio Berçot. In 1997, the designer moved to Tokyo. His creations based on original tailoring techniques and impromptu shows at a shopping arcade in Shimokitazawa and the Komaba student dormitories at the Tokyo University resonated with a younger generation of aspiring Japanese designers. Today, Arakawa's activity mainly consists of designing motorcycle apparel for Honda.

3 Takayuki Suzuki studied graphic design at Tokyo Zokei University and taught himself dressmaking skills. After a period of making theater costumes and presenting his sartorial creations as works of art, Suzuki started his eponymous label "suzuki takayuki" in 2002 characterized by handcrafted details and the use of sustainable, organic materials.

4 In 1999, during his fourth year at the prestigious Waseda University, Keisuke Kanda sent out invitations and train tickets to journalists and presented an unauthorized, impromptu show aboard a moving train of the Keio-Inokashira Line departing from Kichijoji, Tokyo. The show by Kanda's fashion label Candyrock was held during the quiet hour on a holiday. The spectators watched the models walking down the aisle from the comfort of their seats. The show ended successfully, but upon arrival at the terminus of Shibuya, Kanda was arrested by the railway police. Thanks to the intervention of a journalist from the newspaper *Asahi Shimbun* who attended the show, Kanda was soon released.

5 Candyrock was the title of the seminar courses taught by Keisuke Kanda's mentor and professor Shoji Nishitani. Kanda got permission from his professor and named his label after it.

6 "Karasu-zoku" (the Crow Tribe), a term coined by Japanese mass media in the mid-1980s, was a tribe of fashionable youth dressed head to toe in black. Black became a very popular color in Japan after the success of Japanese labels such as Comme des Garçons and Yohji Yamamoto on the Parisian fashion scene. Other domestic labels emulated their style, and the all-black look became the rage in the 1980s. "Takenoko-zoku" (Bamboo Shoot Tribe) was the name of a group of young men and women dressed in colorful ethnic-inspired costumes from the Boutique Takenoko on Takeshita-dori street in Harajuku. Since the beginning of the 1980s, the group gathered at the pedestrian-only promenades between Harajuku station and Yoyogi Park and danced to disco music.

COLLECTIONS

Spring/Summer 2006, ***Handsewn dress.*** A one-piece suit made from old rice bags. Making use of the texture of distressed fabrics to give dresses a romantic appearance remains one of Keisuke Kanda's favorite methodologies.

Spring/Summer 2007, ***Denim School Uniform.*** School uniforms form a steady part of Kanda's collections. Some are uniform coats with stand-up collars, others include sailor-suits, cardigans, V-necked sweaters, shirts, and duffel coats. These items themselves are familiar to anyone, but Kanda changes their meaning and sweeps away their stiff and prosaic style. What results are beguiling dresses that have never existed before. Shown here is a male student's uniform coat made from pieced-together worn-out jeans. It is typical of the brand that this is a coat in denim, yet not a denim jacket.

Spring/Summer 2008, ***Piko Piko Blouse.*** A series that was produced under the theme of "Dresses in the world of computer games." The analog feel of a handmade item and the digital feel of computer design coexist in same clothes, whose outline and lace were designed and cut to look like dots.

Autumn/Winter 2009-2010, ***Trouser of the Imperial Japanese Army.*** While American and European second-hand clothes remain popular, Japanese prewar clothes are hardly thought of as fashionable. This may stem from a general sense of aversion to militarism in Japanese society. Keisuke Kanda, however, exhibited his new collection by consciously employing the term "Imperial Japanese Army," which could be understood as his desire to shake off taboos of all types. The trouser of the Imperial Japanese Army is transformed into something entirely new thanks to the addition of various lovely details.

2011 S/S

2010-2011 A/W

2011 S/S

2011-2012 A/W

Autumn/Winter 2010-2011, ***Gingham Aran Sweater.*** Some of the classic items by keisuke kanda are the horizontally striped or block-checkered t-shirts and sweatshirts printed entirely by hand. Shown above on page 78 is a second-hand aran sweater printed with gingham check, which modifies the bulky sweater's rough image. Seen below: "Children's wear combines into a skirt." From early on, Kanda has been making clothes for adults by piecing together those of children. Their small sizes and cheap details add touches of humor by playing with opposites.

Spring/Summer 2011, ***Sailor suit made from Antique Lace.*** A school uniform designed by Kanda, much like the boys' cardigan and uniform. Though taking the shape of a sailor suit, the item is made from antique lace that lends it a romantic and rustic aura. The selection of fabrics is a top priority.
"Uragoizoku's Choker." keisuke kanda launched "Uragoizoku" as a line of ethnic costumes targeted at girls who adore cute things. Characteristic is their extreme lightness and loveliness, thanks to pastel colors and plastic ornaments and the toning down of bright colors and hefty, folksy colors.

Autumn/Winter 2011-2012, ***Handsewn Jeans.*** Although vintage and vintage-looking jeans are commonplace, each pair by keisuke kanda is one of a kind; two pairs of ripped Levis are sewn up with misalignment, or the lining is striped, and so on. Tailoring by hand renders the form of these jeans suitable for wearing.

keisuke kanda

Designer's profile:
keisuke kanda / Keisuke Kanda

Keisuke Kanda was born in Kagoshima in 1977. He taught himself how to make clothes in 1998 while a student at Waseda University. After graduation, he founded Candyrock Ltd. in the fall of 2005. His first store opened in Koenji at the end of 2011.

Brand history:
2005 Candyrock Ltd. founded.
First collection presented at Tokyo Tower in collaboration with ANREALAGE.
2006 First solo exhibit in the attic of a yakitori restaurant in Nakameguro, Tokyo.
2007 One-man live Anti-Fashion Anti Creation by Keisuke Kanda at the Club Grapefruit Moon.
2008 "National exhibit tour" started from SS2009.
2009 Opening of Snack A.T. Field, an experimental store in a part of his studio.
2010 Broadcasted an independent radio program "We don't belong anywhere."
Presented The First Love Terrorist, an apparel label for pop idol-esque costume.
Presented Uragoizoku, an ethnic costume dedicated to would-be pop idols.
2011 Keisuke Kanda starts communicating through Twitter.
First snack counter store opens in Koenji.

matohu

まとふ
堀畑裕之
関口真希子

matohu
Hiroyuki Horihata
Makiko Sekiguchi

matohu

Hiroyuki Horihata

Makiko Sekiguchi

まとふ
堀畑裕之
関口真希子

"Oribe" is the first collection theme by matohu, launched in 2005. The designers approached the world by deciding themes for ten seasons, all revolving around Japanese aesthetics. Their signature nagagi design has been part of every collection since the start. This two-piece long coat with a kimono structure is symbolic for the philosophy of matohu.

matohu / Hiroyuki Horihata, Makiko Sekiguchi

Creating New Styles of Clothing Based on Common Threads Found in Japanese Aesthetics

Interviewed by Yoko Takagi

In 2005, Hiroyuki Horihata and Makiko Sekiguchi established their fashion brand, matohu. The brand's name, 'matohu' is derived from a Japanese word that has an identical phonetic sound and two different meanings: "to wear" and "to wait". The name of the brand reflects the designers' slow and thoughtful process of creation and presentation of work by these designers. At the launch of their label, they imagined ten collections to be presented over the following five years, all based on the theme of "The Beauty of Keicho". These ten collections were named: Oribe I, Katabira, Kodaiji-makie, Sagabon, Nanban, Shino, Keicho-kosode, Tsujigahana, Kabukimono,and Oribe II. These collections resulted from their painstaking research on the culture, arts and crafts of the Keicho Period (1596-1615) of Japanese history and exuded a profound understanding of the spiritual essence of this era. In 2010, the designers initiated their second long-term series of collections, this time around the theme of "The Japanese Eye". They gave the title "Kasane" (Layers) to their autumn/winter 2010-2011 and spring/summer 2011 collection. The following collection, autumn/winter 2011-2012, was titled "Muji no Bi" (The Infinite Beauty of Plainness). In the summer of 2011 they opened their first flagship store in Aoyama, Tokyo.

Transition from studying philosophy and the constitution of Japan to becoming fashion designers

_ Mr. Horihata, you studied Kantian philosophy at the post-graduate program of Doshisha University. Ms. Sekiguchi, you studied human rights theory at the Kyorin University. When did each of you first become interested in fashion?

Horihata: I went to an all-boys high school, and my senior schoolmates used to ask me to go shopping with them. I accompanied them to the Nanba district in Osaka and gave them my opinions on what looked good on them or how to match different clothing items. They liked my fashion advice so much that I got asked to go shopping with them all the time. Up until that point, I was neither interested in fashion nor familiar with fashion magazines. Perhaps these experiences of giving style advice to others opened my eyes to the fun aspect of fashion.

Sekiguchi: I have always loved dressing up, ever since I was a little girl. Back in the day, *So-en* magazine used to include paper patterns for making your own clothes in the back of each issue, so I made my own clothes using these patterns. I've also been reading *Hanatsubaki* magazine since I was in middle school. The artful connection between the act of creation and the act of wearing clothes is something I've always been aware of.

_ Could you tell me how each of you chose to become a professional fashion designer?

Horihata: I studied German philosophy rigorously in the graduate program and I intended to become a researcher eventually. I even wrote a letter to a professor in Germany and planned to study abroad for a while. But I was uncertain about my future career. Philosophy is a deeply introspective discipline, and it was a hard subject to share with others. I specialized in a certain aspect of Kant's writing, "The Critique of Pure Reason", and there were less than ten people worldwide that I could speak with about this subject. I wanted to work in a field where I could communicate with more people. I loved philosophy, but I wasn't sure if the research work within the field of philosophy should become my life-long career. I started feeling lost and empty. Around this time, I went to a special exhibition called "Japonisme in Fashion" at the National Museum of Modern Art in Kyoto. This was the first time I encountered the world of fashion in such a large-scale setting, and I was deeply moved by the works of Yohji Yamamoto, Issey Miyake and Comme des Garçons. After this experience, I became increasingly interested in fashion. I was fascinated by the writings on fashion by the Japanese philosopher Kiyokazu Washida. I felt the desire to pursue my career in the world of fashion when I finally saw the clothes by Yohji Yamamoto and Comme des Garçons in person and watched the video footage from their runway shows in Paris. Up until that point, my life was about sitting at a desk and thinking about philosophy. I started wishing that I could create something with my own hands.

Sekiguchi: I had been making my own clothes since I was in high school or college. My sewing skills were at the point where I needed to study at a technical college in order to take my techniques to the next level. My major field of study at the university was constitutions. While I was comparing the constitution of Japan to that of Germany, I formed my opinion that an individual's pursuit of happiness was essential to the construction of a healthy society. Although this idea might not be directly related to fashion, it became the foundation for our brand's mission to contribute something positive to society at large.

_ The two of you met each other in April of 1995, on the first day of school at the apparel design department of Bunka Fashion College. You were both in the same foundation class.

Horihata: We got along well from the first moment we met each other. Starting from the summer of our first year in school, we collaborated on creating costumes for the theater and 'hairstyle' shows, plus wedding dresses and dance costumes for Kota Yamazaki's contemporary dance troupe. After school, we used to go to performance sites and venues to create outfits together.

_ In your third year, you studied in the men's fashion design department and learned various traditional skills for making clothes such as tailoring, forming and cutting. After graduation, Mr. Horihata, you got a job working as a patternmaker for women's clothes at Comme des Garçons.
Ms. Sekiguchi, you started as a pattern maker for men's clothes at Yohji Yamamoto and continued working there for the next five years. Could you share some of the memorable moments from your time working for these designers?

Horihata: Our jobs as patternmakers allowed us to have tremendous creative freedom, but at the same time, we had to start at the bottom. We were working in an apprenticeship system, so each of us spent the first two years watching and learning from our seniors while assisting them with sewing and patternmaking. It was a very tough period for me because I had no opportunity to create my own work. In hindsight, though, I appreciate the opportunity to acquire all those fundamental skills. I am a much better fashion designer today because of the experiences I gained during my early days as an apprentice. After I was given more hands-on experiences at work, I learned

The third collection in the "Beauty of Keicho" series for Autumn/Winter 2006-2007 took shape under the theme "Kodaiji-makie." Bamboo leaf was printed on a black Nagagi dress using techniques from "makie", lacquer-ware making.

about the two important qualities that a fashion designer must have in order to create something truly remarkable: a persistent work ethic with the discipline to make corrections over and over again, and an uncompromising attitude towards perfection. Comme des Garçons has won critical acclaim and created controversy at each and every show in Paris. Those creations were not works of art instantly created by a genius - they resulted from the staff's steady and persistent efforts and labor. Each of those jackets and dresses represented an ultimate form of 'beauty' that they arrived at after long hours of trial and error.

Sekiguchi: I was working in the men's clothing department, so I received even stricter tutoring on the fundamental skills of apparel making. These techniques included hand-stitch tailoring, various sewing techniques and patternmaking skills. In men's clothes, the quality of the tailoring equals the 'design' of the garment. My job didn't permit me to make any sloppy mistakes, so it taught me the difficulty and the enjoyment of creating something of the highest quality. I was mainly working as a patternmaker for men's clothing, but I also helped in the women's department when they needed an extra set of hands. I helped them finish their final pieces for the fashion shows, and I helped them mend various parts with a sewing machine. I learned the differences in the apparel-making techniques for men's and women's clothing. While I was helping out at the women's clothing department, I gained many invaluable lessons by comparing and contrasting the different approaches to garment construction in men's and women's clothing.

Horihata: Our jobs at these fashion houses were very tough, so we really had to love what we were doing. These houses created some of the most innovative and creative designs in the world. We worked extremely long hours, from early morning to midnight every day. What sustained us through those tough times was our love of the craft. It was very important for us that we had fun doing our jobs. Our attitude remains the same today. Even when we work under tremendous pressure to meet deadlines, we still enjoy the act of creating something new. We often remind each other how much we love our creative work as designers.

The concept behind the brand

_ So, the two of you were employed at two different companies. Then, for one year, both of you went to London to work under designer Bora Aksu. After your return to Japan, you established the label matohu. Could you elaborate on the concept behind your brand: "Creating new styles of clothing based on common threads found in Japanese aesthetics"?

Horihata: Until we started our label, there was no brand in the fashion industry that dealt with traditional Japanese aesthetics, culture, and history. Major Japanese designers such as Kenzo Takada, Issey Miyake, Yohji Yamamoto, and Rei Kawakubo incorporated elements of these into their collections, but they never pursued Japanese aesthetics as the long-term framework for their brands' identities. We decided to create a brand that existed outside of the Western historical context but which was not based on a 'deconstructive' philosophy. We wanted to pursue new forms of expression using non-Western apparel making techniques. The word "original" comes from the word "origin". We wanted to create clothes that would allow wearers to feel connected with the past while satisfying their desire to wear something contemporary and timeless. We were not interested in designing fashionable apparel for trendy consumers.

_ Today, it has become much easier to share information with others worldwide, and as a result, our cultures have become increasingly homogenized. At the same time, unique regional aesthetics are slowly fading out. What made you start paying attention to Japanese aesthetics?

Horihata: One day in the past, Sekiguchi, my business partner, suggested that we wear kimonos just for fun. She bought me an antique kimono. I was surprised because I've only ever worn a kimono on New Year's Day. Since then, I started wearing a kimono on my day off. When I wore my kimono out in the street, I felt like a foreigner. Even though I was wearing the indigenous costume of Japan, people kept staring at me. At the same time, I noticed that there were particular physical sensations and experiences that were different from wearing any other types of clothes. Rather than "wearing" the garment, it felt as though I was being "enveloped" by a piece of cloth. I could feel the air moving through the fabric against my skin. Also, I found out that a kimono's existence was based on principles completely different from that of regular clothing. A kimono culture has had its own unique use of materials and colors.
I came to realize that the majority of people in Japan today wear only Western-style clothes. I also noticed that kimonos provide a completely different physical sensation than Western-style clothes. This realization changed the way I view the world. Historically speaking, it has only been thirty to forty years since Japanese people switched to Western-style clothing and left their kimono culture behind. In contemporary Japanese society, we are witnessing the disappearance of the traditional aesthetics that have been built over centuries. We are also losing the special textile production techniques and our intimate knowledge of wearing kimonos. Unless we know how it feels to wear a kimono, we cannot truly understand our cultural heritage. We are facing a turning point in our history where we either continue or discontinue our relationship with our kimono culture.

_ With matohu, you integrate certain Japanese aesthetics into the designs of your Western-style clothing, and you have also introduced alternative forms of presentations outside of the industry's conventional system. For example, when you started the label in March of 2005, you simultaneously announced the ten future themes of your coming five years' worth of work. These collections were all based on the theme "The Beauty of Keicho". In a fashion world where a new collection of today's mood is presented in a runway show every six months, your show was highly unconventional.

Horihata: By announcing the theme for ten seasons beforehand, we made it easy for ourselves to plan our long-term projects, especially for manufacturing our fabrics and materials. We were able to source the materials that we planned to use in our collections three, four years down the line. Also, we were able to place special orders with our textile makers several years in advance so we could ensure the highest possible quality of materials. Even though we couldn't change the semi-annual cycle of the fashion industry, we could still adjust our stance and take as much time as necessary for preparing our show. The

name of our brand, "matohu", has the double meaning of 'wearing' and 'waiting'. We want our audience to recognize that it takes a long time to create something good. We'd like to continue our producing from a long-term perspective, going against the fast-fashion trends and the frantic pace of the world today. We believe that it takes more than one day for an individual's aesthetic to grow and mature. Therefore, we need to have a relaxed, patient attitude and let our works evolve slowly.

_ You have created Nagagi, a novel clothing item that is neither a kimono nor

"The Beauty of the Keicho era." Booklets and invitations to be bound in a scroll were distributed individually for each of the 10 seasons, over the span of five years. The booklets formed the basis for the "Beauty of Keicho" exhibition at Spiral Garden in Aoyama, Tokyo. The exhibition then traveled to a museum in Kumamoto, Kyushu, where sets of the booklets, complete with scroll and packaged in a paulownia box, were sold.

The Nagagi dress, which matohu proposes as an intermediate garment between the kimono and Western clothes, remains unchanged. The piece with a collar is to be worn over another without a collar as an exercise in color matching. The two can also be worn separately. They make an appearance every season, allowing for a variety of combinations.

Both pages show a Nagagi dress from the Autumn/ Winter 2011 collection "The Beauty of Solid Color." It can be worn by women and men alike depending on how one fastens it. The front can left open or closed with a belt.

Western-style clothing. It is a two-in-one garment that has an inner layer (robe) and an outer layer (coat).

Horihata: We regard our Nagagi robe not as our 'classic' item, but our 'fixed-form' item. When kimonos are laid flat, they all have the same geometric form, just like a haiku poem. The main concept of our Nagagi robe is that we leave its original form unchanged, but we modify everything else to add a sense of variation and playfulness. This concept of a "fixed-form" allows us to create a timeless piece of clothing. For the wearers, their "Nagagi" robes will never look outdated because they can buy additional new Nagagi robes in different textiles and change the looks of their old robe by mixing and matching the inner and outer layers. We make our Nagagi robes based on our personal point of view of fashion. The concept behind our clothing is completely different from a principle of fashion that changes every six months.

_What is the difference between a "classic" and a "fixed form"?

Sekiguchi: When you call something classic, the shape and the taste/look of the item stays the same. In contrast, with a Nagagi robe, you can drastically alter its appearance by switching the fabrics of which it is made. When it's made of a certain material, it will look like formal wear. Made of some other material, it may look like a cardigan or like a dress. Depending on whether it was knitted or dyed, the function of a Nagagi robe will be completely different. We do not treat our Nagagi collection as our 'classic', but instead, we regard it as an endless opportunity for experimenting with various fabrics. Just like a kimono, a Nagagi robe has the same standardized shape and form. However, by wearing, layering and juxtaposing different textures and colors, a wearer can make his or her Nagagi robe unique and one-of-a-kind for himself/herself. Depending on how a wearer mixes and matches different layers, a Nagagi robe will always remain fresh and contemporary.

_What kind of responses did you receive from your first collection?

Horihata: We presented our Nagagi collection in an exhibition format. We didn't have the time and money to have our pieces fabricated by sewing factories, so we ended up making less than forty samples by ourselves. We were so busy that we had to sleep in our atelier. Some of our old classmates from Bunka Fashion College volunteered to help us with the sewing.

Sekiguchi: People from neighboring apparel companies called us and said, "We'd like to come over and help you after we get off work." They ended up working with us well past midnight, until the last trains left the nearby train station.

Horihata: Our exhibition was small in scale, but we received so many great reactions. It made us feel confident and positive about our future.

Sekiguchi: I was most concerned about how people would respond to our first collection. We initially started our brand as a women's clothing label. However, we had many male customers trying on the Nagagi robes at the exhibition and placing orders personally. We quickly adjusted our business policy and made our Nagagi collection suitable for both men and women. It was so encouraging to know that our ideas were understood and appreciated so much by these people.

Horihata: On the other hand, we received a lot of harsh, negative criticism from the buyers for various retail shops. Some of them were unhappy that our Nagagi was too different from our previous collections. They were also concerned about how to match a Nagagi robe with other conventional clothes. Some people were entirely dismissive of the Japanese aesthetics in our work. If we had listened to all the criticism from these buyers, we probably would have discontinued our Nagagi.

Sekiguchi: A lot of buyers told me that it was impossible to display our work next to other brands in their stores. Also, they wanted to know which other brands I would like to have next to the Nagagi robes in their retail shops. Anyway, because this was our inaugural exhibition, it was a relatively casual affair. Many of our friends brought their acquaintances to our exhibition. Unlike those retail shop buyers, people who wanted to purchase the Nagagi robes for their own personal use had little or no bias against them. Since we didn't have a store at the time, they placed individual orders at the exhibition. We ended up receiving a huge number of orders for new Nagagi robes. Since then, we have adopted the business model of taking special orders for Nagagi robes directly from our customers.

The secret of creativity - matohu's apparel making processes

_Could you talk about matohu's apparel-making processes?

Sekiguchi: We often have discussions about the abstract nature of beauty and how we can translate it into specific materials, colors, and forms in our designs. Also, we collect literature and reference materials, go to exhibitions, and research the various themes that we happen to be working on. When we reach the stage of actually making our clothes, we talk about materials and their draping/stretching qualities, as well as the main colors for our designs.

Horihata: We take the finished fabric, wrap them around a bodice and play around with drapes. We do not make sketches. Instead, we come up with our designs and patterns based on our experiments with draping. The specific nature of each fabric determines the overall silhouettes of our garments. Each of us makes samples of clothing based on our own designs, which we then critique together by being brutally honest with each other. We make adjustments to our designs until we get them right. We are a married couple, so we discuss our work even at home. It would be a lonely process if we didn't have each other. It's wonderful to have a partner who can give me constructive criticism and objective opinions on my designs.

_You mentioned that you let the fabrics determine the silhouettes of your designs. Materials play a key role in your work. Do you make your own original fabrics?

Sekiguchi: About eighty percent of our fabrics are specially made for us. We want to involve ourselves in the manufacturing process of these fabrics as much as possible. Since we are not the experts on textiles, we consult with professional weavers, look through their catalogues and make our requests for custom-order textiles.

_matohu does not seem to have a specific gender and age for the brand's clientele. Who is your main clientele?

Horihata: Our female clientele ranges from those in their 20s to those in their 60s. On the other hand, our male clientele is relatively young, mostly in their 20s and 30s. Our male customers are often stylish and idiosyncratic, and they are mostly people in the fashion industry or the art world, musicians, and young students who are extremely passionate about fashion. They tend to be aware of their own uniqueness and capable of expressing their own individuality through fashion.

Sekiguchi: Many of our most loyal customers are men. There is a gentleman who loves our Nagagi collection so much that he has purchased a new Nagagi robe at every exhibition we've organized.

_What do you think of your brand's image and the way it has been perceived by others?

Horihata: Some people misunderstand our brand, thinking it's based on traditional Japanese decorative motifs. Our designs do not include any decorative motifs and patterns that you see on traditional Japanese kimonos. Instead, we want to create a contemporary yet timeless piece of clothing that can only be made by using a Japanese sensibility. We are very careful about our brand's PR. We have to make sure that people do not mistake our work as simply being about mixing Eastern and Western aesthetics.

_I heard that both of you love Japanese antiques and visit antique shops on your days off. Is it to look for future themes for your collections?

Horihata: I love Japanese antiques, especially tools, instruments and furnishings, but I'm not interested in old Japanese fine art. I like to be able to use these antique items every day. Sometimes, I come up with another use for an antique object and use it as a flower vase, and so on.

_You visit antique shops that have selected inventories, rather than going to flea markets and finding a diamond in the rough.

Sekiguchi: We like to visit antique shops owned by eccentric people. Many of these shops carry items whose original purposes are unknown but which were selected by the owners for their inherent beauty. We like to come up with our own unique ways of using these items in our everyday lives.

_In January of 2010, you held an exhibition titled "matohu: The Beauty of Keicho" at the Spiral Garden Gallery in Tokyo. It encompassed matohu's collections from the last ten seasons (five years) and your sources of inspiration. You juxtaposed the arts and crafts of the Keicho Era with your own work as a way of explaining the process of creating your designs. What do you think about the fact that you will be showing your work in an art museum this time? When we had an initial meeting with all of the ten participating brands, you mentioned that you would like to set up a fitting room in your exhibition space.

Sekiguchi: We are thrilled to show our work within the unique space designed by Ryuji Nakamura. It will be interesting to see how each fashion brand will express its identity and use its allocated exhibition space. We came up with the idea of a fitting room because we wanted to provide museum visitors with a tactile experience of our clothes. We believe that this sensory experience will add dimension and meaning to our creations. It will be meaningful for museum visitors to wear our clothes, so that they can deepen their understanding of our designs.

Horihata: In our exhibition, we would like to share with the visitors our ideas of what is 'fresh and contemporary' at this moment.

In July 2011, matohu's first retail shop opened on Omotesando, Tokyo. Mitsuru Kiryu was in charge of designing the shop. Thanks to diagonal lines and plain wood set in transversal lattices instead of stark walls, the shop radiates the feel of Japonism, which distinguishes it from usual clothing boutiques.

At the runway show for Spring/Summer 2010 "Oribe II," the venue was separated into three sections using curtains of thin fabric. Each stage had a quiet atmosphere like a teahouse. The playfulness and the unique askewness of the brand were expressed in the shoes, the combination of colors in socks, the slouched wigs, and the clack of cups, as well as the shapes of clothes. The show was staged to crown the whole series.

COLLECTIONS

2005-06 A/W

2006 S/S

2006-07 A/W

2007 S/S

2007-08 A/W

matohu was launched by defining daring themes for ten seasons over five years, under the theme of "The Beauty of Keicho." Horihata and Sekiguchi decided to make clothes that are informed by Japanese aesthetics, and chose as their reference point the Keicho era - from the late Momoyama period to the early Edo period - when new aesthetics came into existence. They gathered characteristic topics of the time and made them into themes. "The Beauty of Keicho" was the combined name for the ten collections..

Autumn/Winter 2005-2006, ***Oribe*** (the series, through Spring/Summer 2009, was exhibited at ICHYS GALLERY in Aoyama, Tokyo) formed Matohu's first collection. The theme derives from Oribeyaki, a traditional form of artistic pottery named after Oribe Furuta (1544-1615), a samurai and tea master. The collection included uniquely designed clothes in green and black glaze, distorted shapes, and bold geometric patterns.

Spring/Summer 2006, ***Katabira.*** The Katabira is an unlined summer kimono. Horihata and Sekiguchi found the pale blue katabira worn by Shogun Ieyasu Tokugawa, printed with white crabs, humorous and set out to make a modern version by designing a Nagagi dress decorated with pictures of Japanese ginger.

Autumn/Winter 2006-2007, ***Kodaiji Makie.*** Makie is a Japanese lacquer craft technique in which a picture is painted with lacquer and sprinkled with gold flakes before it dries. The zenith of Kodaiji Makie can be found in Momoyama-era decorations of autumn plants and flowers. Matohu introduced this technique into their collection.

Spring/Summer 2007, ***Saga Book.*** The theme was a beautifully decorated book published in the years of Keicho. The patterns xylographed on woodblocks were printed with mica on fabrics reminiscent of the Japanese paper-type called washi. This formed the first occasion where a

2008 S/S

2008-09 A/W

2009 S/S

2009-10 A/W

matohu collection was exhibited by means of a runway show.

Autumn/Winter 2007-2008 ***Nanban—Barbarians.*** A reference to the first encounter and cultural exchange between Japan and Europe during the 16th century. Horihata and Sekiguchi incorporated the way kimono culture was influenced by the West, though the use of a mantle, a hat, velvet, laces, a cross, and others elements.

Spring/Summer 2008, ***Shino.*** Under the theme "Shinoyaki," pottery created according to original aesthetics from the Momoyama period, Horihata and Sekiguchi recreated simple but delicately varying looks of potteries characterized by an ivory and blue-grey glaze and rust-colored brushwork strokes.
With some dresses drawn by using actual iron rust prints, the collection exuded serenity as well as depth.

Autumn/Winter 2008-2009, ***Keicho Kosode—short-sleeved kimono.*** Keicho Kosode is a style of kimono that was in vogue in the late Keicho period. The collection formed an elaborate collage through tie-dyeing the figured satin with gold foil and adding embroidery.

Spring/Summer 2009 ***Tsujigahana.*** Tsujigahana is a technique of tie-dyeing that flourished in the Momoyama period. It is a specifically Japanese method done by narrowing down designs with high technology and inking the outlines. It had been kept alive only through the Yuzen dyeing method of silk printing, but is now re-evaluated.

Autumn/Winter 2009-2010, ***Kabuki-mono*** (EBISU 303). The verb "Kabuku" stemming from "Kabuki-mono" (which translates roughly as "dandy") means living with a free spirit and the courage to stand out from the crowd. The collection demonstrated a spirit of joy and a wildness expressed through the

color black, associated with avant-garde groups that preferred to be different during the Keicho period.

Spring/Summer 2010, ***Oribe II*** (Tokyo Midtown Hall). The final collection bearing the same name as the first of their ten collections suggests matohu's strong affection for their debut works. While the first Oribe was designed in black with a Japanese flavor, Oribe II worked delightful colors and patterns into modern designs.

Autumn/Winter 2010-2011 ***Kasane Irome—The look of layered colors*** (Tokyo Midtown Hall A).

A "Japanese insight" gleaned from a book by Soetsu Yanagi provided Horihata and Sekiguchi with the inspiration to start a new series of ten seasons. The designers' will to pursue Japanese aesthetics free from direct Western influence was clearly indicated by focusing on a color sense unique to Japan.

Spring/Summer 2011, ***Kasane Irome—The look of layered colors Spring/Summer*** (Tokyo Midtown Hall A). The designers continued to focus on the colors of Japan. The collection consisted mainly of light clothes, with Japanese coloration provided through prints and layering.

Autumn/Winter 2011-2012, ***Beauty of Solid Color*** (presented through images). Focusing on the meaning of solid colors in the context of Japanese aesthetics - profoundly different from that in the West - Matohu presented woven and knitted fabrics in simple yet nuanced colors, demonstrating the delicate beauty of their complexity. Seen was a variety of colors in white, gray, beige and black.

matohu

Designers' profiles:
matohu / Hiroyuki Horihata, Makiko Sekiguchi

Hiroyuki Horihata was born in Osaka. He received his M.A. in philosophy from Doshisha University in 1995. After graduating from the fashion creation department of Bunka Fashion College in 1998, he worked as a patternmaker in the womenswear section of Comme des Garçons for five years.
Makiko Sekiguchi was born in Tokyo. After receiving her B.A. from the faculty of law and political science of Kyorin University, she went to the fashion creation department of Bunka Fashion College. After graduating from college in 1998, she spent five years in the menswear section of Yohji Yamamoto as a patternmaker.
After resigning from their jobs, Horihata and Sekiguchi went to England in 2003, and worked on the FW2004 collection of Bora Aksu. They returned to Japan in 2005 and launched matohu under the concept of "the Japanese aesthetics that underlie newly created clothes."

Brand history:

2005 matohu founded under the concept "the Japanese aesthetics that underlies newly created clothes."
Themes for ten seasons over the next five years were decided on the premise of "The Beauty of Keicho."

2006 Debut at the Japan Fashion Week.

2008 Involved with the new brand "ten," bridging European and Japanese clothes, sold at awai, a kimono dealer with branches in Roppongi and at Isetan department store.

2009 Awarded the Mainichi Fashion Grand Prix Newcomer's Prize and the Shiseido Sponsorship Award.

2011 Exhibition "matohu: The Beauty of Keicho" at Spiral Garden in Aoyama, Tokyo. and at the Contemporary Art Museum in Kumamoto.
A fashion show held at Marugame Genichiro-Inokuma Museum of Contemporary Art.
Opening of a store on Omotesando, Tokyo.

ミナ ペルホネン
皆川 明

minä perhonen
Akira Minagawa

minä perhonen

Akira Minagawa

皆川 明

ミナ ペルホネン

Clothes by minä perhonen are made of originally designed fabrics and emanate daily life. Their forms are somehow nostalgic; they look ordinary, but demonstrate elegant touches in the length of sleeves and in round shoulders. Moreover, much of what the clothes exude is down to the materials. Each fabric has a name, and all these names come from the drawer of Akira Minagawa's memory. The photo shows "chorus", presented in 2010.

mina perhonen / Akira Minagawa

Special Daily Wear

Interviewed by Yoko Takagi

In 1995, Akira Minagawa launched minä perhonen, initially named "minä". The aim of his label is to provide distinctive clothing that can be worn daily, that does not fade away with the passage of time and heightens the spirit of the wearer. Since the beginning, Minagawa has created textiles based on his own original designs: hand-drawn sketches that are woven, dyed, or embroidered. He collaborates with domestic and international textile manufacturers to innovate new materials and techniques for creating his own original designs.
In 2000, his first boutique "minä" opened its doors in Shirogane, Tokyo. In 2003, the label was renamed minä perhonen, meaning 'I butterfly' in Finnish. Minakawa frequently traveled to Scandinavia and found that its cultures and lifestyles appealed to his sensibilities. The name of his label, minä perhonen, reflects the two aspects of his aspirations; 'minä (I)' for hoping that the wearer will be true to herself, and 'perhonen (butterflies)', for wishing that his design motifs would be as beautiful as butterfly wings, and as lyrical as their movement.
Today, minä perhonen's work encompasses a wide range of products such as furniture, textiles, and tableware. All patterns and graphics from the previous collections are carefully archived, and many of the past designs are reproduced in the current collection.

The launch of the label

_ What was the factor that drew you into the world of fashion? Was it your trips to Scandinavia?

Minagawa: My first encounter with the world of fashion happened in my late teens. Up until then, I was not particularly interested in fashion. I worked as a part-time assistant at the Paris Fashion Week and this experience gave me an intuitive appreciation for fashion and its profoundness. I became convinced that I would build a career in fashion for the rest of my life.

_ I am surprised that Paris was where you first came into contact with fashion. What were the exact circumstances?

Minagawa: I was staying in Paris for two months to attend a language school. My classmate asked me to assist him at the fashion show of a Japanese brand. He was working as part of their staff. I was an amateur, so all I did was act as assistant. But I remember how thrilling it was to be backstage at the Paris Collection. I found it challenging and rewarding. After I went back to Japan, I started to attend the evening courses at Bunka Fashion College. It was a two-year program. It took me three years to graduate, because I was traveling a lot and couldn't earn sufficient credits to finish school on time. I traveled to Europe every time I'd earned enough money from my part-time job.

_ Did any fashion designer in particular inspire you at that time?

Minagawa: When I was in school, I had classmates who were dressed in designer brands as if they were trying to out-do each other. Not that I have a negative opinion of this, but I wasn't interested in clothes that made a loud statement like these designers' labels. I was more interested in making clothes that enhanced the subtle beauty of the wearers.

_ When did you decide to become a fashion designer?

Minagawa: I actually wanted to be involved in production rather than design. I started by working at a sewing factory. It was a fur and leather workshop, and I worked there as an assistant patternmaker for three years. I did basting and learned about patternmaking and human anatomy. After that, I worked at a small textile production workshop and exhibited the textiles at galleries. For three years, I was an assistant to a patternmaker and a production control manager. It was a small business with a few employees, so we had to do everything ourselves. After acquiring sufficient skills for sewing, patternmaking and textile production, I was ready to make clothes on my own. In May of 1995, when I turned 27, I started 'minä.' I produced an original fabric and sewed shirts, blouses and dresses. I exhibited these creations by hanging them under the eaves of the office where I worked. Usually, you need to have a presentation for retail shop buyers several months before the start of the new season. I wasn't even aware of this because I had never worked in the apparel industry. In the beginning, I went from store to store trying to sell my hand-made clothes.

Ordinary clothing that enhances the beauty of the wearer

_ What is the philosophy of minä perhonen?

Minagawa: I would like to make soulful clothes that the wearers can cherish for many years, instead of changing every season under the unspoken rules of fashion cycles. Fashion doesn't have to be plain to be timeless. I would like to make clothes that can make a strong impression on you and yet are able to stand the test of time. Since I create the original designs for our textiles, I would like to re-use the same designs in various collections for an extended period of time. There have been almost no other labels that use the same material for more than one collection. It is normal to treat a design as outdated after it is used for a season's collection. It is not common to reuse materials from the previous season. I would like to challenge this notion to see if any of my designs will look dated. I want to create designs that last and make clothes that are for everyday use. Although my label has gained a certain level of recognition, I wouldn't want minä perhonen to become a luxury brand. I would like to continue providing something special within the realm of everyday life.

_ "Soda Water" from spring/summer 2001 is a good example of a textile design that never looks outdated. It is a woven textile with a pattern of simple, randomly overlapping polka dots. The dots seem to stand out from one another, because the twilling of each and every dot has a different weave direction.

Minagawa: "Kakurenbo" from spring/summer 2008 is a tubular textile. The motifs appear only when you cut open the outer fabric with scissors. The appearance of the fabric changes depending on the position and the number you cut open. It's interesting because it's a mass-produced item, but it becomes one of a kind when the wearer interacts with it.

minä perhonen's designer and its team

_ You always use the plural form "we" when you talk about minä perhonen. What's the form of relationship between the designer and the team within minä perhonen?

Minagawa: I design the textiles and silhouettes. I also collaborate with our patternmakers on the pinwork of our clothing. For the textiles, I not only create the surface designs but also develop, with a team of five people, the actual materials from the weaves to the dyes. I let my team know the collection's theme and my vision. Beside myself, I have another designer who draws designs for minä perhonen. This designer creates the drawings based on her interpretations of my vision. I rarely give a precise direction on the motifs or the colors. I will give her my opinion, if she asks for it, but I rarely give her any instruction. I give her full responsibility for completing the work. Otherwise, she will get used to relying on someone else's opinion when she works on her own projects in the future. In the creative domain, you need to be able to work without your boss's opinions. This is how I nurture the next generation of designers and ensure the longevity of the label, even after I retire from the job. It is imperative that everyone on the team fully understands the philosophy of minä perhonen. As long as our designs stay true to the core identity of minä perhonen, it's not important whether the designs come from Minagawa or from others on the team. I am interested in finding various means of presenting the philosophy of minä perhonen.

Going against the course of trends — Setting a goal for the next one hundred years

_ Please tell me about your business principle.

Minagawa: From a management point of view, it is important for us to solve problems within our own cash flow. We don't do any commissioned work and we don't bring in external funds through investors. We are constantly facing the risk of a zero balance on our checkbook, depending on the outcome of our work and how it's received each season. We have chosen to grow slowly with our own means, instead of borrowing a big investment fund and trying to return the money through our business.

For us, defying social conventions was the key to stabilizing our business. While a large facet of the fashion industry lowered the cost of production in response to the recession, we refused to do the same. We would stand out from the crowd if we continued making a substantial investment in materials while everyone else was cutting the cost of production. We have always gone in the opposite direction of the major trend. In fashion, everyone is seeking new business opportunities by adopting the current trend. It becomes a feeding frenzy. In our case, we studied the trends so that we could avoid them all together. We sought an alternative concept, not trends, for creating something attractive and exciting.

_ What made you decide to go in the opposite direction of the trends?

Minagawa: Well, there are millions of adult women in Japan. We have the production capacity that can cater to one-one thousandth of them: our business will be fine if one out of every one thousand people finds it worthwhile. It takes the pressure off of me when I realize that one tenth of a percent of the consumers is all I need for our business to succeed. I do not have to conform to the major trend in order to continue doing what I love to do.
I believe that my work has a positive meaning if it is completely different from what is being done by the majority. Being different is a valuable quality for a designer. This is a small business that anyone with a sewing machine can start. It makes sense that minä perhonen is

photo:sono (bean)

"Kakurenbo" (Spring/Summer 2008) looks like a finished garment dotted with circle patterns in the same color, but butterflies appear when these are cut open.

here for the non-conformist consumer with a distinctive taste.

_ Since the very beginning, it has been your policy to develop and produce your original textiles for the brand. This is unique to your label. Were you conscious of the manufacturing environment in Japan when you came up with this policy?

Minagawa: Basically, my vision for the future dictated what I decided to do at the beginning. My goal was to be able to collaborate with the best factories around the world for at least the next thirty years. I believed that we could forge strong relationships with the best manufacturers if we presented the factories with the best archives of our works. For that to come true, our textiles needed to be of the highest quality. I would like the quality of our textiles to form the distinctive value of our brand. And I would like to pass that value on to my successor when I retire in thirty years. A huge amount of thought and care have gone into the creation of our textiles. We are very obsessive about ensuring the highest quality of our textiles so that they cannot be imitated.

_ Does it mean that you already had a picture of your career up to your retirement when you started out?

Minagawa: My objective is to create a brand that will keep on going even after the end of my term. A business venture won't last long unless its organizer plans beyond his or her term. I think of myself as one of the contributing elements to the brand's longevity. I wanted to know if it would be possible to create a domestic label that would last for at least one hundred years. Knowing that I would be in charge for the first thirty years, I was thinking of what I could do specifically within this time frame. Half of my term has already passed. I would like to maintain a good relationship with reliable suppliers and continue having tangible results for several more years. For my successor, I would like to set up a manufacturing environment that can create all sorts of original textiles.

Foreign Operation

_ How do you perceive the identity minä perhonen as a Japanese label?

Minagawa: I think the borders between Japan and the rest of the world do not exist anymore. Having said that, I know about Japanese artisans and the excellent manufacturing environment here. I want to cherish this and continue to collaborate with them. In the West, designers tend to use pre-manufactured fabrics for their work. In Japan, designers are in a position to

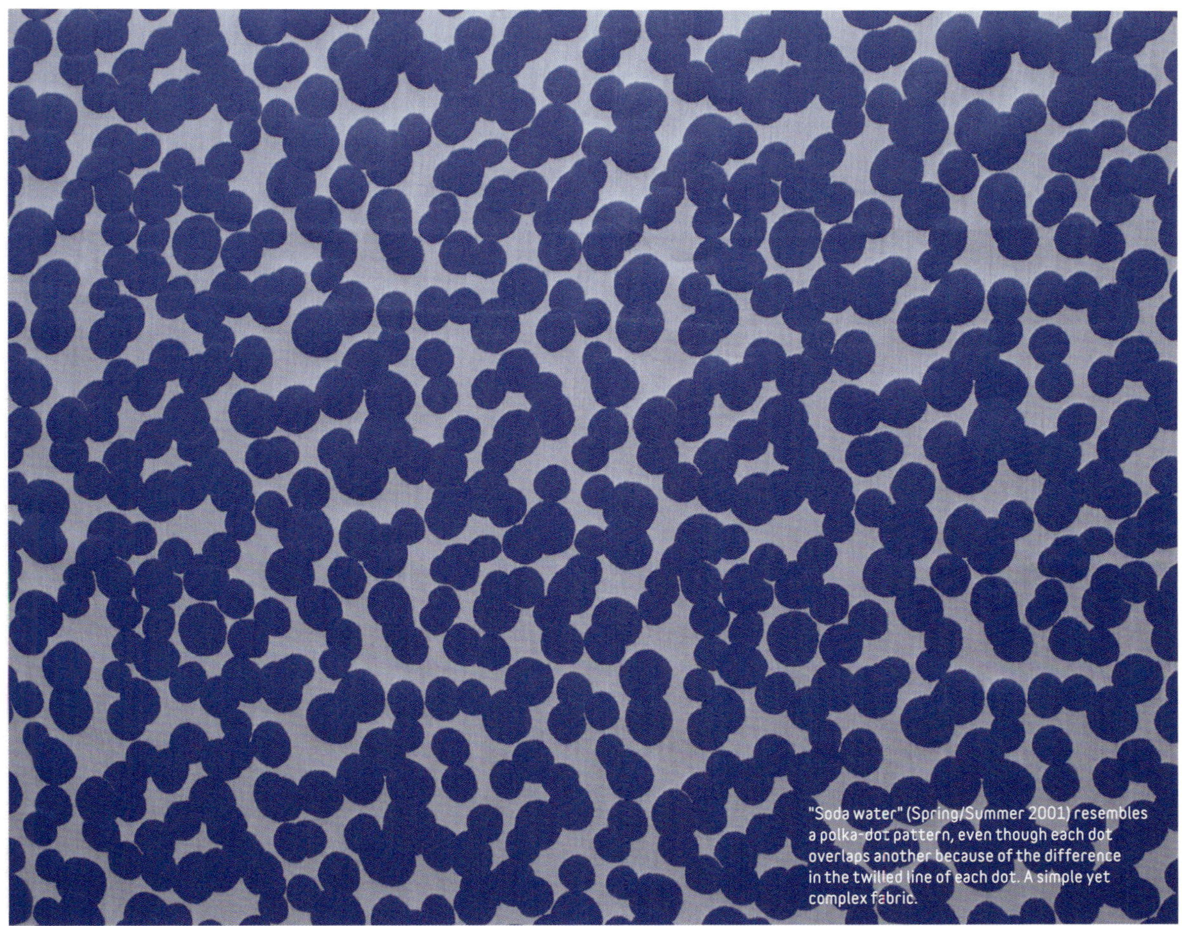

"Soda water" (Spring/Summer 2001) resembles a polka-dot pattern, even though each dot overlaps another because of the difference in the twilled line of each dot. A simple yet complex fabric.

order specific kinds of fabrics for their creations. The manufacturers and the designers are able to collaborate on developing new products together. This close relationship with their clients is something unique to Japanese fabric manufacturers. For Japanese designers, they are one of the most valuable resources.

_ Is it difficult to create fabrics from scratch in other countries?

Minagawa: We have been working with a certain factory in Italy for the last 10 years. This factory is known as one of the world's best producers of cashmere textiles. Certain parts of Europe have great textile manufacturers. However, in terms of the complexities of the weaves, patterns, or processing treatments, I hardly discover anything new from them. In Europe, fabrics and textiles are often produced within a single factory's integrated system. This system ensures a consistent perfect quality of products, but there is hardly any room for experimentation. In Japan, different manufacturers are in charge of various stages of fabric and textile production, such as weaving, dyeing, and processing. We have an ideal environment for creating made-to-order materials.

_ Instead of a runway show, you regularly present your new collections in your boutiques, in the format of an exhibition or publication. How do you present your work abroad?

Minagawa: In Paris, we were curious to see how our work would be perceived in a different cultural context. We wouldn't be showing abroad unless our work brings something new to the international market. In Italy, women's clothing seems to be about emphasizing femininity. Our designs are not necessarily sexy, but we presented our work in Italy because I wanted to know if Italian women would find our clothes relevant to their lifestyles. Now, the majority of our foreign buyers are from Italy.

_ Italy? I thought that Germanic-language speaking countries would be your main audience because of your brand's name and the sense of structural forms in your designs. Wearing your clothes is not about being sexy.

Minagawa: In general, many buyers are interested in ordering from well-known labels, instead of seeking a brand based on their own critical judgment. I guess that minä perhonen was accepted in Italy because the Italian buyers wanted to introduce something new from Japan. Worldwide, we have twenty-two stores that carry our label, and six of them are in Italy. It probably has to do with the fact that Italy has a number of moderately

woolly ball 2009-10 A/W
Mrs. Cloud 2009 S/S
wataridori 2003-04 A/W
necco 2007 S/S
tambourine 2000-01 A/W
wind 1999 S/S
fir tree 2009-10 A/W
rain chukka 2007 S/S
before 2010 S/S
forest parade 2005 S/S
celebrate 2010-11 A/W
jungle relief 2008-09 A/W

sized cities like Milan, Rome, Florence, and Venice. These former city-states have sufficient commercial districts. In France, on the contrary, Paris is the only city that really stands out.
Our sales overseas count for less than ten percent of our overall sales. We are happy with this figure. Otherwise, we would have to deal with more uncertain factors. For our overseas market, we carry European sizes 40 and 42 in addition to the 36 and 38 sold in Japan. For the American market, we make clothes in size 44.

_ What about the Asian market?

Minagawa: We have retailers in South Korea, Taiwan, and Hong Kong. China seems to be the next big market that everyone is focusing on, but we don't feel China's retail environment is quite ready for our type of clothing.

_ Again, it looks like your decision is based on your policy to go against the current trend. Now, let me ask you about your customers. What is your customer base?

Minagawa: Our customer base consists of women of all ages. Our typical customer is someone who focuses on our design and the quality of the materials. The name of our label is not the primary reason for their purchases. In stores abroad, the age of our customers tends to be older because the prices are slightly higher. Our clothes can be repaired even after several years of use. Because of this, minä perhonen appeals to an individual who is interested in a sustainable lifestyle. It's not for someone who goes after trends. We often hear about daughters who inherit minä perhonen clothes from their mothers.

_ How do you manage the PR?

Minagawa: The magazine *So-en* has been writing about us regularly since 2001. Casa Brutus, Bijutsu Techo and Geijutsu Shincho also ran articles about the furniture and various industrial products by minä perhonen. We don't have a budget for advertisement in magazines. We use our catalogues as the main marketing

The fabrics on the left are some examples from the vast numbers in minä perhonen's archive. Each fabric has its own name, which indicates that it carries the same importance as designs and collection themes.

Autumn/Winter 2007-2008 Paris collection. The fashion show took place at a gallery under the theme of "A festival at a small village." Minagawa drew trees on the floor using adhesive tape and used a recording of his own whistling as background music. The show featured fifteen models in colorful clothes.

photo:Makiko Takehara

tool. We would like to spend that money on materials, rather than for advertisement. As far as our PR in the future is concerned, it is becoming more and more important for me to tell the story behind our clothes, the intangible values behind the materials.

Exhibition in an art museum

_ I saw the exhibition "minä perhonen - fashion & design" at Audax Textielmuseum Tilburg in the Netherlands. The show and the catalogue did an excellent job informing the audience about your label's philosophy. The museum referred to you as a designer of textiles, clothing and furniture.

Minagawa: If I think about my job title, it would be more appropriate to call myself a product designer. I've been working in the field of fashion the longest, but I also design furniture and tableware at this point.

_ You once mentioned that your designs are for living, not for art. What do you think of this exhibition taking place in an art museum?

Minagawa: In this exhibition, I hope that spectators will have an emotional experience by getting to know the concept of our label and the philosophy of our design. I don't expect the audience's reaction to be about the beauty of the clothes or their wishes to try them on. I believe a museum is a good venue for appreciating the background of an object, beyond its material value. We will present many different parts of our clothes and photos taken during the manufacturing process. We would like to show the techniques and thoughts that go into the various stages of production. Our brand is unique in the sense that we are involved in every step of the manufacturing process. So much emotional investment and thoughts have gone into the creation of each item, especially the clothes. A single item passes through a number of expert hands before it ends up at a retail store. In this exhibition, we wish to express the hope that our clothes will be loved and worn for many years to come.

On the left: the exhibit "minä perhonen—fashion & design" at the Textile Museum in Tilburg, The Netherlands (October 2009 - February 2010). The walls were plastered with not only Minagawa's clothes but also other product designs.

photo:Tohru Yuasa(B.P.B.) drawing:Akira Minagawa

The booklet "Monkicho" has been published every season since Autumn/Winter 2007. Each booklet is finely edited by a different art director.
Top row, from left: Fumio Tachibana, Atsuki Kikuchi, Daijiro Ohara.
Middle row, l-r: Masayoshi Nakajo, Naomi Hirabayashi, Yuri Suyama.
Bottom row, l-r: Issei Kitagawa, So Hashizume, Takayuki Fukuda.

Two-piece outfit "Monkicho" from Autumn/Winter 2010-2011. The photo shoot took place at studio "Nomad," owned by a photographer Ayako Mogi on Awaji Island. Yuri Suyama served as art director. The picture on the right shows the "Monkicho" from Autumn/Winter 2007-2008, by art director Atsuki Kikuchi.

photos: Ayako Mogi

photo:Yoshiharu Koizumi

COLLECTIONS

1996-97 A/W

1999 S/S

2000 S/S

2001 S/S

2001-02 A/W

2002 S/S

2000-01 A/W

2002-03 A/W

2003 S/S

2003-04 A/W

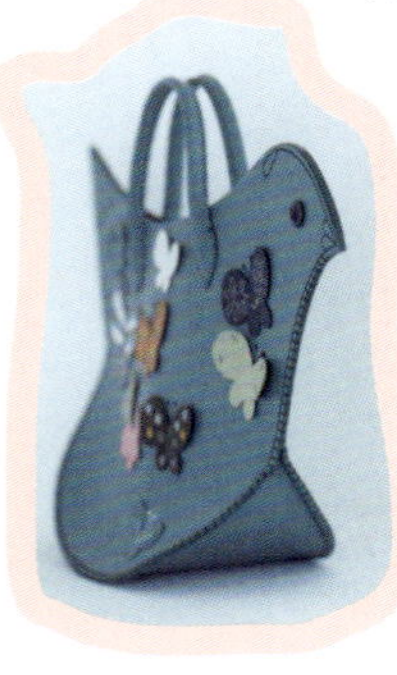

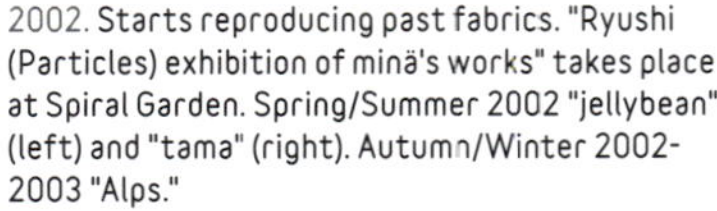

1995. Minagawa founded "minä" and founded his own studio in Hachioji, Tokyo. He started working from his original aesthetics by distancing himself from fashion trends. His stance has always been to design simple and pursue originality in textiles. Each fabric is named.

1996. Launch of the "Mini bag," still in production today. "Nanten," Autumn/Winter 1996-1997.

1997. Launch of the "Egg bag."

1998. The studio relocates to Asagaya, Tokyo. Minagawa becomes interested in product design and launches the original "Giraffe Chair." Spring/Summer 1999 "shabondama."

2000. The studio relocates to Shirokanedai, Tokyo, and the first retail store is opened. Launch of the "Tori bag" (below left). Minagawa starts a long-running serial in *So-en* magazine. Spring/Summer 2000 "bird." Autumn/Winter 2000-2001 "twist."

2001. Launch of a line of men's clothing. Spring/Summer 2000 "mori-no-umi." Autumn/Winter 2001-2002 "sunny rain."

2002. Starts reproducing past fabrics. "Ryushi (Particles) exhibition of minä's works" takes place at Spiral Garden. Spring/Summer 2002 "jellybean" (left) and "tama" (right). Autumn/Winter 2002-2003 "Alps."

2003. The brand's name changes to "minä perhonen." "Perhonen" is the Finnish word for butterfly. Minagawa intensifies his focus on fashion design. His participation in the London Fashion Week means the worldwide breakthrough of minä perhonen. Danish house Fritz Hansen introduces the Egg Chair, Swan Chair, and Seven Chair, all designed by Arne Jakobsen and upholstered with

2004 S/S

2004-05 A/W

2005 S/S

2005-06 A/W

2006 S/S

2006-07 A/W

2007 S/S

2007-08 A/W

2008 S/S

2008-09 A/W

fabrics by minä perhonen (below center). Textiles by minä perhonen are registered with the Scottish Tartan Authority. Minagawa's writings are pubished in book form: "Fractions of Travels" (Akira Minagawa, Bunka Publishing Bureau), "Ryushi particle of minä perhonen" (planned and edited by the Executive Committee of Ryushi Exhibition, Bruce Interactions), "Let's wear minä and travel around" (Akira Minagawa, DAI-X Publishing), etc. Spring/Summer 2003 "moonflower." Autumn/ Winter 2003-2004 "twig" (left) and "wataridori" (right).

2004. Minagawa presents his collection in the form of an exhibition. He supplies wardrobe, stage design, and direction for the dance exhibit "wonder girl." Spring/Summer 2004 "nap" (left) and "papaver" (right). Autumn/W nter "sun bird" (left) and "forest girl" (right).

2005. Minagawa presents his collection as a runway show. Spring/Summer 2006 takes place in Paris, for which dancers are hired. The venue was meticulously staged, with careful selection of music, while a beautiful "minä-like" story unfolded. Photo: Makiko Takehara. Launch of the original design "perhonen chair" (produced by Tendo Mokko).
2006. Akira Minagawa wins the Mainichi Fashion Grand Prix., Danish textile manufacturer Kvadrat introduces fabrics designed by Akira Minagawa. Launch of the sale of original fabrics. Autumn/ Winter 2006-2007 "swan." Spring/Summer 2007 "twins"; the image on the right is from a presentation show at the same gallery in Paris. The runway was decorated with flowers, and the background music was supplied by traditional Japanese street performers. (Photo: Kumi Kin)

2007. First appearance of the season booklet "Monkicho" (pale clouded yellow). Autumn/Winter 2007-2008 "fogland" (Left: from "Monkicho," photo: Yoshiharu Koizumi). Right: from the presentation in Paris (photo: Makiko Takehara).

2008. Launch of a collection of original coffee cups (page 110). Spring/Summer 2008 "hanaco." Autumn/Winter 2008-2009. From photos for coordinates (Photos: Norio Kidera)

2009. The third retail store "minä perhonen arkistot" opens in Kyoto. Launch of original furniture "perhonen shelf" and "bagel stool"., The Liberty department store in England introduces items designed by Akira Minagawa as a part of its Autumn/Winter 2010 collection. "minä perhonen fashion & design," a solo exhibition held at Audax Textiel Museum in Tilburg, The Netherlands. Spring/ Summer 2009 "cats & dogs" (left) and "twitter" (right). Autumn/Winter 2009-2010 (photo: Norio Kidera).

2010. Two shops, "arkistot" and "piece," open in Tokyo after the opening of "piece" in Kyoto. Exhibitions take place at museums and galleries. At "the future from the Past" (21st Century Contemporary Art Museum, Kanazawa [upper right]), the walls were impressively covered with "soda water." Exhibition by minä perhonen "in progress" (Spiral Garden), Spring/Summer 2010 (Photos: L.A. Tomari). Autumn/Winter 2010-2011 "chum." Spring/Summer 2011 "sometimes lucky."

2011. Publication of the 15th anniversary compilation book "minä perhonen?" (BNN Inc.). Autumn/Winter 2011-2012 (photos: Norio Kidera)

Designer's profile:
minä perhonen / Akira Minagawa

Akira Minagawa was born in 1967. He launched minä perhonen (initially minä) in 1995, and runs the brand as its chief designer.
He has designed textiles for KVADRAT in Denmark (2006-) and LIBERTY in England (2010-11A/W), stage artwork and costumes for contemporary dance, as well as pottery and furniture. He is currently a visiting professor at Kyoto University of Art and Design and at Tama Art University. He wrote *Fractions of Travels by Akira Minagawa* (Bunka Publishing Bureau) and *Let's wear minä and travel around* (DAI-X publishing).

Brand history:
1995 minä launched.
2000 Opening of a flagship store in Shirokanedai, Tokyo.
2002 First solo show Ryushi at Spiral Garden, Tokyo.
2003 Renamed his brand minä perhonen.
2004 Prêt-à-porter debut in Paris.
2006 Awarded the 24th Mainichi Fashion Grand Prix.
2007 Opening of a second store in Kyoto. Starts to publish the booklet *Monkicho* every season
2009 Opening of the minä perhonen arkistot store in Kyoto, which exhibits and sells past work.
Exhibition at Audax Textiel Museum in Tilburg, The Netherlands
2010 Opening of the shop minä perhonen piece in Kyoto, which sells items produced at an attached studio.
Opening of the shop minä perhonen piece in Jingumae, Tokyo, and minä perhonen arkistot in Shiroganedai, Tokyo.
Solo show at the 21st Century Contemporary Art Museum, Kanazawa, and Spiral in Aoyama, Tokyo
2011 Published the book minä perhonen? (BNN Inc.).

photo:Tohru Yuasa(B.P.B.)

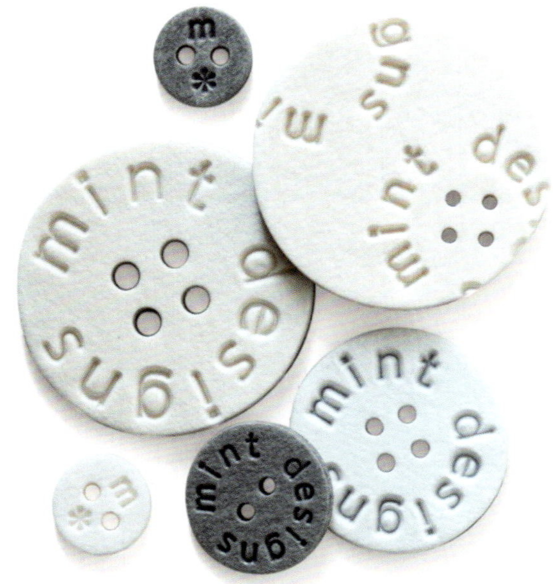

mintdesigns

ミントデザインズ
勝井北斗
八木奈央

mintdesigns
Hokuto Katsui
Nao Yagi

These paper buttons are symbolic for mintdesigns. They were the first product by the brand that aims for fashion to become a form of product design in its own right. Despite being made of paper, they are washable, undeformable, and light. Over the past ten years they have been used in coats, jackets and shirts designed by mintdesigns.

mintdesigns / Hokuto Katsui, Nao Yagi

Creating Clothes As Design Products

Interviewed by Hiroshi Narumi

mintdesigns is a fashion label founded by Haruto Katsuki and Nao Yagi in 2001. After graduating from Central Saint Martins College of Art and Design in London, the duo established their brand based on their vision of designing and creating products that transcend short trend cycles and become a long-term part of the wearer's life.
The designers of mintdesigns have manufactured their own original fabrics and printed patterns, and they have created fashion designs based on colorful palettes, bold patterns and simple, yet distinctive shapes and forms. Their playful approach to design is reflected in their signature decorative motifs, such as a little girl holding a pair of scissors or original buttons made of paper. Besides designing clothes, the duo creates a variety of products including bags, wallets, pencil cases, and chairs. Their design of masks that mimicked the nose and mouth of a woman and an ape became a sensation when they were showcased at Salone del Mobile in Milan in 2009.
In 2008, mintdesigns was invited to the São Paulo Fashion Week, and in May 2011, it held its first retrospective exhibition at the Museum of Contemporary Art in Taipei. The duo has expanded its presence abroad and received international acclaim for their work. mintdesigns won the prestigious Mainichi Fashion Award in 2010 and continued asserting its power on the contemporary global fashion scene.

Studying in Great Britain

_ Both of you went to Central Saint Martins College in London. What made you decide to pursue the careers that you have today? Mr. Katsui, your father is a graphic designer. Did he have any influence on your career choice?

Hokuto Katsui: I was more interested in fashion than graphic design. I was born and raised in Tokyo, and my father had his office at our home near Omotesando. The boutiques of Comme des Garçons, Yohji Yamamoto, and Issey Miyake were just a stone's throw away from our house. That neighborhood was my playground. Perhaps my experience of growing up in the Omotesando area had an effect on my choice of career.
I thought about going to a professional training school to study fashion, but I was more drawn to art school because I thought there would be more interaction with people in other fields like architecture and industrial design. At the time, I became acquainted with someone who was attending Central Saint Martins College of Art and Design (CSM), and it made me want to fly to the UK right away. But I first went to Kanazawa City in Ishikawa Prefecture to attend a school that was affiliated with Parsons the New School for Design in New York. Afterwards, I moved to the United States to attend Parsons in New York.

_ Ms. Yagi, you went to a high school in London.

Nao Yagi: Yes, though I didn't really know what I wanted to do there. I just wanted to get away from Japan. When I was still in middle school, I naively thought that things would be more exciting in London. My motive for moving there was really simple. I graduated from high school in the UK and got into to Doshisha University in Japan, majoring in aesthetics. I was interested in art criticism and curatorial studies, but I didn't believe that I had enough talent to pursue these for the rest of my life.
I come from a family with a creative background, so I felt that I might be better suited to follow a creative line of work. I chose fashion because I knew I would always be excited about it and I would never get tired of it. Fashion was something tangible for me because I would be able to see a person wearing a dress and moving in the dress and leaving an aesthetic impression on me.
I know that I made the right choice for my career because I still approach my

work with a fresh perspective and a lot of enthusiasm.

_ Then you went to CSM. What was your impression of London?

Yagi: London during that period, in the late 1990s, was a very exciting place to be. There was so much going on in fashion and contemporary art. In terms of fashion, Alexander McQueen was just arriving on the scene. In the contemporary art scene, Damien Hirst was much talked about with the controversial exhibit "Sensation."

Katsui: The first school I went to abroad was Parsons, which primarily taught the orthodox rules of building a fashion business. It seemed very similar to professional training schools in Japan. Their focus was on teaching business skills and various dressmaking techniques. I was fascinated by the energy of New York, which was quite different from Europe. But one day, I saw a magazine article featuring the new "Brit Movement". It made me want to go to London, so I transferred to CSM.

Yagi: I had the impression that, in the UK, fashion didn't exist just for the sake of fashion itself. It had its place somewhere between art and 'la mode' in the Parisian sense. I never thought about going Paris to study fashion because, in my mind, Paris was a place to learn the technical skills involved with fashion.

_ I often hear that CSM emphasizes students' creativity, and it is quite different from dressmaking schools in Japan.

Katsui: Right after we entered the school, we were given our first assignment, called the "white project". We were required to make clothes in sheeting fabric or felt, but I was unable to hand in my assignment. Initially, I planned to make a doll as a model and create clothes for it, but I ended up running out of time and only had the doll to show the class. My teacher put me on the spot in front of everyone and told me that I should have enrolled in the sculpture department if I didn't want to make clothes.

Yagi: I remember going to a bar with classmates after that critique and exchanging words with Katsui for the first time. We'd hardly talked to each other until that point.

"to be someone"
Mask exhibited at
"Tokyo Fiber 09 Senseware,"
Milano Salone 2009

photo:Nacasa & partners

Katsui: Yagi and I took the same womenswear course during our first year, but halfway through the year I transferred to the fashion design/printed textile course. It was a course where you learned about textile manufacturing as well as dressmaking. I became interested in textiles after I'd made my first silkscreen T-shirts. Hussein Chalayan and Wakako Kishimoto of Eley Kishimoto are two of the graduates of this textile course.

_ Who was your biggest influence?

Katsui: Rather than a specific fashion designer, I was influenced by contemporary culture, including various movements in music, like Brit Pop, in art and in fashion.

Yagi: I was inspired by Hussein Chalayan and Alexander McQueen, Nicolas Ghesquiere at Balenciaga, and also Viktor & Rolf. People tend to be more susceptible to influences when they are young students. But I quickly realized that it wasn't really about emulating these designers. I figured that I would have to use my own method to do something original.

Katsui: In London, I often went to various kinds of street markets. There would be flowers or antiques, depending on the day of the week. I loved browsing those markets.

Yagi: I admired the product designers Naoto Fukasawa and Kenya Hara. I also loved Tokujin Yoshioka's spatial design that he created for the exhibition "ISSEY MIYAKE Making Things" at the Cartier Foundation in 1998. I found the works by these Japanese designers very inspiring.

Katsui: In those days, the Japanese lifestyle brand MUJI was really popular in London. Naoto Fukasawa designed a lot of products for them and he was attracting so much international attention. It was refreshing for me to see Japan through the eyes of international audiences.

Yagi: For people in Great Britain today, the predominant image of contemporary Japan comes from Japanese street fashion. However, it was the Japanese modern design that was recognized here first. In London, I was exposed to the image of Japan through Japanese contemporary design.

Product ideas

_ mintdesigns seems to draw ideas from industrial design rather than fashion. Your apparel design follows the rules of fashion, but your perspective is based on the discipline of industrial design. Your paper buttons are a case in point.

Yagi: In fact, when we established our fashion brand, we decided to approach fashion as one of the disciplines within the field of product design.

Katsui: The paper button was our very first product. We made them even before we made our first clothes. We are still very particular about our buttons.

Yagi: Those buttons were made of a pulp material called vulcanized fiber, which is normally used to make suitcases. They

Okuda dye-works factory in Hachioji, Tokyo, specializes in serigraphy. The factory produces mintdesigns's print designs.

photo:Kentaro Oshio

are durable and water-resistant. Of course, they will become sodden if they get soaked in water, but they won't fall apart. They become hard again once they dry up. They can be washed the regular way and you can dye them as well. We use the same material for all the buttons on our clothes.

Katsui: In our first collection, we presented clothes made of sheeting fabrics and decorated with paper buttons. We rented the Junzo Sakakura Memorial Gallery (Gallery Saka) behind Tokyo Midtown to use for our presentation.

Yagi: We sent out invitation cards with buttons attached to them, because we thought that this was the best way to illustrate our brand's concept. We wanted to show people that designing a button held just as much significance for us as designing clothes.

_ What kind of feedback did you get from your first presentation?

Yagi: For some reason, a lot of editors of art magazines came to our presentation. Some people came thinking that it would be an exhibition of buttons. In hindsight, we didn't even know who to send our invitations to. We thought that retail buyers would find their own way to our show.

Katsui: Although it was supposed to be an autumn/winter collection, our clothes were made with sheeting fabrics only.

Yagi: We were simply clueless. We were too naive and optimistic.

_ How do you collaborate on making your clothes?

Katsui: We create our fabrics at the same time as designing our forms. We are more likely to start with fabrics, though.

Yagi: People often ask us if our textile design comes first, before our fashion design. By working on them simultaneously, these two aspects tend to influence one another, which allows us to formulate new designs. We don't necessarily begin with a seasonal theme. Sometimes, we will still be in the middle of discussing our theme when we start designing and making fabrics. We typically have two to three weeks to work on our fabric design. We design forms and surface designs for our clothes at the same time, so we occasionally come up with new motifs for our textiles in response to the form we have just designed.

Katsui: When we come up with a new motif for our textiles, we usually need to adjust its design according to the style and the form of our clothes. Depending on the size, layout, and density of the motif, the textile design would look different on the actual clothes.

_ Between the two of you, you don't divide tasks. Instead, you take every decision together. How do you come up with your seasonal themes?

Katsui: We basically stock up on ideas. The repertoire of our designs has grown larger and larger as our experiences continue to grow. Our theme for the season depends on our mood or our reactions toward certain circumstances in society at that time. Sometimes we know ahead of time what we want to do for the next season.

Yagi: At mintdesigns, we've had two major types of themes in our collections. The first type is based on techniques and materials. An example would be our denim collection titled "Almost Blue" (spring/summer 2011) or our lace collection called "3D Lace Project" (spring/summer 2006). We also focused on using a particular material in our first three collections. Sheeting fabric was used for our first collection, followed by jerseys in our second collection, and finally knitwear for our third collection. The second theme is based on our worldview. "Fashion Surgery" (fall/winter 2011-12), "A New Hope" (fall/winter 2011-12), and "Dame-ni-ikiru (Living the life of a loser)" (spring/summer 2007) are examples of this type.

Katsui: Usually, a winter collection by a designer consists of various materials such as wool, knitwear, and leather. But in our case, we don't use different kinds of materials because we are adamant about making our original textiles and because our knowledge of materials and financial resources is limited. This is why we decided to concentrate on using a single material per collection. In doing so, we've been able to learn about an entire spectrum of different materials and their production background. We expand our knowledge of materials each season and as a result, our label grows stronger. Our denim collection was the result of our long-standing wish to make denim fabric from scratch. Nine years had passed since we launched our label, and we felt it was the right time for us to create clothes in denim.

Yagi: When we pick a material as the theme of our collection, our work becomes more like research and development. When we made our own lace, we searched for the kind of lace that could reflect who we were as a brand. For each material we have worked on, we've done a substantial amount of research on its production background. Through trial and error, we've come up with a unique approach to manufacturing our original materials.

Their policy on the apparel making process

_ You really adhere to your policy of creating an original product from scratch.

Katsui: When I was working as an intern at a fashion designer's studio in London, I noticed how small the scale of his workshop was in contrast to the huge attention he was receiving from the mass media. Like this designer, I thought that we could keep the scale of our business to a manageable size and still make great products.

Yagi: In the apparel-making industry, it's usually very difficult to develop a new material from scratch unless you have sufficient budget. But in our case, we carefully study how we can produce our own materials within the means at our disposal. We work closely with manufacturers and give them various suggestions so that they can produce our materials in a small batch. We are meticulous about our manufacturing processes. Otherwise we wouldn't be able to get the most out of the material that we researched and produced. Along the way, we learned that we can't afford to have our fingers in too many different pies. If we were to produce new fabrics using an ordinary method, our work wouldn't be much different from other apparel makers. We will always insist on using our particular methods of small-scale production to make our original fabrics. I believe that this sets us apart from other designers.

_ Did you have this idea to create your original fabrics since the beginning of your career?

Yagi: We didn't have to make our own fabrics. But an item of clothing will always look cheap if it's made of an inexpensive, mass-produced fabric. Even if the cutting of the garment was well done, it would still look like something we've seen somewhere else. It is so wonderful to see a garment with

photo:Kosuke Tamura styling:Misa Nishizaki

"Glass balls" - Japanese confectionery made in collaboration with Toraya, a traditional Japanese sweets shop, and launched in October 2009. Small balls of bean paste are confined inside jelly like marbles.

photo:Yoshitsugu Enomoto

Spring/Summer 2011 "almost blue." The first collection of blue jeans bymintdesigns

Fabrics and swatches for Spring/Summer 2011

a perfect harmony of great cutting, design, and graphics. We can't focus on a single one of these aspects. For example, Cristobal Balenciaga's past works are truly distinctive because he perfectly matched his fabrics with his cuttings.

_ In the beginning, who did you think was your clientele?

Katsui: We wanted our work to be received by a wide range of audiences. We were hoping that our clothes would be sold not only in clothing boutiques and department stores, but also in museum shops and interior design stores.

Yagi: To put it simply, I wanted our label to be recognized by people who are into design. I wasn't too interested in getting attention from people who are into high fashion.

Katsui: I hope that people who have their own sets of values and who love fashion, not trends, will wear our clothes. These are people who choose to wear certain clothes because they simply like them and find them beautiful.

Yagi: I would hope that people who are not only interested in the trendy fashion of the moment but also curious about various creative disciplines such as architecture and graphic design, make mintdesigns a part of their regular wardrobes.

Japan and overseas

_ Are you self-conscious about being a Japanese fashion label?

Katsui: We don't have an inferiority complex toward the West. Interestingly, while I was at school in London, I met a lot of fashion students who were influenced by Japanese designers and admired their work. I even remember one of my classmates asking me how to get a job at Comme des Garçons.

Yagi: Katsui and I also admire Issey Miyake, Rei Kawakubo, and Yohji Yamamoto. We respect them so much that we don't want our work to be like theirs. Even if we tried to emulate their design methods, we would be unable to compete against the original. Our work can only be authentic if we put our own soul into it.

_ How is mintdesigns received by audiences abroad?

Yagi: Japanese people share similar skin colors, body types and even their taste in fashion. This is not the case overseas. Everyone has a different point of view. When I lived in the UK, people appreciated my Japanese sensibility as something unique. At CSM, people described my work as "Japanesey". When we returned to Japan and established mintdesigns, we were surprised to hear Japanese people characterize our brand as 'Scandinavian'. Our international audiences find our brand typically Japanese, but our domestic audiences think our brand has a European flavor.

On the left, the exhibit "'happy mistake!'—pattern on pattern". mintdesigns put up their own exhibition featuring characteristic textiles such as "Dot Dolls" and "Zig Zag," and installation works including "Trash, Slash & Flash!" at the Museum of Contemporary Art in Taipei, Taiwan, in May 2011.
On the right, from "'happy mistake!'—pattern on pattern, Kyoto version", held at a gallery of Osaka Seikei University, where the designers teach as visiting professors. This was a selection of items from the last ten years, newly coordinated without regard for the seasons, which bathed the whole space in the colors of mintdesigns.

CURWEN
BELLE
STOPIT
DONAL MACDOUGAL
HARVEY
GODFREY JAMES
MATINEE
"JUST A COMEDIENNE"

Autumn/Winter 2011-2012, "fashion surgery." While many brands decided to refrain from showing their collections after the earthquake of March 11th, mintdesigns carried out their runway show at "TABLOID," a former printing factory on the seashore of Tokyo's Minato Ward. Like the fluorescent light that beamed down on the venue, elaborate headdresses made from light-emitting diode illumination seemed to form a ray of hope at this beautiful show.

photo:Yoshitsugu Enomoto

Our work has been recognized in Japan mainly for the use of multiple, subtle colors. But when we were invited to Brazil to do a fashion show, we found that Brazilians didn't really care about our use of colors, because Brazil already has so many fashion designers who use colorful designs in their work. Instead, they were drawn to the weaving and cutting techniques in our garments, as well as the conceptual and poetic aspects of our work.

_ Would you like to expand your business overseas?

Katsui: First, we would like to take our work to Asia. We have already done a fashion show in Beijing and a solo exhibition at the Museum of Contemporary Art Taipei in Taiwan. We have so much in common with neighboring countries like China, Thailand and Singapore.

Yagi: We don't feel obliged to go to Paris or to New York. Instead, we would like to take our work to the rest of Asia and let Asian people know more about our label. There is so much we share in terms of physiques and skin tones, so I am sure Asian people will understand the strength of our designs when they actually wear the clothes that we have made. Sometimes I think Salone Internazionale del Mobile in Milan might be a great venue to show our work again instead of Paris, considering that our work isn't limited to the realm of fashion design. We're celebrating our tenth anniversary this year, so we are already looking ahead toward our next decade. We would like to plan our strategy for showing our work abroad.

Katsui: The Japan Fashion Week is an occasion mainly for professionals, like buyers and journalists. In terms of a fashion event, I find a public event like Design Tide Tokyo interesting, so I hope to gain some inspiration from it. Two years ago, we participated in Salone Internazionale del Mobile in Milan. It was great to see the general public mingling freely with professionals. They made it into a really festive event. Perhaps we can make fashion more fun if we create more events like this.

COLLECTIONS

Autumn/Winter/Spring 2002-2003, ***happy mistake!*** (Gallery Saka). The first collection, consisting of sheeting, was displayed at a gallery in Roppongi in the form of a presentation show.

Spring/Summer 2003, ***happy mistake! vol.2*** (bio ojiyan cafe). First presentation of a collection in the form of a runway show. The dolls pattern that has come to symbolize the brand originated with this season.

Autumn/Winter 2003-2004, ***knitting project*** (AUX BACCHANALES CAFÉ). The café that was the venue for this runway show no longer exists. The collection consisted exclusively of knitted fabrics, and the venue decorated with objects like cups and baguettes, all covered with knitting, attracted a lot of interest.

Spring/Summer 2004, ***printing project*** (THINK ZONE). This experimental show featuring the designers and several craftsmen performing silk screen printing live, became one of representative collections of their early career.

Autumn/Winter 2004-2005, ***triangular project*** (TAMADA PROJECT ALTERNATIVE SPACE). This collection featured fabrics with bold geometric pattern.

Spring/Summer 2005, ***tri-colombian project*** (CLASKA). A total of 33 models were directed to appear simultaneously at the gallery of HOTEL CLASKA. The theme name is a composite of the word tricolor and Columbia Market in London.

Autumn/Winter/Spring 2005-2006, ***moving in square*** (KUWASAWA DESIGN SCHOOL). A long corridor in a (now defunct) building of Kuwasawa Design School was used as a runway. Furoshiki—a square piece of cloth for wrapping things—was the main source of inspiration for the collection.

Spring/Summer 2006, ***3D lace project*** (Meiji Memorial Picture Gallery TOKIWA). The show,

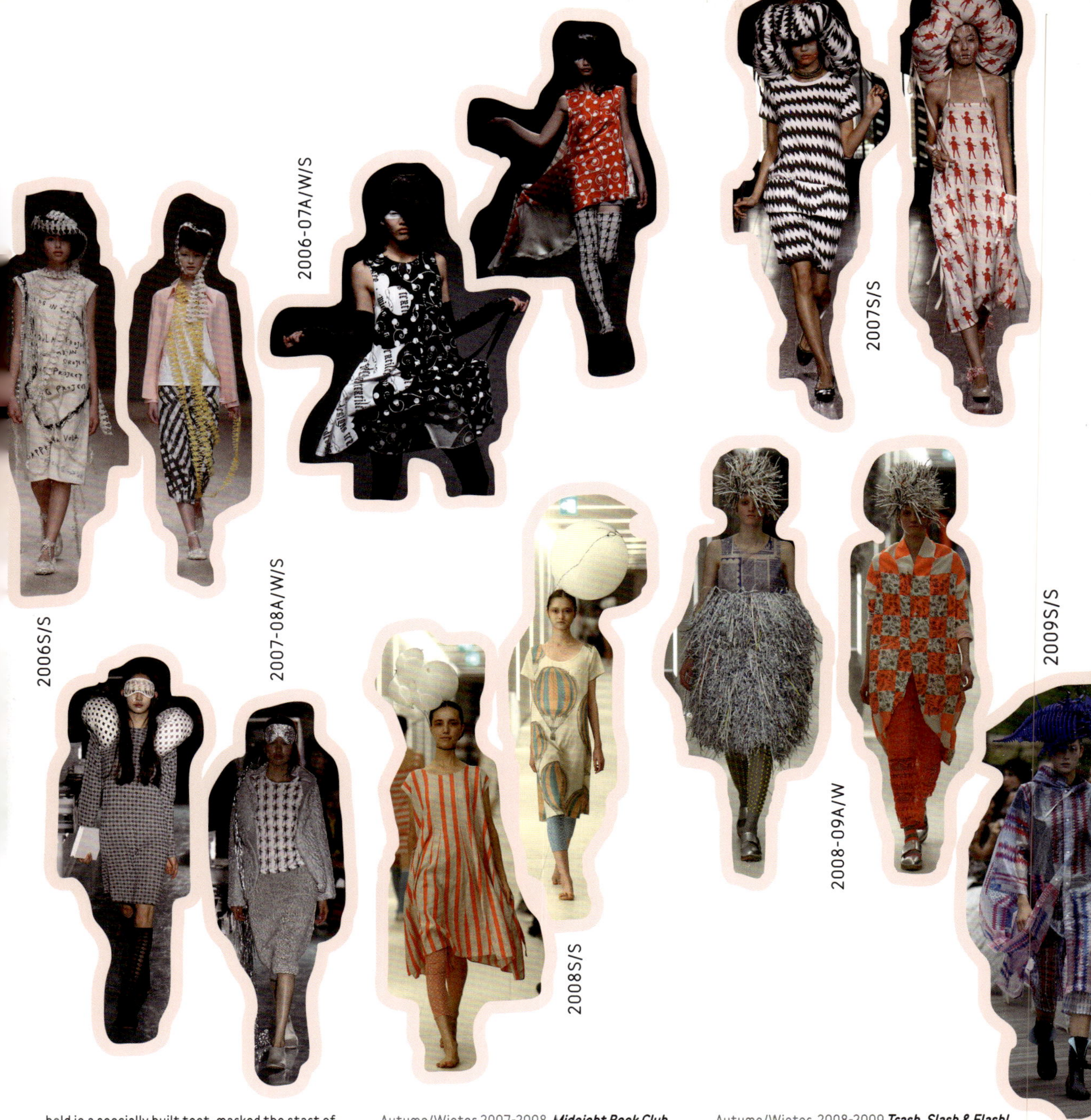

held in a specially built tent, marked the start of Japan Fashion Week. The staff wore T-shirts by mintdesigns and sat opposite the audience.

Autumn/Winter/Spring 2006-2007, ***composing project*** (Meiji Memorial Picture Gallery TOKIWA). Music, score, soiree, and waltz formed the image sources for the collection.

Spring/Summer 2007, ***To pathetically live*** (Jiyugakuen Myonichikan). The collection attracted interest thanks to the iconic zigzag patterns, headpieces, and painted makeup. After this season, themes developed into expressions of the designers' attitude toward the world.

Autumn/Winter 2007-2008, ***Midnight Book Club*** (Shibuya Parco Part1 B1). This fashion show took place at Shibuya Parco to celebrate the opening of the Mint Designs retail store. The bookshop on the same floor was transformed into a Mint Designs world with their books and posters.

Spring/Summer 2008, ***The Flying Girls 1808*** (Salon de Shu Sanctuary). The collection, focusing on civilization and information 200 years ago, took place at Salon de Shu Sanctuary in Tokyo Midtown. The long corridor gave the show a fantastical touch.

Autumn/Winter, 2008-2009 ***Trash, Slash & Flash!*** (Salon de Shu Sanctuary). Like its predecessor, the collection was held at Salon de Shu Sanctuary. The shredder served as the image source, but also for configuring the venue. Waste products were shredded and reused in the designs presented at this collection.

Spring/Summer 2009, ***Death Pop*** (Tokyo Midtown Galeria B1 Wood Terrace). The first exterior show consisted of original en-tout-cas, rain boots, and rain wears. The collection's designs resulted from being imaginative with bones.

Autumn/Winter 2009-2010, ***The rebellious stage of mintdesigns*** (Tokyo Tower Parking Center). Rebellion against society has become too slick and controlled; their rebellion is also against laws of designing and the past images of mintdesigns . The show expressed their understanding of rebelling in a positive way that is typical of mintdesigns.

Spring/Summer 2010, ***twinkling, shining, fluttering, fluffy, sheer, smooth*** (The Gallery of Horyuji Treasures, Tokyo National Museum). Modern elegance was rarely expressed as lightly as here. The collection demonstrated a new and experimental side to offset the sense of darkness exuded by the previous collection.

Autumn/Winter 2010-2011, ***A NEW HOPE*** (National Olympic Stadium). Instead of being particular with details, the designers aimed at a simple and powerful style with patterns that were so large that they seemed to spread beyond the fabric.

Spring/Summer 2011, ***almost blue*** (ARTS CHIYODA). The show revolved mainly around the brand's first original jeans. The use of ethnic patterns suggested a transnational style of denim. The finale saw the last model enter the stage into a blue room.

Autumn/Winter 2011-2012, ***fashion surgery*** (TABLOID). A new meaning and patterns, and the power of silhouettes formed the result of experimentally combining and then reassembling symbolic and plain motifs—circles, lines and as such—plus different materials. The theme was the recreation of beauty from an ensemble of basic matter. Headpieces, made from light-emitting diodes, echoed the motif of dresses with curvy lines and provided the symbol of linear beams of light.

mintdesigns

Designers' profiles:
mintdesigns / Hokuto Katsui, Nao Yagi

Hokuto Katsui was born in Tokyo in 1973. After studying at Parsons School of Design in New York, he moved to London and graduated from Central St. Martins College of Art and Design. Nao Yagi was born in Osaka in 1973. After studying art criticism at Doshisha University, she graduated from Central St. Martins College of Art and Design.
After graduation they both returned to Japan, where they launched mintdesigns in 2001. They defy the boundaries of wardrobe and aim to improve living spaces and daily life by defining clothes as designed products.

Brand history:
2001 mintdesigns launched
2002 Tokyo Collection debut with SS2003.
2005 Moet et Chandon Designer Debut Award.
2006 Involved with Uniqlo's Designer Invitation Project.
2007 Opening of a mintdesigns garage store at Shibuya Parco.
2008 Participated in São Paulo Fashion Week SS2009 in June. Became visiting professors at Osaka Seikei University.
2009 Exhibition "to be someone" at Tokyo Fiber 2009 in Milan, Italy.
2010 Awarded the 28th Mainichi Fashion Grand Prix.
2011 "Happy mistake! Pattern on pattern" exhibition at MOCA Taipei in Taiwan.
The Kyoto version takes place at the gallery of Osaka Seikei University.

SASQUATCHfabrix.

SASQUATCHfabrix.

Wonder Worker Guerrilla Band

Daisuke Yokoyama

Katsuki Araki

サスクワァッチファブリックス

ワンダーワーカーゲリラバンド

横山大介

荒木克記

SASQUATCHfabrix.

Wonder Worker Guerrilla Band

Daisuke Yokoyama

Katsuki Araki

サスクワァッチファブリックス

ワンダーワーカーゲリラバンド

横山大介

荒木克記

The "Tairyo-Kimono", with its "INRI" motif, features dynamic graphics combining Japanese and Western styles, and is typical for SASQUATCHfabrix. This work was shown at the exhibition "THE PARTY GROUND", under the concept of "God's playground", held at the select shop "VICE VERSA" in Fukuoka.

SASQUATCHfabrix / Daisuke Yokoyama, Katsunori Araki (Wonder Worker Guerrilla Band)

"We want to be like a Sasquatch: an elusive, mysterious presence in the world of street fashion."

Interviewed by Mariko Nishitani

SASQUATCHfabrix is the only men's fashion label represented in this exhibition. It was Daisuke Yokoyama and Katsunori Araki who established the label in 2003. The brand's aesthetic is deeply rooted in the Tokyo street fashion of the 1990s, which was these designers' formative period. Yokoyama and Araki studied architecture and textile design at the Nagaoka Institute of Design in Niigata Prefecture. Since then, they have shared their love of American casual clothes, vintage items, denim jeans, and the Japanese subculture called "Urahara boom".

The Tokyo fashion of the 2000s cannot be discussed without mentioning the domestic menswear brands and their great success. Labels such as Undercover and Number (N)ine led the way, followed by N.Hoolywood, Kolor, John Lawrence Sullivan, White Mountaineering, VISVIM, FACTOTUM, PHENOMENON, and Unused. While there were very few common denominators among women's fashion, these menswear designers shared similar aesthetics and attitudes. The aesthetic they shared was decidedly casual. They also studied, analyzed, and emulated the 'cool factors' of vintage clothing. Over the course of several years, this accumulation of knowledge resulted in various interpretations of casual and vintage-inspired fashion, broadening the range of stylistic options for consumers. The international fashion world has since taken notice of the richness and diversity of Tokyo menswear fashion.

SASQUATCHfabrix belongs to this group of successful Japanese menswear brands. However, the label distinguishes itself through its use of powerful graphics and the designers' interest in an eclectic mix of tribal and ethnic cultures from around the world. Unlike many other brands, SASQUATCHfabrix does not limit its aesthetic to American casual style, and it takes its inspiration from everywhere. Their signature style can be called "tribal-casual", mainly based on Native American motifs. The designers have also adopted aesthetic elements from Mexican, Tibetan, African, Scandinavian, and even Japanese sources.

The early days: Obsessive consumption of clothes and the love of the 'Urahara' style

_ Could each of you talk about your first encounter with fashion?

Yokoyama: For me, it was around 1995 or 1996. I was probably in middle school or high school then. I was attracted to vintage and outdoor clothing. Music also influenced my wardrobe choice. I remember buying a pair of Ben Davis pants, like the ones the Beastie Boys were wearing.

Araki: In my case, I remember buying a pair of cargo pants and parachute boots when I was in the sixth or seventh grade. It was before I knew anything about fashion brands, magazines or trends.

It was the very first time my parents let me buy my own clothes. I thought the details on the army cargo pants looked really cool. But I had no idea how to wear them properly. They were too big for me even after my mother did some alterations on them. A lot of clothes just didn't look right on my body, and I have always felt dissatisfied with the designs of these store-bought items. That was when I started feeling the need for fixing and improving the designs of ready-made clothes.

_ Both of you studied at the Nagaoka Design Institute. Did you grow up in the city of Nagaoka as well?

Araki: I grew up in Yokkaichi City in Mie Prefecture. I moved to Nagaoka for college, because I wanted to be as far away as possible from my hometown.

Yokoyama: I spent my childhood in Niigata Prefecture.

_ When did you start reading fashion magazines?

Araki: I was probably in the eighth grade. It was around the time I stopped doing after-school sports activities.

Yokoyama: I was reading magazines like *Men's Non-no*, *Check Mate* and *Popeye*.

Araki: I also remember *Hot Dog* and *Boon*. I wasn't too selective about which magazines to read. I pretty much read everything.

_ So, were you learning about fashion through these magazines?

Yokoyama: Not really. I learned about fashion from urban street cultures. I was more influenced by what I saw on the streets than in fashion magazines.

_ Your taste in fashion was largely based on the American casual style. You were not interested in high fashion, right?

Yokoyama: Right. I was not into someone like Masaki Matsushima.

Araki: Me neither. Back in the day, everyone was wearing Dirk Bikkenbergs, but not me.

_ You didn't find them interesting.

Araki: I didn't know why, but they just weren't my style.

Yokoyama: Of all the high fashion brands, Comme des Garçons was the only label I found fascinating.

_ What was your perspective on Comme des Garçons?

Yokoyama: I thought that Comme des Garçons was easy to adopt into my regular wardrobe. Their clothing items, such as knit cardigans, were based on the 'American Traditional' taste and reminded me of street clothes.

Araki: Perhaps we were influenced by Hiroshi Fujiwara's opinion. He was a charismatic fashion figure who advocated Comme des Garçons. I bet a lot of people in our generation followed his taste and shared his love of Comme des Garçons. He wrote a magazine article, saying something like "I just bought this particular Comme des Garçons's shirt in all three colors."

_ Did you go to any of Comme des Garçons's boutiques?

Araki: I trekked all the way to Nagoya Prefecture to shop at one of their boutiques. I remember the really edgy haircut on all of the female shopkeepers there.

Yokoyama: Besides Comme des Garçons, Vivian Westwood was really popular even in Niigata Prefecture where I lived.
I used to hang out with the cool people who knew a lot about fashion and culture. I learned everything from them.

Araki: Those cool people would tell you what was hip, and you went out and bought the items they recommend, right?

The "Mexican Skull," first presented at the Mexico-themed Spring/Summer 2005 collection, has appeared in different guises over the years. The version shown here was produced in 2008 for the temporary "SASQUATCHfabrix, Guerrilla Shop" at THE CONTEMPORARY FIX, a specialty store in Aoyama, Tokyo.

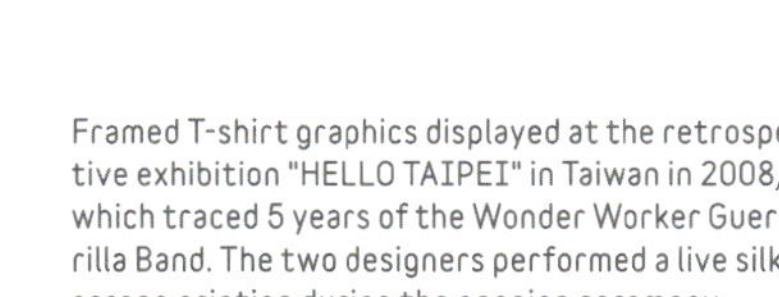

Framed T-shirt graphics displayed at the retrospective exhibition "HELLO TAIPEI" in Taiwan in 2008, which traced 5 years of the Wonder Worker Guerrilla Band. The two designers performed a live silk screen printing during the opening ceremony.

Yokoyama: It was like the hierarchical relationship in a Japanese high school sports team. The captain of the team told you what was hip and what was out, and you just followed their instructions (laughs).

Araki: They gave you their rules of fashion. As you discovered your own rules, you started developing your own sense of style.

Yokoyama: There were so many kinds of cool people. The London style, the American style, the Continental European style...the list goes on.

_ Did you belong to the group with the American style?

Yokoyama: I wasn't in any of them.

Araki: This was the beginning of the era in which everybody was mixing different styles.

_ When you first met at the Nagaoka Design Institute, what kind of clothes were you wearing?

Yokoyama: I was really into a fashion label called Good Enough by Hiroshi Fujiwara. It was one of those brands that only a minority of fashion insiders knew about. As it turned out, Araki was also into Good Enough.

_ What a coincidence. What exactly were you wearing?

Araki: It was just a jersey parka.

Yokoyama: It had a GE logo on it (laughs).

Araki: This brand was the precursor to the 'Urahara boom.' That logo with the letter G was very precious to me. I loved it so much that it was almost a matter of life or death.

Yokoyama: This is what you mean by "being crazed" by a brand. You didn't even know if it was stylish or not anymore.

_ And did you wear a pair of jeans with it?

Yokoyama: Yes. I wore a pair of vintage denim. And I matched them with a pair of sneakers by Jack Purcell, All Star Converse, or Red Wing.

Araki: Wow, you were so specific.

_ Would you call your look a typical 'Urahara' style?

Yokoyama: Back in those days, there were only three or four options (for menswear styles): the Outdoorsy style, the American casual style, hardcore vintage style, or 'Urahara' style.

Araki: A lot of my friends had disposable incomes from their part-time jobs, so some of them went and bought clothes that were really 'out there'. Fashion brands like Beauty:Beast and W< had just come out at the time.

Yokoyama: In the suburbs, many thuggish kids were also into fashion. They would wear vintage clothing and hang out in a group. Do you remember "Air Max Hunt"? Those pairs of Nike Air Max 95 shoes were so rare that you couldn't wear them in the street unless you wanted to get mugged by these kids.

_ How did Undercover and NIGO affect your style?

Araki: I think they came about a year after Hiroshi Fujiwara's Good Enough.

Yokoyama: Undercover was insanely popular.

Araki: For me, Undercover was a part of my high school experience. I remember standing in line before the opening of the boutique, waiting for the new release products to hit the shelf. The storekeepers of these fashion boutiques used to be so stylish and charismatic. There was a huge difference between the way these shopkeepers and their customers dressed. But then, many of the domestic brands used poor-quality materials, and their products were cheap looking. I couldn't believe that they asked for 8000 yen for a flimsy T-shirt. I forced myself to look beyond the poor quality in order to buy their products. I still felt compelled to buy them even when I didn't like what I saw. I was caught in the frenzy.

Yokoyama: We were caught in the frenzy for only a year or two. Then we fell off the wagon, so to speak.

_ What made you so crazed about their products?

Araki: Back then, these domestic brands

On the left: "BUY OR DIE" was produced as a limited edition for Autumn/Winter 2004-2005 and sent out through direct mail. It contained illustrations of all the items for the season. Page 134 and 135 featured all their past exhibition invitations. When seen side-by-side, one of the most striking features is the dazzling variety of native elements SASQUATCHfabrix have incorporated into their collections over the seasons.

represented the perfect mix of casual aesthetic and the edgy styles of punk rock and rock bands. It was hard to find fashion brands that represented our favorite youth culture. It didn't matter to us how poor the quality of these products was. Today, Jun Takahashi (the designer of Undercover) would be horrified to see how cheap his products used to look. But back then it was acceptable. Everyone was cutting corners when it came to product quality. Because of this, the fashion designers from our generation are really obsessive about getting everything right. Anyway, I used to spend a lot of money on clothes.

Yokoyama: They were really expensive. But in hindsight, none of those pricey things were made to last. Several pairs of denim pants and some portable electronic goods are the only things I still have with me.

_ Fashion has so many interesting facets.

Yokoyama: That is probably why I work in the fashion industry.

Araki: Fashion is not only about the quality of the products. It's about creating passion for those products. My mother couldn't believe how much money I splurged on a pair of torn-up jeans.

Yokoyama: I used to have a pair of Levi's 501 XX and my grandmother put a patch on the hole. I got so mad that I thought I was going to die (laughs).

Araki: Those grown-ups never got it.

Yokoyama: We used to go clubbing wearing our favorite clothes. Our subculture was all about wearing certain styles of clothes to match the scene we were playing in.

Establishing the brand in Tokyo

_ The two of you met in college, and you started the fashion label together in Tokyo.

Yokoyama: At first, I had no intention of establishing a fashion brand. After graduating from college with an architecture degree, I moved to Tokyo to work at a design firm. By that time, I was no longer obsessed with buying clothes.

Araki: I got a job at a product planning company for a big box apparel maker in Tokyo. When I graduated from college, I wanted to become a fashion designer, but I had no idea how to proceed. I thought that working in the apparel industry would be a step toward my goal. But I had lost interest in domestic clothing brands. There were too many of them that were mediocre, and I got fed up with them.

Yokoyama: Those domestic brands were boring derivatives of the 'Urahara' style.

_ Could you tell me the process of starting your own brand?

Yokoyama: After living and working in Tokyo for two years, I was comfortable at my job and had a plenty of time to make new friends. These friends were from the street fashion scenes. I started making newsletters, writing about cool happenings in and around Tokyo. I took the copies of my newsletters all over Tokyo, and before I knew it I was surrounded by really interesting people. They inspired me to do something creative. Then I ran into Araki on the street and we decided to make T-shirts together. We were really happy with the way they came out. In a way, our level of confidence was unfounded.

_ You not only made the graphics, but also the T-shirts themselves.

Araki: We were determined to create T-shirts with the highest quality of materials. We didn't want to repeat the same mistakes that the earlier domestic brands made. But our wholesalers didn't do a very good job selling our T-shirts.

Yokoyama: We assumed that it would be easy to sell at least one hundred T-shirts. Back then, many T-shirts were made in a limited production number of one hundred.

Araki: I thought consumers would go crazy for anything in a limited number production.

_ How did you sell your products? Did you hold an exhibition?

Yokoyama: No, we did not. We had no idea.

Araki: We were not business savvy at all.

Yokoyama: We made a boxed set of our T-shirt, our newsletter, the art magazine we wrote, and a music CD that we designed the jacket for. We put our original sticker on the box and made a bunch of sample box sets. Then, we looked up the names of well-known wholesalers in Japan and sent them the samples, totally unsolicited. We enclosed a cover letter saying, "Please contact us if you are interested." Miraculously, we got responses from ten wholesalers.

_ So your business started out in a pretty crude manner.

Araki: In the end we received two or three faxes with orders. For the next three years, our inventories sat in

photo:Shunya Arai styling:Keita Izuka hair:Kaneda(Image) make-up:Michiko Funahiki model:Cyril

photo:Takemi Yabuki styling:Keita Izuka hair:Kazuya Matsumoto make-up:UDA model:Valentin

Since Autumn/Winter 2009-2010, Wonder Worker Guerrilla Band has been responsible for directing and designing visuals for SASQUATCHfabrix. Their fantastical imagery seems as borderless as their clothing designs. Top left is Autumn/Winter 2009-2010's "TOKYO AIR RUNNERS" and bottom left Autumn/Winter 2010-2011's "CONTEMPORARY PIRATES 2." On the right is Spring/Summer 2011's "ZENARCHY."

photo:Muga Miyahara styling:Keita Izuka hair:KANADA make-up:Miharu model:Fenton

our apartments. We had to stare at a mountain of cardboard boxes before we went to sleep every night (laughs).

Yokoyama: Regardless of the lackluster sales, I believe we made a huge impact in the Tokyo fashion scene with our graphic logos. I might even say that we changed the history of graphic T-shirts! Our graphics were not original, but they were mostly parodies of pre-existing logos.

Araki: In the past, graphic designers did the graphics on T-shirts, and they didn't know how to make them look good when they are actually worn on the body. There was a sense of disconnection between graphic designer and fashion designer.

Yokoyama: We wanted to solve this problem.

_ Where did the name "Sasquatch" come from?

Araki: "Sasquatch" means Bigfoot, the legendary monster in the snowy mountains.

Yokoyama: We have two reasons for the name of our brand. First, we met each other in Nagaoka, an area with lots of snow. Second, we wanted to say that our designs are rare and special, like an encounter with a Sasquatch. We wanted our customers to be shocked by our creations, just like when they bump into a Sasquatch!

Araki: A Sasquatch is a mythological creature. We wanted our clothes to look eccentric enough to stand out in the crowd. The name "SASQUATCHfabrix" embodies the 'randomness' of finding our products and the 'rarity' of our designs.

_ You have kept the same name for your brand since you started making the T-shirts.

Araki: Our concept was clear from day one.

Towards a new branding strategy: Employing 'Primitive' design elements

_ I think the most fascinating feature of SASQUATCHfabrix's design is the mixture of diverse cultural influences and the ways you let them interact with each other. You have chosen your themes and motifs from such a wide range of sources such as the Native Americans, Tibetans, and Eskimos, Mexico, Africa, Nordic countries, Hawaii, and so on.
You have also incorporated the hippie aesthetic, Ivy League style, arabesque motifs, and even pirate and ninja motifs. It's intriguing to see how many motifs you have adopted without any sense of restriction.

Yokoyama: The Native American motif is not the only theme for our design. We are open to anything. Our basic stance is to take inspiration from whatever we thought was 'cool' at that time. We tend to be drawn to indigenous cultures because their aesthetics are unique to certain locales. There is something mysterious about these indigenous cultures that no 'outsider' will ever fully understand. Japanese kimonos are one example. There is a sense of richness and depth to an indigenous culture because it is born out of a unique history and the specific climate of a region. We were first drawn to Native American aesthetics because we were personally into Native American jewelry and rugs. We were trying to figure out how to add our own twist to these indigenous cultural styles and make them our signature styles.

_ How did you move on from making T-shirts to doing a full collection of clothes?

Yokoyama: "Buy or Die" (autumn/winter 2004-2005) was the first collection we presented. The title of the collection had nothing to do with the theme of our designs. We used a lot of military/hunting camouflage on the clothes. There were MA-1 Air Force flight jackets, leopard rings, eagle-claw necklaces, and even the facial portraits of Prince, Freddie Mercury and Bootsy Collins. We used them as graphic motifs because they looked great in leopard prints. Our first collection was really outrageous, and we were heading in a direction that was the complete opposite of the mainstream trend. The world of high fashion was all about being chic, like Dior Homme and Raf Simons.
For our next spring/summer 2005 collection, our main theme was Mexico, and we used a lot of skull motifs.

_ You have used Mexico as the theme, and then you moved on to Tibetan Esoteric Buddhism.
Yokoyama: It started when we used the Chinese Mandarin gowns in our design. Also, the inspiration came from books, tchotchkes, and vintage clothing. We let everything inspire us. We have the same attitude when we make our own music. Psychedelic rock, funk, house, hip hop — we absorb everything from a neutral point of view. When we adopt elements from other cultures, we always study their cultural roots so we know how far we can go to 'deconstruct' them.

Araki: It is our "stance" that makes our brand 'cool', not the details of our design. Today, there are so many other brands with hybrid aesthetics. It's become common to see young people mix vintage, 'American Casual', European, and ethnic clothing. We want to move further away from these hybrid aesthetics because they've become too familiar to ordinary people.

Yokoyama: We want to contradict the trend. We want to do something that no one else can do.

Araki: Which doesn't mean that we'll start making outrageous designs just for the sake of it. We want the cool people to identify with our designs and adopt them into their wardrobes. These people are quick learners, and their sense of style is constantly evolving. So it's important for us to continue making designs that seem to be one step ahead of them.

Yokoyama: Rather than making clothes, we are making "fashion".

What are the types of clothes that only Japanese designers can make?

_ Where do you locate your identity as a Japanese fashion brand?

Yokoyama: I think there is a certain atmosphere that only Japanese brands can create, and it is something that no other international brands can emulate. Japanese designers have a special talent to create their own version of the hybrid, casual style of clothing. Maybe it's the same with contemporary Japanese music. It's neither original nor artistic, but it's easy to take in and fun. We could take inspirations from American and European sources and make a new hybrid design that would resonate with both American and European sensibilities. It's like we have no aesthetic/cultural roots of our own, so we will interpret other people's roots in our imagination and create something completely new. There is a sense of cultural misunderstanding when a Japanese person tries to interpret other cultures. The result is something really interesting and totally unique to Japan.

Araki: We grew up during the end of the 1970s, and we lived through the time of economic prosperity, even though the Japanese economy was at the end of its rapid growth. We were able to absorb so many influences from other cultures while growing up, and this allowed us to build a huge archive of diverse cultural imports in our brains. Now, we are able to export our own version of hybrid cultures. However, we worshipped the American cultural imports too much, and we neglected to appreciate the value of traditional Japanese arts and crafts. All I was thinking about were a pair of blue jeans and sneakers. That was such a mistake. I think our generation is in a way responsible for killing the traditional Japanese arts and crafts. Perhaps we were manipulated by the media. As a result, Japanese culture has lost so much of its distinctive flavor and instead it's turning into strange subcultures like "Harajuku" and "Akihabara".

Yokoyama: It's interesting that many people of our generation don't admire the West the same way the previous generation did. For example, I have no desire to visit the United States or to move there. I'm more fascinated by the West seen through the Japanese perspective and the unique Japanese interpretation of foreign cultures.

Araki: I agree with you. But I still think Japanese people lack a basic appreciation for their own cultural heritage. The French and the British are much better at it.

_ Perhaps you can create a new Japanese culture based on the perspective from abroad?

Yokoyama: Yes. That is actually what we are working on now. I want to create Japanese designs from a foreigner's point of view, so that young Japanese people will find them hip and attractive.

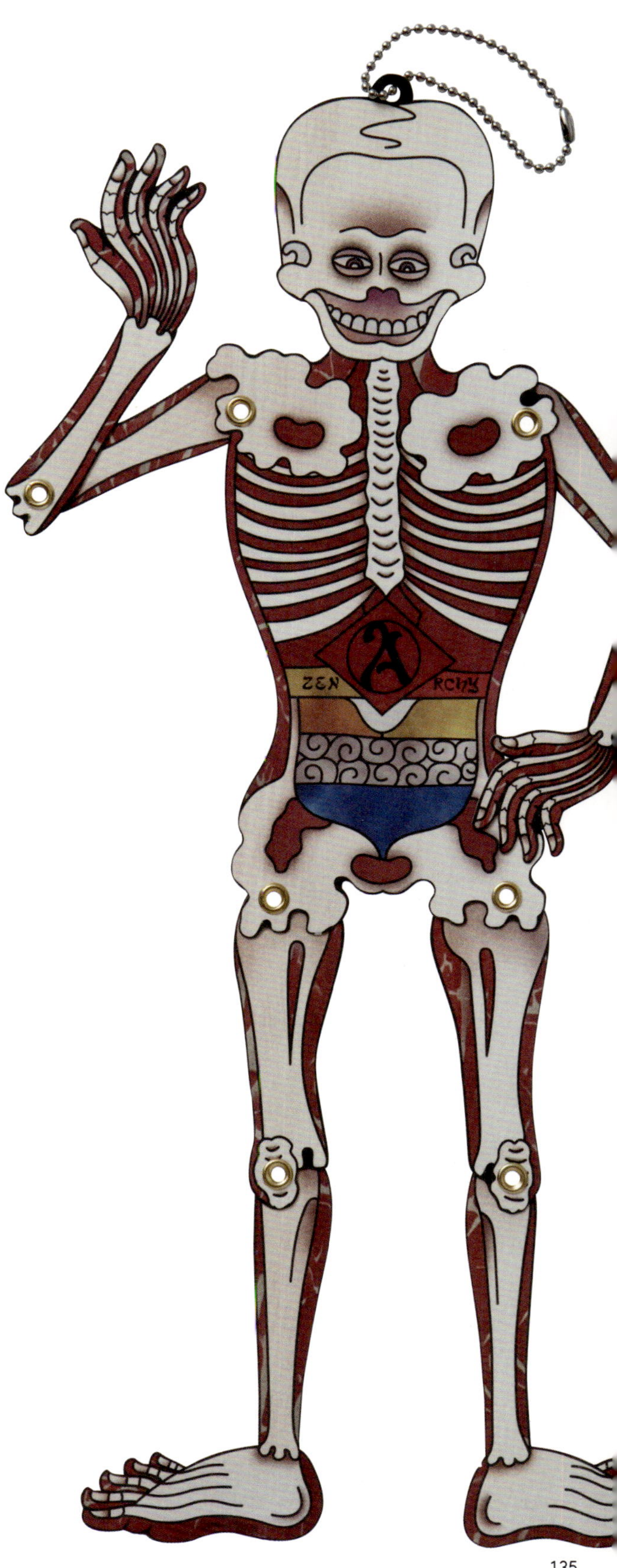

Spring/Summer 2005, ***Fancy Dress.*** A style with trad elements such as embroidery patterns, vintage metal buttons, and patches found in American second-hand clothing, mixed with Mexican elements such as skulls and hemp. The clothes were extremely elaborate and exuded a Mexican flavor, making them both vigorous and fun.

Autumn/Winter 2005-2006, ***FRONTIERSMEN.*** The clothes looked used as a result of the method of fabrication and the patterns, featuring uniquely Native American flavors combined with elements from traditional work clothes; Chino, flannel and denim were processed to look like vintage work clothes that are both functional and well made. The designers were responsible for not only the fabrics, with their cable design and Native American patterns, but also accessories such as conchos and embroidered patches. Their preoccupations could be seen in iconography of frontiersmen—invaders, intruders and colonizers of America—and in the "Amekaji" American casual style of flannel shirts and chino pants.

2006, ***JUNK MODE.*** The collection was defined by the worn-out texture of Vietnamese, Hawaiian, Asian, and store-brand used denim. These give off an aura of junk but are somehow elegant at the same time. This is what's meant by "JUNK MODE;" it is an encounter between American and Southeast Asian daily wear, with elements embedded in aloha, Western and Native American styles.

Autumn/Winter 2006-2007, ***SLACKER.*** The slacker: someone who is laid-back, obsessed with something trivial, and living his life in a big city without being bound to social rules. This season was defined by a blend of military and work elements under the "SLACKER" theme. The casual items and military-look clothes were rendered elegant by subduing their earthiness. Conversely, the formal clothes and items were rendered more casual by adding military and work wear elements. Some of their dressy items with military taste include the satin A-2 flight jacket, whose armholes, sleeves and width were reduced in size. Their jacket with lapels was tailored to a denim-like style with a top fabric of stretch wool and an underlining layer of wool in border print. The paired slacks, designed to look

2010-11 A/W

Sasquatch fabrix.

EOTOTO

2011 S/S

Sasquatch fabrix.

EOTOTO

like painter's overalls, consist of dress-down formal items.

Spring/Summer 2007, ***SLACKER.*** The "SLACKER" theme continued from the previous season, with the addition of the circle paisley motif.

Autumn/Winter 2007-2008, ***TORA TORA TORA.*** Formal clothing made of high-quality fabrics were spiced up with the motif of the Tibetan tiger—a guardian deity—creating a great example of Yokoyama and Araki's original world. The style looks neither too casual nor too formal thanks to its oriental feel, and playfulness was characteristic for the collection as a whole.

Spring/Summer 2008, ***ILLEGAL PLAYERS.*** Based on school tastes, basic items like blazers, button-down shirts, and drizzler jackets were updated with fluorescent colors and graphics containing strong messages. The collection expressed youth's sense of longing for something illegal.

Autumn/Winter 2008-2009. From this season, the items infused with Native American tastes were introduced separately as the "EOTOTO" line. Eototo is the father of the Katsina spirits from the Hopi's spiritual pantheon; he exists above all Katsinam, has knowledge of all kinds of rituals, and controls the seasons.

Spring/Summer 2009, ***HOMING-chama cha amani.*** Under the motto "Let's go home," the collection was named after "CHAMA CHA AMANI," an African expression meaning "peaceful people," and proposed daily wear colored with flamboyant African graphics.

Autumn/Winter 2009-2010, ***TOKYO AIR RUNNERS.*** In the late 1980s, styles changed rapidly; techno and house music appeared at a time when American casual clothes and a style exclusive to Shibuya were popular, prompting people to start arranging main items by layering or wearing a bandanna. The collection was intended as a catalyst to trigger a movement like the DC boom, the used-wear boom and the Harajuku street boom. It also launched the

Sasquatch fabrix.

message "It's time to do fashion seriously!" to a staid Japanese fashion world where reproduction of European styles and American used wear dominate.

Spring/Summer 2010, ***CONTEMPORARY PIRATES*** (photos on page 140). Over the past dozen years or so, the fashion culture in Tokyo has been segmented by the pursuit of various styles and world cultures. The designers interpreted youth's capacity of enjoying fashion instinctively and without rules as "pirates." This collection was therefore titled "CONTEMPORARY PIRATES" and proposed the "Viking" style, a mix of 1980s London culture and the style of pirates—incorporating black metal, death metal, and Viking metal—rooted in Scandinavia.

Autumn/Winter 2010-2011, ***CONTEMPORARY PIRATES 2*** (photos on page 141). The collection was titled "CONTEMPORARY PIRATES 2" as a continuation of the previous season. A more aggressive, violent flavor was mixed in with last season's style.

Spring/Summer 2011, ***ZENARCHY.*** The term "ZEN-ARCHY" is a composite of zen and anarchy originally coined by The KLF, the house music unit consisting of Bill Drummond and Jimmy Cauty; it means to achieve spiritual awakening without rigorous training. The designers used the term to create a story, which they expressed in their clothes. The oriental feel of zen lay in the copious use of denim, the Japanese-inspired graphics, tie-dyeing and bleaching.

Autumn/Winter 2011-2012, ***MODERN NINJA*** (above). The collection was influenced by the freedom of ideas for evolving designs in high-tech sneakers. It is the style of a modern ninja, associated with suppleness and speed; details of riders' wear like stretch fabrics and bellows were incorporated with an old-school taste. While layers of colors and intricate designs become more common, the designers dared to try out the black tone for the first time in their work.

Photo:Tohru Yuasa(B.P.B.)

Designers' profiles:
SASQUATCHfabrix / Daisuke Yokoyama (right), Katsuki Araki

Daisuke Yokoyama was born in Niigata in 1977. He graduated from Nagaoka Institute of Design with a degree in architectural design. After working for a graphic design company in Tokyo, he launched SASQUATCHfabrix with Araki in 2003.
Katsuki Araki was born in 1977. He graduated in textile design from Nagaoka Institute of Design. He worked as a salesman for a mass retailer of children's clothing before launching SASQUATCHfabrix with Yokoyama in 2003.
They run SASQUATCHfabrix while creating graphic designs for the fields of fashion and music under the name Wonder Worker Guerrilla Band. In addition to their main brand, they offer two subsidiaries, EOTOTO and SASQUATCHfabrix. Chilling. Since the start of their brand most of their products have been made with original fabrics.

Brand history:
2003 SASQUATCHfabrix founded.
2004 Produced skateboard decks and bangles for furniture manufacturer Tendo Mokko.
2006 Involved with "Japan Pop Culture T-shirt Project" for the opening of the Uniqlo store in Soho, New York City, directed by Kashiwa Sato.
2007 Exhibited a solid structure for the first time at "The Royal House" under the concept "Bed Room."
Design a "funny bike" for kalavinka, a ,manufacturer of racing bike frames.
2008 First exhibition as Wonder Worker Guerrilla Band, "HelloTaipei!!"
Debut of the EOTOTO line featuring Native American styles.
2009 Worked for Hot Chocolate, a collaboration brand with Uniqlo UT.
Involved in the layout of the UT store in Harajuku.
Debut of SASQUATCHfabrix. Chilling.
2011 Exhibition of their installation works at LN-CC, a specialty store in London.

photo:Sinya Keita(Rollup Studio)

SOMARTA

ソマルタ
廣川玉枝

SOMARTA
Tamae Hirokawa

SOMARTA
Tamae Hirokawa

ソマルタ
廣川玉枝

"Robin" from the body wear series called "Skin" released in 2006 by SOMARTA under the concept of "the possibilities of bodywear." Its delicate lace, programmed to fit seamlessly around a woman's body, symbolizes the brand.

SOMARTA / Tamae Hirokawa

The Evolving Form of Knitwear for the Future

Interviewed by Mariko Nishitani

Tamae Hirokawa graduated from the department of apparel design at Bunka Fashion College. After working for Issey Miyake, Hirokawa created her own fashion brand, Somarta. As a regular participant in the Tokyo Collections, Hirokawa won the Newcomer's Prize at the Mainichi Fashion Grand Prix and the Shiseido Sponsorship Award. Lady Gaga famously wore Hirokawa's bodysuit for her live performance in Tokyo in April 2010. Tamae Hirokawa has led a very successful career in fashion. Yet she is clearly different from the typical fashion industry insider. Hirokawa is disarmingly unpretentious and considers her label Somarta as one of the design projects of her own design firm, Soma Design. Hirokawa specializes in creating seamless knitwear made with the precision of both a craftsman and a mathematician. On the runway, she presents the narrative elements of her designs in a film projection created by Soma Design. Her clothes feature the most cutting-edge technology in textile manufacturing. For the name of her label, Hirokawa took inspiration from her own name, Tamae, a bejeweled branch from the legendary island of Horai and applied the Sanskrit words soma and amrta. Hirokawa's distinctive creations transcend time and open an innovative path toward the future of fashion.

Entering Bunka Fashion College to become a designer

_ What initially attracted you to the world of fashion?

Hirokawa: When I was in high school, I was intrigued by all the beautiful images I saw in magazines. My interest in fashion grew from there.

_ Were you interested in visual images of fashion rather than dressing yourself up in stylish clothes?

Hirokawa: I had a part-time job during my last year in high school, and with the money I earned I bought clothes. By that time, I started to hope that my future career would have something to do with the concept of 'women's beauty'. I learned several foreign languages to prepare for my career. I also loved drawing, but instead of pursuing fine art, I wanted to work in a field where I could bring joy to people by creating something that they could directly interact with. I thought I had no choice but to become a designer.

_ You entered Bunka Fashion College after you finished high school. Why did you choose to study in the apparel design department?

Hirokawa: Many famous designers have studied in this department, and I also liked the iconic round architecture of the school building. I was not good at sewing at all, and I knew that I was behind my classmates. I spent my freshman year desperately catching up with them and learning the basics of dressmaking.

_ Many of your fellow classmates have emerged as successful fashion designers, such as Hiroyuki Horihata and Makiko Sekiguchi of matohu, Yoshiyuki Miyamae of Issey Miyake, Cabaret Aki of Gut's Dynamite Cabarets, and Iku Furudate of Commuun.

Hirokawa: Yes, indeed. We hardly spent time with each other outside of school, though. We had too many assignments. When I had some extra time, I went to theaters with my classmates. I had a friend who was into contemporary dance, so I often went to see performances by Saburo Teshigawara, Pappa Tarahumara, and Dump Type. These experiences opened my eyes to various forms of theatrical expressions. My time at Bunka Fashion College was very inspirational. All of my classmates were really hardworking. We competed with each other for various awards and learned a lot from each other.

photo:Mitsuaki Koshizuka

"PROTEAN" was the theme for Somarta's second collection, Autumn/Winter 2007-2008. The stitched lace body wear was encrusted with Swarovski diamonds, expressing "the glistening body," as could be witnessed from the way it reflected the stage lights. This piece was later worn by Lady Gaga.

"The Secret Garden," an installation presented in collaboration with Canon at the NEOREAL Exhibition of the Milano Salone 2008 in Italy. A set-like space was created using the digital output technology, which formed the basis of the exhibition – unveiled here for the firs time. It also formed the introduction of the "Skin+Bone Chair."

_ Did you apply for the So-en Awards?

Hirokawa: Yes, I did. I made clothes that featured concealed fasteners.

_ Where did you get the idea?

Hirokawa: I was thinking of clothes that could be worn in many different ways. I sewed the fasteners onto a sheet of water-soluble vinyl. In the end, I melted the vinyl away and left only the draping of the fasteners. When the fasteners were opened, the inner layers of colors were exposed, creating a surprising contrast. I was so happy to receive feedback from Mr. Yoshiki Hishinuma who was one of the jury members, that I continued entering various contests. My designs became more playful and I received a lot of valuable advice from designers such as Nobuo Nakamura, Junko Koshino, and Mitsuhiro Matsuda. Mr. Issey Miyake was a judge in the last contest I entered before graduation. It was Mr. Miyake's last time as a jury member in this contest, so I did my very best to be on the shortlist. I became one of the finalists and was able to show my work to Mr. Miyake at the Miyake Design Studio.
I vividly remember the atmosphere of his studio during this visit. This experience gave me a chance to learn about Issey Miyake's work and made me want to work for him in the future. I identified with his approach to apparel making which was based on his broad perspective of design as an expressive medium. Even though I didn't win any prizes, entering those contests gave me a lot of meaningful experiences.

Encounter with knitwear

Hirokawa: I first worked at the Miyake Design Studio, and then spent 18 months as an assistant to Mr. Kosuke Tsumura in the Miyake-affiliated company A-net. Subsequently, a senior colleague retired and I took over her position in the knitwear department. That was my first encounter with knitwear.

_ This was around 1999?

Hirokawa: Exactly. I discovered many fascinating characteristics of knitted fabrics. I also learned a lot by visiting factories and talking to artisans. A regular fabric usually becomes a three-dimensional form through the process of drawing patterns, cutting and sewing. In the case of a knitted fabric, we can choose a yarn and design the form as well as the textile at the same time. I thought, "Great, what an efficient material!" I became deeply engaged in learning about knitted fabrics through trial and error. Next, I was transferred to the menswear department of Issey Miyake. That was when I met my future business partners, Takashi Mori and Takeshi Fukui. Fukui was in the graphic design department of Issey Miyake, which took care of everything from product packaging, prints, and displays to advertising for both the women's and men's collections.

_ You were not involved in A-POC.

Hirokawa: I was interested in A-POC, but I was on a different team. I was working under Naoto Takizawa who was designing the main collection line of Issey Miyake. I designed men's knits and jerseys. At first, it was difficult for me to design within the vocabulary of basic menswear. I always tended to overdo my designs because I've been a big fan of eye-catching theater costumes since I was a student. But in the end, I discovered infinite possibilities with menswear design. Issey Miyake created experimental menswear apparel with playful dyes, embroideries and prints. I learned about many different ways of treating fabrics as well as knitting and 'cut-and-sewn' techniques. After this, I was transferred to the women's apparel department. I continued designing knitwear, using my past experiences from working in the menswear department. I discovered seamless knitting techniques while I was working on projects outside of the main collection lines.

Seamless knits

_ Soon afterwards, you launched your label, Somarta. You made a series of bodysuits using seamless knits, which became an iconic product for Somarta. What was it about seamless knits that fascinated you as a designer?

Hirokawa: I discovered the term "second skin" when I was a student. This expression stayed in my heart. I also learned that, in the history of fashion, many designers including Issey Miyake used the concept of the second skin as their theme. I have always been interested in studying human anatomy through fashion, and I dreamed of designing my 'second skin' when I became a designer. Seamless knitwear became my own interpretation of the second skin; it's supple and elastic, and it fits the contours of a body exactly like skin. Seamless knits have an ideal structure and infinite possibilities. I was sure that incorporating a clothing item like a skin would enrich the vocabulary of my fashion design. Seamless knits also produce a minimum waste because they allow me to make clothes without sewing together different parts. I believe that I can find applications of Somarta's "Skin" series in various fields other than fashion.

_ In the Skin series, you have some items that have sleeves. Are those also made without any seams?

Hirokawa: It depends on the designs. Sometimes the knits are cut and sewn afterwards. I think that Japanese people are great at inventing a flat and simple structure, like the kimono. A woman's body consists of curves created by her bust, waist, and hips. When you make clothes using a regular fabric, your cutting skills will determine the result. In the case of a knitted fabric, however, we can change the very structure of the fabric and make it stretchable or shrinkable. It's fascinating that a fabric itself can determine the shape of clothing. I think of knits as our modern-day kimonos.

The launch of Soma Design and Somarta

_ You established your design studio, Soma Design, in conjunction with your label Somarta.

Hirokawa: I had always thought about bringing in associates when I was going to set up my own label. I wanted Soma Design to function as a design firm. Fukui would handle a wide spectrum of design work ranging from graphic design to art direction. Our projects went far beyond brand management. In the beginning, I drew a chart of our organization and positioned Somarta as a fashion project within Soma Design. Takashi Mori is in charge of music for all of our shows. He used to be a fashion designer with his own label and a musician before he became my associate. Also, I found Mr.

Hanabusa who was proficient in motion graphics so that we could strengthen our visual presentations.

_ Did you pool your resources to establish Soma Design?

Hirokawa: Initially, I was on my own. I rented a small apartment and asked for assistance from factories and friends in making my samples. For my first collection, I only had a few models of clothing made from three different materials, as well as some unique knitted items.

_ Could you tell me what "SOMARTA" stands for?

Hirokawa: SOMARTA is derived from the words "soma" and "amrta" in Sanskrit. My name is Tamae, which means a jeweled branch from the island of Horai, a mystical island from a legend. The branch produces a dew of immortality called "amrta". I crossed it with the word "soma", which stands for moon, and coined the word "Somarta". In English, via New Latin from Greek, "soma" means "the body". I think I came up with a very good name.

_ How did you build your brand's concept?

Hirokawa: In the very beginning, I built a three-year plan and decided the themes for the next six seasons. I wanted SOMARTA to be principally a knitwear label and produce bodysuits that resemble a "second skin". I would like to continue SOMARTA's "Skin" series as my lifework.

_ Did you have any particular muse for SOMARTA?

Hirokawa: Not really. I wanted to make clothes that I would like to wear. I had just turned thirty when I started the label, so I could say that my target audience was women who are mature. In the beginning, nobody on our team had a clear understanding of how to run a business, so we were incapable of making any business-oriented decisions. When I was working for a company, I had no professional network outside of that company. I didn't know anybody in the profession who could help me put together a fashion show.
Mr. Horihata of matohu, who already had his own label, was kind enough to introduce me to hair and make-up artists and PR agents. Gradually I started to get to know more people. One contact led me to another. One of the hair and make-up artists introduced me to Mr. Kaiji Moriyama, the contemporary dancer who ended up working on collaboration with us several years later. Mr. Moriyama then introduced me to Miu Sakamoto, the wonderful singer who sang at one of our shows.

_ I find the movie projections in your shows impressive. Are they made by Nobuyuki Hanabusa, your associate who is in charge of motion graphics?

Hirokawa: I come up with an original idea based on the concept of each collection and discuss this with Mr. Hanabusa, working out the various details of camera-work and imagery.

_ You are privileged to have these talented people working for you. It is also amazing that you can come up with great ideas all the time. Fashion is not only about clothes but also about creating certain feelings and opening up a new horizon for creative expression. Otherwise, fashion would be just about people with decent dressmaking skills.

Hirokawa: Soma Design is in charge of the branding of Somarta and the construction of the brand's world-view. I am grateful to have so many talented people working for me. Perhaps I have a talent for getting brilliant people involved in my projects.

Encounter with Noritaka Tatehana

_ You collaborated with the shoe designer Noritaka Tatehana for spring/summer 2011 and autumn/winter 2011 - 2012. How did the collaboration start?

Hirokawa: I first found out about him through a picture of Lady Gaga that I saw in a magazine. She was wearing Somarta's bodysuit and Noritaka Tatehana's shoes. Next, another photograph of a model wearing Somarta with his shoes appeared again in the American magazine Vanity Fair. When I saw that, I started thinking that perhaps we have something in common. The feeling of affinity for the human body is at the core of Somarta's philosophy. Likewise, I felt that Noritaka's shoes are very close to the anatomy of human feet, as though the feet were transformed into his shoes. Later, I had an opportunity to meet Noritaka at his exhibition and found out that he was also curious about SOMARTA. We decided to collaborate on SOMARTA's spring/summer 2011 collection. Noritaka made us his signature 'heel-less' shoes, but in SOMARTA's version, the shoes were easier to walk in because their soles were covered with a larger platform surface. They were also made to coordinate with the colors and motifs on the outfits from the "Skin" series. The theme of our autumn/winter 2011-12 collection was about the transformation of plants and flowers over time, so he made us shoes that featured some botanical designs, such as slits that looked like leaf veins. Noritaka is a great shoemaker, so we discuss our ideas and come up with new designs for the shoes together.

Vision toward the global market

_ Does SOMARTA see itself in the global market?

Hirokawa: Last year, we did runway shows in India and Russia. We haven't done any exhibitions with business in mind, but we are definitely interested in having a commercial presence abroad. I hope to be able to step into Europe and the rest of Asia in the near future.

_ How was your show in Russia received?

Hirokawa: We were invited to the Aurora Fashion Week in Saint Petersburg. We recreated the show we did in Tokyo with video projection, and we received very positive feedback. I was happy to see that a foreign audience loved our show. Also, I was surprised when a lady asked me right away after the show, "I want that last dress you showed. How much is it?" Our dresses are quite expensive in Japan and difficult to sell, so I hadn't even prepared a price sheet in Russian currency. In India, a lot of people were interested in the opulent dresses with pleated details. It made me realize that outside of Japan, a woman has more occasions to wear dresses in her day-to-day life.

_ Unlike women in Japan, they have the tradition of the "soirée", of changing and going out for the evening.

Hirokawa: SOMARTA's collections have two major directions: first, I aim at making exciting clothes that embody joy and beauty without any sense of

The size of the universe is in the eye of the beholder. The "WUNDERKAMMER" series of body wear beaded entirely by hand, vividly expresses the idea of "microcosm" that formed the theme for Spring/Summer 2011.

photo: Mitsuaki Koshizuka (MORE VISION) CG: SOMA DESIGN

Opposite page: Projecting images at runway shows to present the designer's world is a SOMARTA characteristic. Seen here is footage from "The Secret Garden," shown with the Spring/Summer 2007 collection. Adapted from the novel of the same title by F. H. Burnett, it was meant as a homage to the author. When the imaginative Mary opens her heart with a key given by a redbreasted robin, she encounters the "Guardian," an inhabitant of the garden. Page 153: Footage shown at the Spring/Summer 2007 collection, "Le Paysage dans le cadre des portières." Sources of inspiration were the poem of the same title by Paul Verlaine and the impromptu "PIANOSTALGIA," a sound project by SOMA DESIGN). A 50-meter wide panoramic screen transformed the runway into a train station platform. The show started with an image of a train arriving at the platform, while the illusion of a moving screen in the latter half of the show surprised the audience by making them feel as if aboard the departing train.

photo:Midori Tsunoda

The theme for Autumn/Winter 2011-2012 was "METAMORPHOSIS." From the concept of WUNDERKAMMER Hirokawa expressed the way flowers bloom from buds and the transformation of larvae into butterflies. She designed leavers lace in smoky and neutral colors by imagining a pile of fallen leaves and poked holes into the knitwear to simulate the texture of a tree trunk. This season introduced the minimal dresses of the "Skin" series, which wrap organically around the human body to evoke the look of a flower bud.

restrictions; second, I want to make modern clothes that enhance the beauty of the wearer, something like daytime dresses that I would want to wear. People in Japan find our dresses expensive, but they are exactly what customers in Russia and India are looking for. I thought we had to do more research on our price setting.

_ Did it make you feel self-aware of your Japanese identity when you showed your work abroad?

Hirokawa: India has a wonderful craftsmanship of dyeing, weaving, and treatment of natural fiber that is comparable to that of Japan. However, its technology in apparel production has yet to evolve, and knitwear is not very common there. Somarta's knitwear thus appeared shocking to our audience in India. Indian fashion journalists and artisans were surprised when they saw our work. In Russia, people found our knitwear and our production methods remarkable. People were especially amazed by the high standard of manufacturing techniques and advanced technology in apparel making in Japan.

_ Today, Japan seems to stand for innovation, rather than for the ancient philosophy of "wa" (harmony) or the well-known concept of "a piece of cloth".

Hirokawa: I agree with you. Perhaps their perception of Japan is oriented more towards our technology. When I was abroad, I rediscovered the richness of Japanese craftsmanship. It is meticulous, sensitive, and full of the artisan's pride. I was born and raised in Japan, so I do not need to be self-conscious about my identity in order to create something that embodies Japanese culture. I would like to expand my experiences and skills that I can only acquire in Japan, and I hope to present them to audiences abroad in the future.

"STEM," the heelless shoes with their leaf vein look, were introduced in Autumn/Winter 2011-2012 as the second collaboration between Somarta and Noritaka Tatehana.

COLLECTIONS

Over the course of three years and six seasons, from Spring/Summer 2007 to Autumn/Winter 2009-2010, Hirokawa set themes aimed at constructing the images of her brand around "Skin," SOMARTA's characteristic range of body wear. Instead of the usual "one season-one theme" approach, she stuck with one theme throughout the year . This allowed her to pursue techniques and subjects in a more profound way between the Spring/Summer and Autumn/Winter collections.

2007 ***The Secret Garden*** was the theme the whole year around. Hirokawa's high-tech knit program was in full bloom, forming the basis for Spring/Summer: "to wear designed skin". "GUARDIAN" dressed the human body in flower patterns; "ROBIN" worked with bird feathers, and "Angelos" took its cues from the garden. The Autumn/Winter collection's keyword was "PROTEAN", while flowers and bird feathers returned to form the motif for the following Spring/Summer. Flowers like clematis and protea found their way into knitwear, creating relief through joining garment to lining.

2008 ***TRIBAL*** was this year's theme. By imagining a fictional tribe, for the Spring/Summer "ENGRAVER" collection Hirokawa knitted the tribal graphics of the moon-dwelling SOMA into her work like tattoos. Using a machine that enabled a completely seamless construction, she also made vertical holes in the areas of hands, feet, and the side of "Skin", for another type of tribal graphics expressing RABI, the guardian of the earth. These continued to evolve in the "L'Oiseau Bleu" collection of Autumn/Winter, with lamé fabrics evoking ice crystals in addition to the tattoo motifs. Further

developments were also made with the use of sparkling knitwear.

2009 For the year-round of ***BODY***, Hirokawa created a new form by studying the structure of bones, muscles, and skin in animals and unknown creatures, as well as that of the human body. Imagining the wide range of elements from skin and bones to fictional structures and cells, she expressed these with seamless knitwear and hand-made knitting. The Autumn/Winter collection was based on "ADAMANTINE" - the extraordinary image of substance and a person's will sparkling like diamonds. She pursued ways to protect the human body against the cold and against enemies with knit garments. A waffle texture realized through compression technology was characteristic for her knit protective gear. Products other than knitwear were also introduced, such as leather with an embossed armor-like effect

Having completed her three-year project, designer Tamae Hirokawa set her collection theme by following her interests and continuing her knitwear project after the rapid development of seamless knitwear. Clothes were created by imagining the world of "Le paysage dans le cadre" by the poet Paul Verlaine; she shot footage based on the poem and designed clothes that, like the images, change with the passage of time. The romantic retro style was a departure from the futuristic and warrior-like image of previous year's SOMA. The Autumn/Winter collection was based on the "WUNDERKAMMER", the cabinet of curiosities or display room for collections of artifacts related to archeology, biology, physics, or anatomy. Such

2010-11 A/W

2011 S/S

2011-12 A/W

rooms were the product of pure curiosity and the results of developments in science and knowledge.

2011 The ***WUNDERKAMMER*** series continued on from last season. With her "inquisitive mind" for knitwear, Hirokawa collaborated with Noritaka Tatehana, and further expanded her activities.

Opposite page, top left: The brand name SOMARTA is derived from SOMA (moon), AMRTA (dew) and the designer's name Tamae, with the logo forming a threefold moiré. Bottom right is the Skin+Bone Chair, whose skeleton resembles a blooming flower, with the cover of lace encasing a body of air. SOMARTA's ideas on clothing give us hope for the creation of a new kind of lifestyle.

Designer's profile:
SOMARTA / Tamae Hirokawa

Tamae Hirokawa was born in Kanagawa in 1976. She graduated in apparel design from Bunka Fashion College. After working for Issey Miyake, she became independent in 2006, establishing SOMA DESIGN, which specializes in fashion, graphic design, sound creation and visual direction, and her apparel brand SOMARTA. She won the 25th Mainichi Fashion Grand Prix Newcomer's Prize and the Shiseido Sponsorship Award a year after her debut at the Tokyo Collection. She continued to develop her brand with the "Skin" series of knitwear, which uses technology capable of completely seamless construction. She was also involved in various fields outside fashion, such as interior design, art, and product design, and her activities have received praise in foreign countries including India and Russia.

Brand history:

2006 Established the design project SOMARTA.
Launched the body wear series "Skin" under the concept "the possibilities of body wear."
Tokyo Collection debut in SS2007.

2007 Won the 25th Mainichi Fashion Grand Prix Newcomer's Prize and the Shiseido Sponsorship Award.

2008 Presented the installations "The Secret Garden" and "ENGRAVER," plus the "Skin + Bone Chair" interior furniture at Canon NEOREAL Exhibition at the Milano Salone 2008, Italy.
Presented Concept Car and installation works at the [iQ X SOMARTA MICROCOSMOS] exhibition with Toyota at Designtide Tokyo

2010 Presented her creations at the First International Jewelry Week in Mumbai, India, in partnership with budding jewelry company CVM Exports.
Invited to the Second Aurora Fashion Week in St. Petersburg, Russia, where she presented her collection.

2011 Designed uniforms for Shiseido The Ginza.

THEATRE PRODUCTS

photo:Nao Tsuda

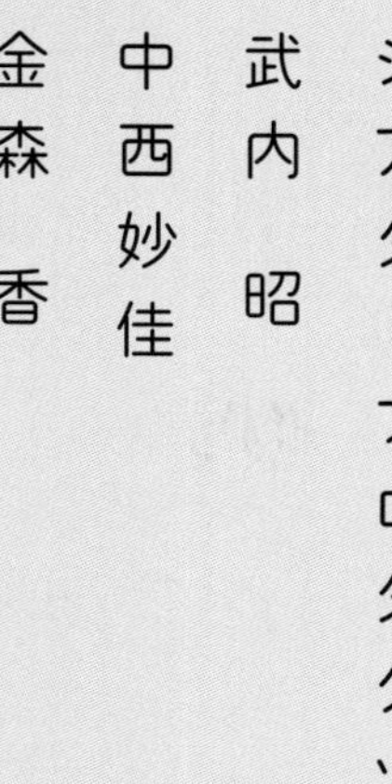

THEATRE PRODUCTS

Akira Takeuchi
Tayuka Nakanishi
Kao Kanamori

THEATRE PRODUCTS
Akira Takeuchi
Tayuka Nakanishi
Kao Kanamori
シアタープロダクツ
武内昭
中西妙佳
金森香

"THEATRE PRODUTS MAIN SHOP", exhibited in 2002 at the RICE GALLERY/G2 in Tokyo, in a building since torn down, was a tent made of tulle laces as a base, overlaid with needle-punched T-shirts and jackets. The tent had the connotation of theater, and the audience could peel off clothes and purchase them, as a result of which the tent changed every day.

THEATRE PRODUCTS / Akira Takeuchi, Tayuka Nakanishi, Kao Kanamori

"The world will become a theater stage if we have clothes"

Interviewed by Hiroshi Narumi

In 2001, designers Akira Takeuchi and Tayuka Nakanishi, and producer Kao Kanamori established Theatre Products with the motto "the world will become a theater stage if we have clothes." In addition to creating and selling clothes, the label also designs elaborate presentations and devises unique ways of bringing their products to customers. Theatre Products turns every aspect of the business of fashion into a spectacle and a work of art.
Their runway shows have often assumed unique and eccentric forms. In 2009, their show was part of the arts festival "Spectacles on the Farm", which took place in the Nasu Highlands. They organized a bus tour on which the audience could watch the fashion show by performers and animals out of their tour bus windows. In 2010, their show "Boutique" had the audience sitting across the stage of the Nihonbashi Mitsukoshi Theater and observing an uncanny spectacle, revealing the entire process of a fashion show, including a group of photographers sitting in a row behind the fashion models. In 2011, with "Housing", they employed AR (augmented reality) technology to create a 'virtual' fashion show. These innovative events have consistently attracted people's attention toward Theatre Products.
Theatre Products has expanded its body of work beyond the realm of conventional apparel making. In their special project, "Cut and Sewn", the trio traveled to various locations worldwide and collaborated with local residents to create knits and jerseys using the indigenous textiles of each region. They also created an art installation entitled "The Work Site of Theatre Products", transposing the day-to-day business operations from their office into the context of an art gallery. In addition to their work in fashion, they run a music label and host musical events on a regular basis. They established the non-profit corporation Drifters International for planning and hosting events that introduce cutting-edge fashion, art, and performance to their domestic and international audiences.

The Original form of Theatre Products

_ Could you tell me how you met each other? Why did you enter the field of fashion?

Takeuchi: I started becoming interested in fashion while I was in a preparatory school for college. In one of our classes, we had a debate on the subject of fashion, and that was when I found out about Rei Kawakubo. I then took some orientation classes at ESMOD Japan and officially enrolled there the following spring. By my second year in ESMOD, I was enjoying making clothes so much that I decided to pursue my dream to become a professional fashion designer. Right after I graduated, I started working at Comme des Garçons but quit after two years to start something on my own. My decision to quit wasn't based on an ambition to establish my own label, but rather because I felt the urge to find my own means of expression. I spent the next year experimenting with various media outside of fashion, such as fine art, costume making for the theater, and planning events at department stores and dance clubs. At the time, I was working with Nakanishi on these projects. When we met Kanamori, the three of us decided to exhibit something together at the art gallery where Kanamori was employed. We came up with the idea of displaying a 'business company'. This became the prototype for Theatre Products.

Nakanishi: Takeuchi and I went to ESMOD together, though I was one year behind him. I've wanted to become a fashion designer since I was little, so it was a natural choice for me to attend a fashion college. While I was a student there, I didn't have a clear idea of what kind of clothes I wanted to make, let alone in which direction I should take my work. After graduating I spent two years working as a corporate designer. I left that job to start working with Takeuchi on various projects, such as art installations and making theater costumes.

Kanamori: Until I met Nakanishi and Takeuchi, I'd never been in direct contact with the world of fashion. I'd been a painter and intended to go to an art school, but I lacked the aspiration to become a professional painter. I vaguely thought that I would like to be involved in some kind of creative activity. I was also interested in musical events, so I decided to study theater and performance in summer classes at Central Saint Martins College of Art and Design (CSM) in London. There were a lot of interesting things happening on the arts scene in Great Britain, and I became drawn to contemporary art. So instead of theater classes, I enrolled in the newly established contemporary art courses at CSM.
At the time, I met a lot of Japanese students at the fashion department at CSM and I started to appreciate the power of fashion as a form of corporeal expression. But I was primarily interested in exploring methods of theatrical performance. I experimented a lot and did numerous performances. I once attached a film projector to my bicycle and rode it around the city. After I returned to Japan, I started working at the publishing company Little More and met Takeuchi and Nakanishi at their exhibition. Shortly after that, we discussed the idea of creating a company together.

_ How did Theatre Products begin?

Takeuchi: We wanted to create a company that wouldn't only make clothes but also show the backgrounds behind those clothes. We were interested in revealing various facets of fashion beyond selling the forms, colors and designs of our products. In the beginning, we focused on the idea of different kinds of emotions that people experience when they get new clothes. We took a hint from an earlier exhibition we did together, the 'Tank Top Exhibit'. For this we made an oversized patchwork fabric of about forty to fifty meters long by two to three meters wide. We let the gallery visitors cut out shapes and sew these onto tank tops, which they could take home with them.

Kanamori: It was more like performance art. We left pattern papers in the gallery so visitors could cut their own fabric using these patterns, and two of us were on site to sew the fabrics into tank tops for them. In fact, we're still continuing this performance in our current series of exhibits titled "Cut and Sewn".

Takeuchi: Initially, when I did this project, I wasn't thinking of using fashion as my primary medium of expression. I had some ideas that I wanted to express, and using fabrics happened to be the most straightforward way to get my ideas across to an audience.

Nakanishi: In my case, I just wanted to make clothes. But I was open to being part of anything interesting. Maybe I understood that something good would come out of it eventually.

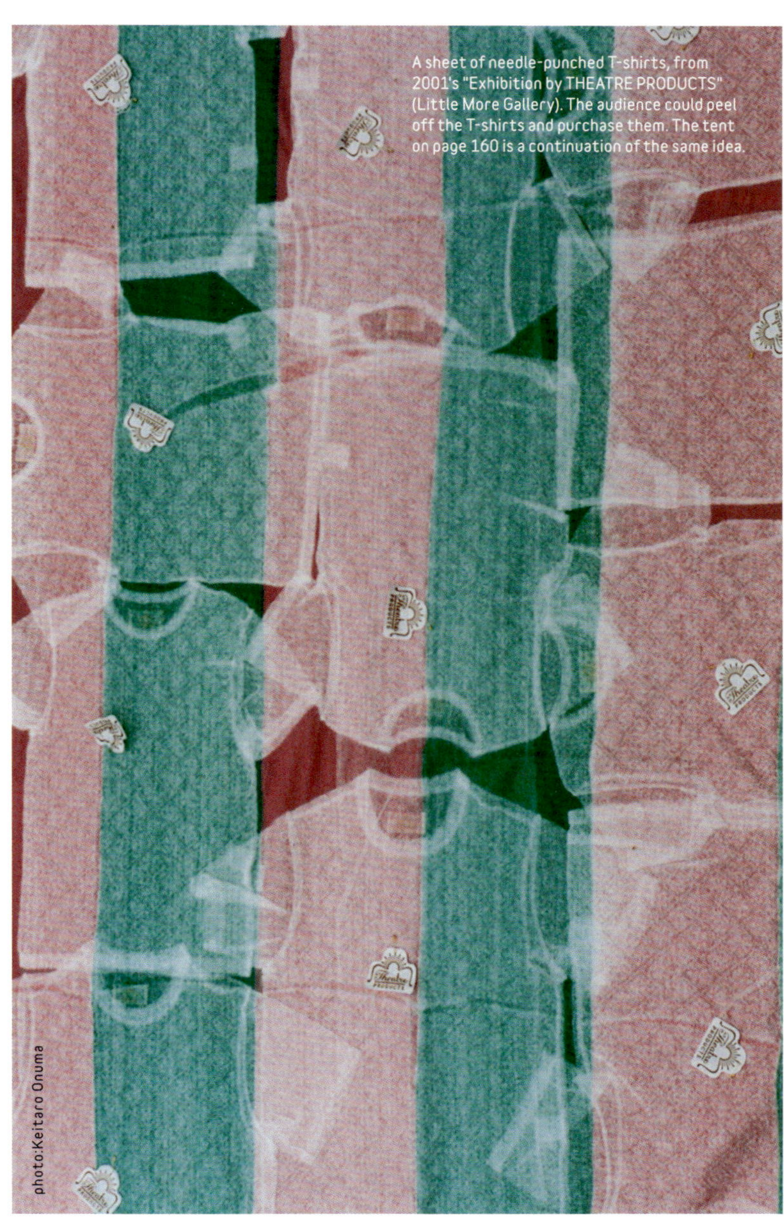

A sheet of needle-punched T-shirts, from 2001's "Exhibition by THEATRE PRODUCTS" (Little More Gallery). The audience could peel off the T-shirts and purchase them. The tent on page 160 is a continuation of the same idea.

photo:Keitaro Onuma

About 180 chairs in storage were brought out and piled up to build a wall at the opening of Theatre Products' shop at Shibuya Parco's Zero Gate in 2004. The chairs were commercial items and the wall became smaller as they were sold.

Kanamori: For this "Tank Top Exhibit", it was really important for us that our final products be pretty and wearable. Even though this project was supposed to be performance art and an experimental installation, I was simply impressed by the fact that the visitors looked really cute in our tank tops. For me, it was a feeling of sheer joy that needed no explanation or words.

Takeuchi: Yes, it is an important feeling to have in all our works.

Kanamori: When we were talking about creating a company, we came up with the idea of establishing a system that would show the final products as well as the process of making them. The idea sounded interesting to me, so I decided to join forces with them. I didn't want to miss such a rare opportunity to create a company from scratch. I didn't think too much about the consequences. I thought, "If this doesn't work out, I'll think of something else to do."

The Concept of a "Company"

_ The idea of presenting your products and your process on an equal platform is pretty unique. But I find it even more intriguing that you managed to create an actual business out of this idea.

Takeuchi: In the beginning, we were interested in creating an apparel making company as a piece of performance art. It was important to us that our company was not fictitious but that it functioned as a business that produces clothes. We planned to show various facets of our business, one at a time, at our shows. Creating an authentic apparel company was absolutely necessary for this to work.

Kanamori: During the first five years, I focused mainly on creating venues and opportunities for Takeuchi and Nakanishi so that they could have a place to express their ideas. I just wanted to share the excitement with our customers. I had no knowledge of how to structure a company, no idea how difficult it would be. After five years, I realized that this was a business and I changed my stance to meet our goals. When we started the company, I had no hesitations because I was driven by my curiosity to see what we would come up with and what we could share with the audience.

Nakanishi: I had a vague image of what I wanted to express and how I wanted to achieve it. By getting together as a group and establishing a company, I was able to materialize this image.

Kanamori: The two designers (Nakanishi and Takeuchi) are responsible for creating the clothes, so I'm not involved in that aspect of the business. But when we established Theatre Products, we talked about how we wanted to demonstrate various theatrical aspects of clothes. That was how we came up with the name of our company. We had no discussion about what age group our clientele would be or how to set up retail environments for our clothes.

Takeuchi: We didn't have a fixed direction for our brand. We think it is important to express what we want to create in the most direct and straightforward manner, one step at a time. We will continue working this way and let the future direction for our company emerge from this process.

_ What did you show at your first exhibition?

Takeuchi: Our first exhibitiona revolved around our collection "Peeling Clothes". Using a needle felting technique, we created a sheet of fabric that had a bunch of our clothes embedded in it. The visitors could peel off a clothing item, buy it, and take it home. The act of peeling was also part of the merchandise. We felt that the act of shopping should bring pleasure to the shopper, so we wanted them to have fun with the act of peeling fabrics. It's difficult to imagine buying 'the experience of peeling', but this experience came with a piece of clothing that you could take home and actually wear. The show was about the fun feeling of shopping and of peeling an object.

Kanamori: We invited a lot of retail shop buyers, journalists, and fashion industry people to this show. Since it took place in an art gallery, we also attracted people from the art world and from publishing companies. The gallery was open to the general public as well.

Takeuchi: We gave this exhibition the title "Tenjikai-Ten" (Exhibition Show). We basically created a tableau of an apparel maker hosting an exhibition of their clothes within the context of an art gallery. But people thought that we had a real exhibition by a real apparel maker. We were caught by surprise when we received orders from retail shop buyers. It was no longer a tableau of an exhibition, but it became a real exhibition.

Kanamori: Representatives of major retailers and department stores came to the gallery. We were in a tricky situation because many of them thought our exhibition was for real. On the other hand, we gained an opportunity to show this work at the Saga Exhibit Space, a contemporary art space in Tokyo.

_ Your presentation was unusual from the fashion industry's point of view. Yet, you received so many positive reactions to this show from people in the fashion world. Why do you think that was the case?

Takeuchi: Perhaps they thought that our clothes were viable as merchandise. Our products sounded very conceptual when we spelled out the process of 'peeling' and 'buying', but when you looked at them simply as clothes, they were desirable and completely wearable products.

Kanamori: Our work looked strange, so people remembered it. Perhaps people in the fashion world were fascinated by the fact that we were operating as a functional fashion label. People in the art world were also drawn to our work and there was a lot of word of mouth. Our inaugural collection turned out to be really popular. I think people's curiosity was piqued by the keyword "theater". Perhaps they responded to the fact that our conceptual performance project produced viable merchandise.

_ Do you make clothes as the props for your performance?

Takeuchi: Actually, it's the opposite. We create performances because we want to deliver our clothes to people. We're not interested in creating performances for their own sake.
Our brand's concept, 'revealing many facets of fashion,' might sound like a performance. At one time, we wanted to present the entire scenery of a typical fashion show to the audience, so we put a row of photographers on the stage and

THEATRE PRODUCTS has produced a significant number of printed items from seasonal DMs to invitations, posters, fliers and books. Ryosuke Uehara has contributed a lot to the creation of their image as art director.

photo:D-BROS

had them photograph the models while the show was taking place. We chose the Nihonbashi Mitsukoshi Theater as our venue, the historic theater where the first fashion show took place in Japan.

_ That theater has a classical interior. When the stage curtain was lifted, we saw the row of seats for photographers on the stage. You did another runway show in Roppongi, where you also had photographers in action as part of the show.

Takeuchi: We divided the audience into two groups: the fashion industry people and the general public. They arrived at the venue separately and seated themselves in two sections opposite each other. We knew that it would have a shocking effect to have the two groups facing each other in a room. When we did our show at the Mitsukoshi Theater, we had the photographers face the audience. In Roppongi, we presented the scenery of a photo shoot in a studio for the runway show.

Kanamori: Basically, we've been putting a spotlight on every aspect of running a fashion label and highlighting them on the runway stage one at a time.

Nakanishi: We believe that fashion is essentially about fun. We want to show our works in such a way that people will naturally feel the joy of fashion.

Various Projects

_ I think it's interesting that Theatre Products combines its art projects with business activities. Could you explain what you did in your exhibition, "Cut and Sewn"? This was not a conventional fashion show.

Kanamori: For our very first exhibition, we used a needle felting technique to create a large sheet of fabric. We took this earlier idea and turned it into our current project, "Cut and Sewn". This project is not a part of our regular collections, but it's a series of workshops held at various locations worldwide. So far, we have been to Indonesia and Iceland. We sourced the fabrics locally and collaborated with local residents to make an oversized patchwork fabric. We then exhibited the fabric and let each visitor cut out a piece of fabric to create a tank top.

Takeuchi: This allowed us to create works that were culturally specific to the places we visited, because we worked with local residents, locally sourced materials and tools that were available there. We would like to continue this project in many other places.

Kanamori: For example, we realized that Iceland doesn't manufacture fabrics domestically, but Scandinavia has an excellent commercial network and we were able to obtain fabrics that were made in Denmark.

Takeuchi: In Indonesia, people mainly use a foot-operated sewing machine as opposed to an overlock sewing machine.

Kanamori: We are planning to take this workshop to a few more locations worldwide and compile a book to be published in the future.

_ You have won recognition for your graphic design work in various printed materials. You also run a music label.

Kanamori: When we express our ideas in a graphic medium, we tend to bring an outside designer's perspective into our work. But we still regard these printed materials as our own work. Our music label Theatre Musica has a separate identity and a different set of values from our fashion label. Depending on our projects, we will let our work in music link to our collections, release records by independent musicians, or plan a special joint project to bring the two disciplines together.

_ Ms. Kanamori, you have established a non-profit corporation called Drifters International and have held lectures and dialogues with audiences under the title, "The Drifter's Fashion Laboratory".

Kanamori: Drifters International was established as a forum to bring together architecture, fashion, and the performing arts, in order to foster interdisciplinary dialogues. I wanted to provide a place for students and professionals to share information, mingle, and share their creations with each other. I was always frustrated by how little information was available when we were searching for our next move as a business. I also felt that my professional network was becoming static. I wondered what my legacy would be and what kind of example I could set for the next generation. That was when I decided to create this non-profit organisation to provide a better working environment for people in various creative disciplines. As for the Drifter's Fashion Laboratory, I wanted to provide a casual meeting place for people in the fashion industry by hosting seminars and various events. I noticed that there were a lot of people who thought along the same lines as I did. Even though I took the initiative to raise the topics for discussions in these seminars, people who attended the seminars had similar perspectives and felt comfortable enough to have lively conversations with each other. They even gave me suggestions for new topics to discuss in future sessions. Initially I thought about hosting one event per month, but I ended up hosting over twenty events in one year. After running it for one year, I've put the Drifter's Fashion Laboratory on hiatus for the moment.

_ It is interesting that you connected your work in fashion with other media and disciplines.

Kanamori: Drifters International came out of our desire to depart from an apparel manufacturer's conventional business cycle of producing, selling and buying clothes. We wanted to effectively run projects that had more artistic and socially conscientious values, like our "Cut and Sewn" projects. Even though this non-profit corporation is a separate organization from Theatre Products, it still functions as a place to host exhibitions by creative organizations, including Theatre Products.

Nakanishi: When we established Drifters International, we were searching for effective methods of running workshops and other non-business related projects within the context of a company. In many ways, because of Drifters International, Theatre Products is able to engage in various projects with a clearer focus.

Scenes from workshops at the "Cut and Sewn" exhibition held in Indonesia in 2008, Iceland in 2009, and at Tokyo's Watarium Museum. The local fabrics were seamed together and displayed as a gigantic cloth. Visitors could cut out a part of it, which one of the students would sew onto a tank top on site.

photos:THEATRE PRODUCTS

From "THE BOOK OF THEATRE PRODUCTS: a method by theatre products" (Little More, 2007).
The wearers are, from left to right; niu, Audrey Fondecave, Maho Shimao, Rie, Mio Yamakawa, Mayu Kitaki, kiki.
THEATRE PRODUCTS introduced its worn clothes in flower patterns during 2004 and 2007.

photo:Fumio Doi

_ In 2009, you planned the special tour of the fashion show titled "Spectacle on the Farm" in the Nasu Highlands.

Kanamori: We wanted to hold a Theatre Products fashion show on a farm. That's how this idea got started.

Takeuchi: At first, we thought we would create a catwalk on the farmland and invite an audience to view our show from a tour bus. We were also planning to have street vendors and stalls. We were imagining something festive for our season's theme.

Kanamori: In the end, we decided to look for a much greater significance for this event from multiple angles, so we sought support from many people and expanded the scale of the event. It also made us realize that Tokyo isn't the only city where you can hold fashion shows. We were thinking about creating a venue where people who were working in different disciplines and media could interact with each other.

About making clothes

_ Ms. Nakanishi, what is your role as a fashion designer at Theatre Products?

Nakanishi: I see my role within the organization as a designer who comes up with 'wearable' clothes. I draw a clear line between something that is wearable and something that is not. In order to come up with a fashion design, I need to be able to imagine the sensation people feel when they come across something they want to wear. The strength of my designs varies, depending on whether I can visualize my designs on people or not.

Takeuchi: Nakanishi is very much in touch with women's sensibilities and what they want from their clothes. It's hard to describe in words, but Nakanishi is able to design clothes that are desirable for women.

Nakanishi: I am always thinking, "What would it feel like to wear this?" I try to visualize it in as much detail as I can. "How does it feel to wear it outside? How does it feel to sit down or walk in it? How would it look on the street? What kind of emotion would it bring to the wearer?" As the label Theatre Products, we have been using methods of creation and presentation that are inspired by ordinary everyday activities. We are fascinated by precious moments that occur in our everyday lives. We hope to share these cherished moments with our customers through the clothes that we have created.

Takeuchi: I believe that the biggest compliment we can get is when a woman tells us, "It is so cute. I want to wear it". The strength of our clothes cannot be fully understood unless one actually wears them. So we focus our energy on reaching out to those people who like our clothes and delivering our products to them.

_ Are you planning to do something abroad?

Kanamori: We just celebrated the company's tenth anniversary, and we've been discussing the potential and various methods for our international activities. Even though we think of Paris and Milan as viable options for showing our work, it is not our goal to show in these cities. In fact, it's more important for us to know 'what' we want to say and 'who' our audience is. Showing in Paris used to be the pinnacle of achievement for many fashion designers, but recently this doesn't seem to be the case. We are thinking about a strategy for our future that makes sense to both our customers and ourselves.

Takeuchi: A company needs to keep growing. Otherwise, it will go out of business. The pace of growth can be slow or fast. Sustaining our work is very important. We are still a small company, so we've only been able to express our ideas up to a certain level. We believe that taking our work abroad is an important step for our future.

The first "Spectacle in the Farm" in Nasu Highlands, 2009, incorporating such events as fashion shows, concerts, and theatrical plays.

For its Spring/Summer 2008 collection, THEATRE PRODUCTS collaborated with Vietnam Airlines. The items shown on the red carpet were titled "a honeymoon" by THEATRE PRODUCTS, and the items shown on the blue carpet were titled "Vietnam Airlines" by KINGLY THEATRE PRODUCTS. The men's and women's collections were therefore shown side by side.

Autumn/Winter 2011-2012. The presentation was carried out by AR—augmented reality. Thanks to a collaboration with AR Three Brothers, it became possible to enjoy this fashion show anywhere, as long as the viewer came prepared with a computer, sheet and internet access.

COLLECTIONS

2003-04A/W UNIFORM for the OL

2004S/S WILD NATURE

2004-05A/W WILD NATURE 2

2005S/S simple TEATRO PRODUZIONI

2005-06A/W ALPENGLOW

2006S/S OPHELIA'S DEEP FOREST AND THE FITTED SYSTEMATIC-KITCHEN

2006-07A/W COMPACT IS BEAUTIFUL

Autumn/Winter 2003, ***Uniform for the OL*** (Okamura factory show room). The first collection presented in the form of a runway show after three seasons of exhibitions and installations. Delightful "uniforms" for office ladies and salarymen were presented at a showroom for office furniture.

Spring/Summer 2004 ***Nature*** (Super Deluxe). The show was held at the then newly opened club in Roppongi. Featuring a performance by magician Mame Yamada, the show had the feeling of a school play. The clothes added to the theatrical ambiance. The objective was to express "Nature," as a contrast to the previous season's show. It proved to be THEATRE PRODUCTS's breakthrough.

Autumn/Winter 2004-2005, ***Nature*** follow-up (Club Heights.) The show at a defunct cabaret was filled with the loaded sounds of Mozart's Requiem. The invitation consisted of a tattoo seal, which the audience was required to wear on their skin as a dress code.

Spring/Summer 2005, ***simple TEATRO PRODUCZIONI*** (CANAL CAFE). Resort wear created by imagining a town on the Italian coast and displayed on the terrace of a waterfront restaurant. As Italian pop music resounded, the models arrived in a small boat.

Autumn/Winter 2005-2006, ***ALPEN GLOW*** (National Stadium). The stadium was selected as venue since the show was to promote a stretch limo Rover Mini, only three of which were ever built. When the red mini arrived, three women (including performer KATHY) emerged from it and the show started. The collection was mainly comprised of formal wear.

Spring/Summer 2006, ***Kitchen Unit in Ophelia's forest*** (Japan Fashion Week official tent "TOKIWA"). THEATRE PRODUCTS participated in the first Japan Fashion Week, reorganized from Tokyo Collection by the Ministry of Economy, Trade and Industry. The show took place at a venue associated with the event. The colors used to depict the forest and pond in Millais's painting of "Ophelia" were contrasted with the cold texture of a kitchen unit. Kingly Theatre Products for men's "Yuya Honda and flags of all nations" was shown separately.

2007S/S NEVER ENDING

2007-08A/W NOSTALGIA

2008S/S HONEYMOON

2008-09A/W CYNDI

2009S/S COUNTRY

2009-10A/W JOY

Autumn/Winter 2006-2007, ***COMPACT IS BEAUTIFUL*** (JFW official venue). The collection revolved around shapes, which was unique for the brand. Compact silhouettes and shapes were created by adding volume to clothes; the compactness was perceived through its balance, while the silhouette revealed the volume inside the clothes, and fair amounts of fur, quilting, and down were used. Vivid colors such as black, ivory, and red were also characteristic.

Spring/Summer 2007, ***NEVER ENDING*** (tent on Isetan Shinjuku roof terrace). Even pastel tones in pink, yellow, green, and blue expressed a fantasy world where nothing exists besides happiness. Most pieces were made of jersey cloth such as plain stitch fabric and nets, including dresses and bags.

Autumn/Winter 2007-2008, ***NOSTALGIA*** (JFW official venue). The landscape you see when the views in your memory are recolored. Bold items dart-seamed in ellipsoidal and radial fashion set the tone. Umitaro Abe at Theatre Musica selected the background music - renowned for his pitch-perfect selections, he offered up nostalgic music from a mix of countries.

Spring/Summer 2008, ***HONEYMOON*** (Tokyo Midtown Hall A). A collection in collaboration with Vietnam Airlines. The designers used Vietnamese fabrics to profess their fascination with Vietnam. The honeymoon theme expressed the longing for a romantic journey.

Autumn/Winter 2008-2009, ***CYNDI*** (Studio Mouris Roppongi). The collection was exceptionally presented at a photo studio, presenting a photo shoot as a show. The theme this time was Cyndi, referrinf to the symbolic power and pop lightness of singer Cyndi Lauper.

Spring/Summer 2009, "***COUNTRY***" (Shinjuku FACE). The collection was presented as a stage musical at a theatre in Kabukicho, Shinjuku. Bales of straw were piled up on the stage, on which the bands EGO-WRAPPIN' and BLACK BOTTOM BRASS BRAND performed, and models were free to enjoy the country-style and Charleston-age atmosphere any way they wanted. Tickets for the show were on sale to the public.

Autumn/Winter 2009-2010, ***JOY*** (Laforet Museum Harajuku). A collection filled with warmth, based on the image of indoor comfort and featuring voluminous knits and fur, colorful boots, and knapsacks. Real-life parents, siblings, lovers, and husbands and wives appeared as models whose intimacy became part of the show.

Spring/Summer 2010, ***BOMBAY*** (VACANT). Inspired by a time when Bombay (Mumbai) experienced a great influx of Western culture, the clothes were designed by imagining the unique details characteristic of a place at the crossroads of different cultures. The collection was superb in its perfect mixture that was neither totally colonial nor totally Indian.

Autumn/Winter 2010-2011, ***BOUTIQUE*** (MITSUKOSHI THEATER). When the heavy curtain opened at the Mitsukoshi Theater, the place where Japan's first-ever fashion show was held, there were photographers standing abreast! In front of them, the elegant and retro show unfolded like a play about the presentation of a new collection at a clothing boutique.

Spring/Summer 2011, ***CAMOUFLAGE*** (Tokyo Midtown Hall A). The stage consisted of two rooms: one with white walls and the other covered in camouflage print. Colors and materials for the camouflage room were chosen to fit into surroundings inspired by the paintings of Édouard Vuillard. The result was a strong statement about the relationship between clothing and surroundings, and the effectiveness of camouflage.

Autumn/Winter 2011-2012, ***HOUSING.*** The collection was presented by means of AR—augmented reality; the audience could see pieces on AR sheets when the web camera was held up to them. Inspired by home interiors of the 1960s, the stage represented a house and the lives of its inhabitants, from different generations and with different interests and activities. Each room was distinct in texture and atmosphere to express differences coexisting in the same house. The collection presented many disparate items , yet demonstrated great coordination.

Designers' profiles:
THEATRE PRODUCTS / Akira Takeuchi, Tayuka Nakanishi, Kao Kanamori

Akira Takeuchi was born in 1976. He is the president and representative designer of THEATRE PRODUCTS. After graduating from Esmod Japon, he worked for Comme des Garçons as a patternmaker, then founded THEATRE PRODUCTS in 2001.
He is an associate professor at Kyoto University of Art and Design. He launched his menswear brand PASCAL DONQUINO in 2009.
Tayuka Nakanishi was born in 1977. She is the fashion designer for THEATRE PRODUCTS. After graduating from Esmod Japon, she worked for Sanei International Co., Ltd. as a planner, after which she founded THEATRE PRODUCTS with Takeuchi and Kanamori.
Kao Kanamori was born in 1974. She works as producer and press officer for THEATRE PRODUCTS. After graduating in art criticism from Central St. Martins College of Art and Design, she worked for Little More Gallery and then joined the foundation of THEATRE PRODUCTS. She became the executive producer of Spectacle in the Farm in 2009 and 2010, and founded the NPO Drifters International in 2010.

Brand history:

2001 THEATRE PRODUCTS founded.
"Exhibition of THEATRE PRODUCTS" at Little More Gallery.
2002 Exhibition "Opening of a flagship store by THEATRE PRODUCTS" at Little More Gallery, graf media gm, Rice Gallery, and others.
2004 Opening of a store at Zero Gate in Shibuya.
2006 THEATRE MUSICA founded. Opening of a store at Parco in Shibuya and of Stripe by Theatre Products at Laforet in Harajuku.
2007 Exhibition "The State of THEATRE PRODUCTS" at Parco Museum.
2008 Exhibition "Cut & Sewn" in Indonesia.
2009 Opening of a flagship store on Omotesando.
An event called Spectacle in the Farm carried out in Nasu Kogen (also in 2010).
Ryosuke Uehara of D-BROS selected for the Yusaku Kamekura Design Award thanks to his graphic designs for THEATRE PRODUCTS.
Takeuchi launches men's brand PASCAL DONQUINO.
2010 The NPO Drifters International founded by Kanamori (with Akane Nakamura and Teppei Fujiwara)
2011 Opening of a store at JR Osaka Mitsukoshi Isetan.
"Spectacle on the Bay" in Yokohama.

writtenafterwards

リトゥンアフターワーズ
山縣良和

writtenafterwards
Yoshikazu Yamagata

writtenafterwards

yoshikazu yamagata

リトゥンアフターワーズ

山縣良和

From the collection #04 "graduate fashion show-0points," shown at HOTEL CLASKA in Meguro, Tokyo in 2009. What appeared were dresses all made of waste materials generated by graduation projects from various schools. "The graduation show really is the fundamental standpoint", in the words of Yoshikazu Yamakake.

writtenafterwards / Yoshikazu YAMAGATA

Yoshikazu Yamagata, poet/fashion designer/philosopher

Interviewed by Yoko Takagi

Yoshikazu Yamagata's work explores the boundary between fashion and art. Yamagata does not regard his work as a fashion designer as being limited to the production, distribution, and sale of his clothes. Instead, he poses himself questions: What is fashion? What kind of creative work can be done in the form of fashion today? During his study at Central Saint Martins College of Art and Design in London, Yamagata gained invaluable experience working as an intern for Ann-Sofie Back and Alexander McQueen. In Paris, he worked as an assistant to John Galliano. Antonio Marras of Kenzo recognized Yamagata's talent and recruited him to create a special Christmas tree decoration for Kenzo at Centre Pompidou. After graduating with distinction and honor from Central Saint Martins, he returned to Japan. In 2007, he established his label writtenafterwards. For his spring/summer 2009 collection, he presented a highly controversial collection of dresses made of crumpled, discarded paper.

Overcoming the inferiority complex: changing from being an F student in Japan to a top graduating student from Central Saint Martins College of Art and Design

_What kind of childhood did you have? Could you tell me when you became interested in fashion?

Yamagata: I was born in Tottori Prefecture, and grew up surrounded by rice fields and mountains. I was never a good student. I had a low self-esteem and poor communication skills. Drawing was the only thing I was good at. I've known that I wanted to become an artist of some sort since I was in elementary school. In middle school I had a popular classmate that I always looked up to. He was always well dressed. He made me realize that being cool is about being stylish. That was when I started becoming interested in fashion.

_You were in middle school, so was this the age when you started becoming interested in girls as well?

Yamagata: I was so shy that I wasn't any good at talking to girls. But I noticed that fashion could also be a form of communication. My self-esteem was low, and I felt that fashion was my only hope of transforming and improving myself. When I entered high school, I became absorbed in reading various fashion magazines. First, I was reading men's street style fashion magazines, then I moved on to women's fashion magazines. My interest shifted to high fashion brands, so I started flipping through magazines such as *High Fashion*, *Studio Voice*, *Ryuko Tsushin*, and *Zyappu*. My friends and I used to compare our knowledge of fashion and fashion brands. Because we lived in such a remote rural community, the world we saw in magazines was nowhere to be seen in reality. So we became even more obsessed with the fantasy world within these fashion magazines.

_What do you remember the most from the magazines you were reading?

Yamagata: It was the dress titled "body meets dress" (spring/summer 1997) by Comme des Garçons, from articles in Ryuko Tsushin. I was about sixteen or seventeen years old then. Without comprehending what it was all about, I thought the dress was simply beautiful. Among people of my generation, Undercover and other 'Urahara' style brands were really popular. I admired Yohji Yamamoto. I was drawn to his charismatic presence as if I was under his spell. I identified with his lifestyle and his work, and I wished to follow in his footsteps one day. For those of us who were teenagers in the 1990s, fashion designers were subjects of respect and admiration. The world of fine art, on the other hand, didn't leave much of an impression. For us, fashion seemed to be the center of a cultural force and to have the power to potentially engulf everything. These fashion designers were at the center of this vortex, exerting their charisma and delivering expressive and creative works.

_ What kind of path did you take to become a fashion designer?

Yamagata: The thought of becoming a fashion designer didn't even occur to me. For me, a fashion designer was someone who was charismatic and important. I thought I could never become someone like that. At the time I was suffering from an inferiority complex and had zero self-esteem. But I still had deep admiration for fashion, so I entered the Bunka Fashion College in Osaka. Even though I wanted to be in the studio program, I thought I could never do it. So instead, I entered the fashion business program. It was foolish of me to think that I could at least become a shopkeeper or a retail buyer. At the same time, I couldn't give up my dream of doing something creative in fashion. I thought about transferring to the Bunka Fashion College in Tokyo, but my teachers and parents were against it. They thought it wouldn't change anything except the name of the city where I went to school. Once again, I asked myself what I really wanted to do, and I decided to become a shoe designer because I loved shoes. I was told about the option of studying abroad by someone who worked in my favorite shoe store. A lot of things were going wrong in my life at the time, and I was feeling lost and depressed. I managed to get out of Osaka and moved to London. First, I went to an English language school so that I could study at the local shoemaking school in London. After about three months, I started to question my decision to study shoemaking. Was I genuinely interested in learning how to make shoes? Or was I making another compromise? I was finally able to admit to myself that fashion design, not shoemaking, was what I really wanted to do. My life had been a series of compromises up to that point. First, I went to Osaka even though I wanted to be in Tokyo. In Osaka, I studied fashion business even though I wanted to do something creative in fashion. Then, in London, I fooled myself to think that I wanted to become a shoemaker. Finally, I made the decision to study fashion design at the school I wanted to go the most, Central Saint Martins School of Art and Design. I started with summer classes, then took some preparatory courses before I enrolled in the Bachelor of Arts in Fashion program. It was a three-year course, but I took a year off in between school years, so I graduated from CSM in four years.

_ You graduated top of your class from CSM, with distinction and honor. In

Collection #05, "the fashion show of the gods" (2009). Painting by Yoshikazu Yamagata for his collection "The Fashion Show of the Gods a gift from the Gods " held at Tokyo Taito Designer's Village.

Japan, by contrast, you'd been considered a 'not-so-bright' student. What do you think of the differences in how you were evaluated? Does Japanese society tend to overlook talented individual like you?

Yamagata: Japan and Great Britain have completely different ideas about education. The way we study various subject matters in secondary schools in Japan, students study references, textbooks and they take exams. Fashion education in Japan follows this style of teaching and learning. The concept of education in Japan is based on the idea of finding 'the right answer' to a question. For example, in my fashion drawing class, we learned to copy human figures exactly the way our teacher drew for six months straight. When I was finally able to make my own drawing in a class assignment, I submitted a drawing of a full-figured body with clothes on. My teacher gave me an 'F' for it.

_ In Japan, learning equals emulating. Copying the works by masters has been the traditional approach to studying art in Japan. Perhaps your teachers in your fashion school were following this traditional model of teaching and learning. In 2008, you established a private school for fashion design in Japan called "Coconogacco". In Coconogacco, you bring together various educational styles of Japan and abroad. I see that your motivation to start this private school was based on your experiences of receiving two drastically different evaluations by teachers. Could you tell me what kind of education you had in Great Britain?

Yamagata: At Central Saint Martins, professors gave very few lectures to students. Independent thinking was given the highest value. As long as we worked on our assignments, we were free to explore our own passion and create anything we wanted. Their curriculum allowed the students to set their own class schedules. So I worked with the London-based Japanese designer Kei Kagami and I did an internship with Ann-Sofie Back (currently the chief director of Cheap Monday) as well as Alexander McQueen. Also, I got a job working at John Galliano's studio in Paris. At that time, Galliano was also the chief designer for Dior, and I was able to witness the process behind the creation of the autumn/winter 2004-2005 collection. By working inside the world's best couture workshop, I gained

"The Emperor and Afterwards (everyone's new clothes)," a drawing by Yamagata for the graduation show at Central St. Martins College of Art and Design.

drawing: Yoshikazu Yamagata

photos:Koomi Kim

a perspective on the standard of work that was capable of winning international acclaim. This experience inspired me to create fashion designs of my own, so I made a series called "A Long Story" and entered it in a juried show in Italy called ITS#3. At the runway show, I presented a storybook about a monster which lived near a village, a mischievous boy who stole a larger-than-life bra and panties, and so on. This was the first time I used a story behind my clothes in a collection. To this day, I design clothes with stories behind them. Anyways, Antonio Marras of Kenzo was one of the judges on this show, and he kindly invited me to create a design for a Christmas tree for the Pompidou Center in Paris. I made a flowing Christmas tree that fused with the blue pipes of the museum's architecture.

_ Could you tell me about your graduation work at Central Saint Martins?

Yamagata: For my graduation show in 2005, I created a collection titled "the everyone's new clothes" in honor of the two hundredth birthday of Hans Christian Andersen. I wrote a sequel to The Emperor's New Clothes. My story was about an empire in which a fashion show of invisible clothes took place every year. My show looked as if it had popped out of a picture book. I received very positive feedback from professors of Central Saint Martins, and it led to my graduating at the top of my class. However, the media's response was mixed. Some people felt confused and questioned whether what I did could be called 'fashion'.

_ After your brilliant academic accomplishments and internship experiences, why did you come back to Japan instead of staying in Europe and working at one of the famous fashion houses?

Yamagata: When I was working at John Galliano's workshop, I found out that I was not very good at following instructions. Things went wrong when I tried to fulfill orders. It made me realize that I was not good at guessing other people's intentions and seeking answers for them. Perhaps I was afraid that I would become a problem student again. I figured that I couldn't work within the framework of a hierarchical relationship in which I would be characterized as 'the bad student' and my boss as my 'teacher'. Also, I got to know how difficult it would be to set up my own business in the UK or France because of the problems with taxes, immigration, language barriers, and racial bias. So I decided to go back to Japan to become an independent designer and establish my own fashion label.

The course of establishing the brand

_ Could you describe the process of establishing your brand after you returned to Japan?

Yamagata: First, I attempted to exhibit my graduation work from Central Saint Martins to figure out how my work would function within society. I happened to visit the Hinohara pre-school in the small town of Hinohara on the edge of Tokyo. Intuitively, I thought this would be the perfect venue for my debut show in Japan. As a symbolic space in which a child's first encounter with society takes place, this pre-school on the outskirts of Tokyo seemed to be the perfect starting point for me. In January of 2006, I presented my graduation show at the school festival there. Then, for one year, I worked with my former classmate from Central Saint Martins, Kentaro Tamai (currently the designer of ASEEDONCLOUD) and we established the label writtenafterwards. I was responsible for coming up with basic concepts, and we collaborated on the designs. We continued working together, designing the next three collections.

_ What was your first collection like?

Yamagata: For the 2007 collection titled "before running away from home", I wanted to do a proper presentation of our products. The idea a 'globe' made of lace material popped into my head, so we made a lace fabric with a map of the world woven into it. Out of this lace we made clothes and we also turned the fabric into a globe by using resin. Our business had the three-prong strategy of selling fabrics, clothes, and the globe. We

Shown on the left is a gigantic brassiere Yamagata produced while a student at Central St. Martins College to apply for ITS#3, the fashion contest hosted by Diesel in Trieste, Italy. Yamagata received three awards for this and another design called "a long story," a work with a storyline. The photo shoot took place in London. Several full-body suits made for the graduation show were used for the shoot, and Naoki Honjo took the photographs. The photo "fake in the fact" (2007) was newly taken for the magazine "Dune No.32" (Art Days).

photo:Naoki Honjo

drawing:Yoshikazu Yamagata 2009

image of 'God' through anime. In this show, I wanted to evoke this intimate yet peculiar image of God. For my sixth collection, "Crime and Punishment", I made a series of clothes that symbolized Japanese society's perception of women. I tried to imagine the ultimate version of a "mature girlie" fashion for immature women of a certain age. The theme for this show was about the 'paradox' of making a mature feminine style for immature women and society's stigma against them.

_ You seem to follow your intuition and impulses in creating your designs. You are an artistic type of fashion designer. What are you trying to express through your collections?

Yamagata: I want to express the truth and essence of fashion, including its superficial, ridiculous side. When I first encountered the book titled Handbook of Fashion by Kiyokazu Washida, I was perhaps in high school or in a community college. The book trigged my interest in learning about the social phenomenon called fashion. Then my interest shifted toward finding the means of expressing my fascination with fashion. I wanted to demonstrate how fashion and fads function in society. My graduation show at Central Saint Martins was a tongue-in-cheek satire of fashion. It was based on the story of The Emperor's New Clothes, and it was about the latest fashion that took the empire by storm: nakedness. It was not just a negative criticism of fashion. I wanted to bring a human side to this social phenomenon and reveal its positive as well as its negative sides. I hope to challenge myself to find various means of expression beyond words and fashion.

_ Have you heard people saying that you are more like an artist who deals with fashion?

Yamagata: It doesn't bother me to hear that. But I've been trying to come up with a better title to describe my job. I coined the term "shisouka" (poet/ fashion designer/philosopher). I always incorporate a narrative element to my designs and create poetry out of an act of 'wearing' garments. I want my occupation to be about disseminating fashion and poetry to people. The name of my fashion label 'writtenafterwards,' originated from the word 'postscript'. Before I start creating the designs for

exhibited this collection at 21_21Design Sight, and thankfully, both the fabrics and the globe were sold. For our second collection titled "sleeping in the book bed", we fabricated a giant bed shaped like a book and a series of pajamas for the models to wear and have sweet dreams. Then we joined the Japan Fashion Week for the first time and presented our third collection titled "prince prince prince". We showed a strange Japanese version of a fairy tale prince on the runway.

_ Your fourth collection, "graduate fashion show" was the first work of yours that I saw in person. Your show took place at Hotel Klaska on March 28th of 2009 during the Japan Fashion Week. You presented a series of dresses made out of discarded, crumpled paper you got for free from students at fashion and architecture schools. These dresses were not only visually striking but also provocative. You explored the outer limit of 'beauty' by clashing two extreme opposite elements: the glamorous form of dresses and the use of abject garbage. This collection seemed to be a reflection of your experiences from working with John Galliano. What was the story behind this show?

Yamagata: I wrote a story called "I am Zero". It was about the main character "Zero" who was a born loser. After being bullied by "Fifteen" and "Forty-three", Zero started smoking and living a self-destructive lifestyle. As the story went on, Zero would attempt to take a positive step forward by searching for his inner strength, and eventually he would find a glimmer of hope for his future and begin his new journey. The theme of this story was based on the question: "Do losers have a second chance?"

_ That sounds like your autobiography. Starting from your fifth collection, "the fashion show of the gods", you become the only designer behind writtenafterwards since your partner Kentaro Tamai left to start his own label.

Yamagata: In this collection, I tried to imagine the origin of fashion. I made up a story about the very first fashion show by the gods that took place on Earth in front of the animals. Two hours before the start of my fashion show, each gods was wrapped by an entire bolt of fabric (50 meters), and the cardboard tube in the center was made into a walking cane. Young Japanese people have been exposed to a particular archetypal my clothes, I construct some sort of story with a set of specific characters and a setting. For each collection, I imagine specific wardrobes for the different characters in my story. The storytelling aspect of my work has been important since my graduation show at Central Saint Martins. I even presented everyone with a picture book that read "Written by Yoshikazu Yamagata".

_ Are you conscious of your identity as a Japanese designer?

Yamagata: My work is based on my memories of growing up in the countryside of Japan and the feeling of admiration I felt toward the West. I don't know if this comes from my personal background or my Japanese cultural identity. The overall aesthetic of my design is cute (kawaii) and childish, rather than elegant. Perhaps this 'cute' aesthetic is particular to Japan. I would like to be able to emphasize my Japanese identity when I exhibit my works internationally. However, this will be difficult to do. I think of myself as lacking certain abilities that people associate with Japanese designers. These would be skillfulness, sensitivity to details, and an ability to cooperate with others. I am not an artisan, and my creative process is not about copying, applying and developing a concept. Instead, I use my passion and emotion to create my work spontaneously. I would like to be able to bring a Japanese sensibility to my work by collaborating with those who have delicate, masterful skills. I would love to recognize the beauty of being Japanese and incorporate it into my work for an international audience. Perhaps I feel this way because of my experiences of living abroad.

_ Do you have a plan to show your work abroad?

Yamagata: I would be thrilled to show my work in Paris, the classic stage for presenting fashion. But it's not that I want to become part of the pre-existing system of the fashion industry. Despite the recent decline of its prêt-a-porter, Paris is still the center of fashion for many people around the world. When my work reaches a certain level of maturity, I would love to exhibit my work in Paris to be reviewed by critics and become a part of fashion history. Also, I aspire to be a creative innovator in fashion so that I would be invited to join the Venice Biennale or other events that lie beyond the realm of the fashion industry.

_ Who are your supporters and clientele?

Yamagata: I try not to be conscious of a specific clientele or specific audiences. I would like my work to be able to reach a universal audience, instead of a specific gender or age group. When I presented my shows about the garbage dresses and the 'Gods', I received so many

Shown on the left is a drawing from Yamagata's illustrated book "I Scored a Zero," displayed at Hotel Claska to coincide with "graduate fashion show—0points—".

Shown below is the collection#0 "2012 S/S by freemaison" held at VACANT in Harajuku, Tokyo on May 5th 2011.

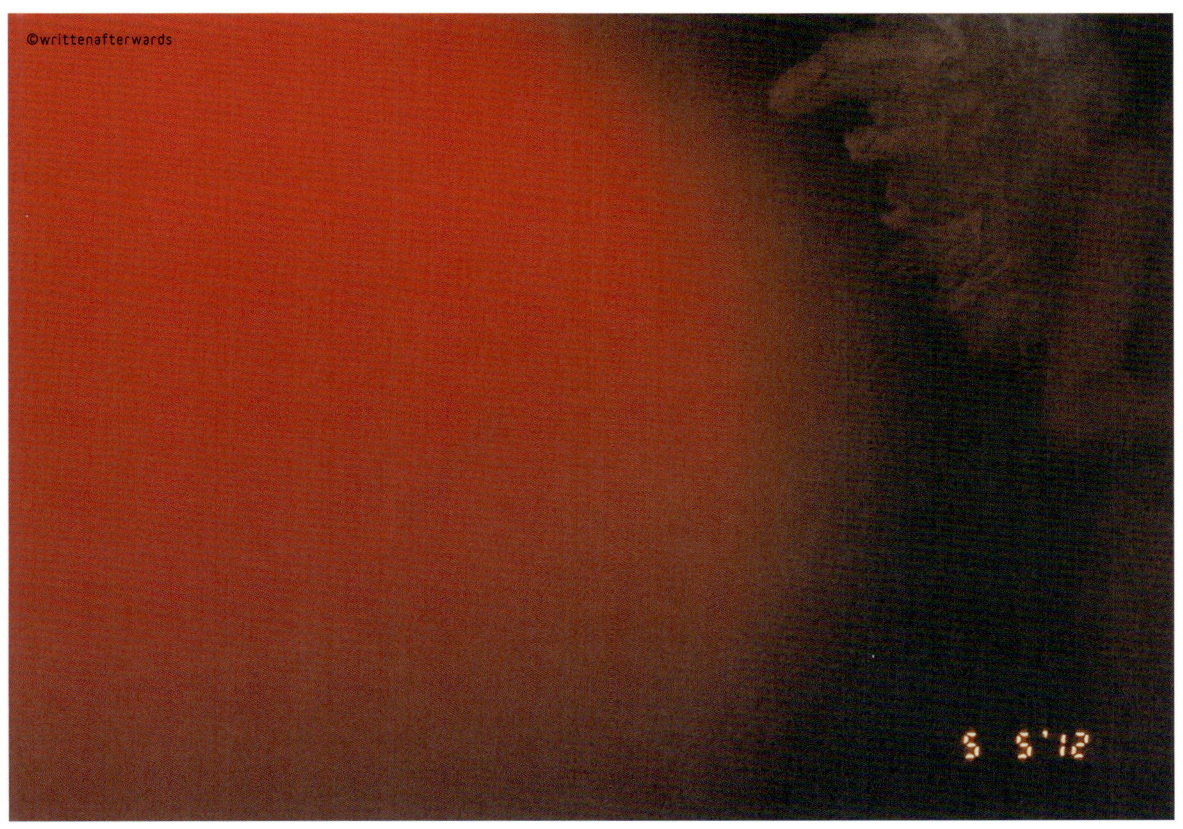

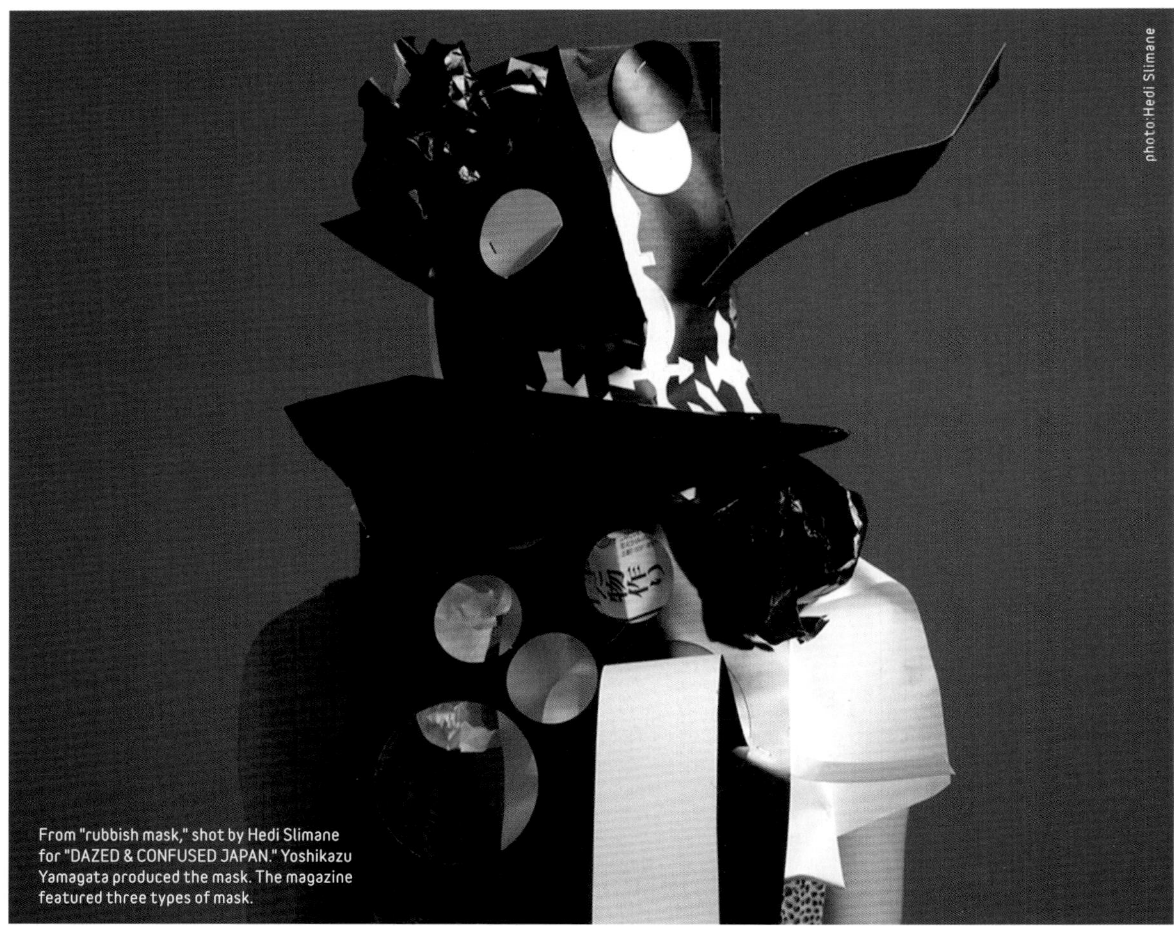
photo:Hedi Slimane

From "rubbish mask," shot by Hedi Slimane for "DAZED & CONFUSED JAPAN." Yoshikazu Yamagata produced the mask. The magazine featured three types of mask.

reactions from people outside of fashion industry. Many fashion designers try to differentiate themselves from others by focusing on the minute details of their craft. Only the insiders of the fashion world can appreciate such details, and people on the outside have no idea what they are. My work tends to elicit a reaction that is beyond a typical love or hate reaction. People have a reaction similar to the feeling that one gets after witnessing an emerging new medium and finding yourself without the criteria for evaluating it.

_ How would you like your work to be received by your audience?

Yamagata: I would like to raise the question in people's minds, "What is fashion?" I would like to provoke discussion and critical thinking on fashion. It's problematic that there has been little practice of cultural criticism in Japan. A society without the practice of critical thinking cannot be healthy. After all, it is not surprising because it has only been sixty years since the history of fashion started in Japan and only thirty years since Japan's fashion reached international audiences.

Creating a context for fashion

_ Your collections seem to be about the criticism of fashion.

Yamagata: At Central Saint Martins, professors and students were expected to discuss contemporary fashion based on the historical context of fashion design. Everyone understood that being a fashion designer required you to create something new while having a dialogue with history. In the past ten years, the world of fashion has shifted its emphasis from luxury brands to low-priced fast-fashion. The prêt-a-porter industry has been shrinking in size while the fast-fashion industry has increased its financial power by integrating high fashion designers into their systems. A garment by a major fast-fashion brand would cost only one-tenth of the same garment sold by a young independent designer. The outcome of this business competition is apparent. Even the quality of materials and construction of fast-fashion garments have been improving steadily. I think it will become increasingly difficult for young designers to start and maintain small and independent businesses. There will be fewer manufacturers that will be willing to accept small-scale orders. An act of creation takes time, effort, and money. We need to set up a fair pricing system for products and labor. The luxury brands have realized the need for setting an alternative value system. In order to counter the cheap fast-fashion products,

Yamagata collaborated with students at his private school "Koko no Gakko" for a photo session using items from his Collection #04 "graduate fashion show—0points—".

photo: Shunichiro Miura

they started to integrate artistic value into their luxury products. A luxury product used to be valued mainly for its craftsmanship. In the future, challenging conceptual fashion will be exhibited in museums and become part of art history, and the value of creativity in fashion will increase even more. I believe this is the natural course for our future.

_I believe that a fashion designer has to understand the historical context of his/her work in order to create a new design. We have assembled ten contemporary Japanese fashion designers for this exhibition. By using installations and an accompanying catalogue, we will attempt to explain a specific historical context where each of these designers came from. Could you talk about your installation?

Yamagata: In my last couple of collections, I explored the 'origin of fashion' as my major theme. For this upcoming installation, the theme will be 'fashion and money'. I had an idea about creating a fabric that has an inherent value, so I will be making a new currency, "zero yen", out of fabric. Fashion and money have been inseparable since the beginning of time. There is a history of using fabric as a form of currency. I am fed up with the common interpretation of fashion as a symbol of capitalism. I want to project a sense of irony into this tired attitude toward fashion.

_In Japan, fashion has been regarded as a commercial activity and marginalized as 'applied arts' by the world of fine art. Public art museums have only recently started exhibiting shows about fashion.

Yamagata: The Hussein Chalayan exhibition at the Museum of Contemporary Art in Tokyo is an important example of the change in the museum's attitude toward fashion. For fashion designers who pursue creativity and innovation, their financial situation will become more and more dire while their public persona becomes more prominent and renowned. In the fashion industry, the twentieth-century business model and value system have completely collapsed. It is outdated to think that fashion designers only engage in commercial activities. This exhibition will place Japanese contemporary fashion in the context of art as seen from an international perspective. I hope that this exhibition will bring an opportunity for generating a renewed appreciation for creativity in fashion.

COLLECTIONS

Collection #01

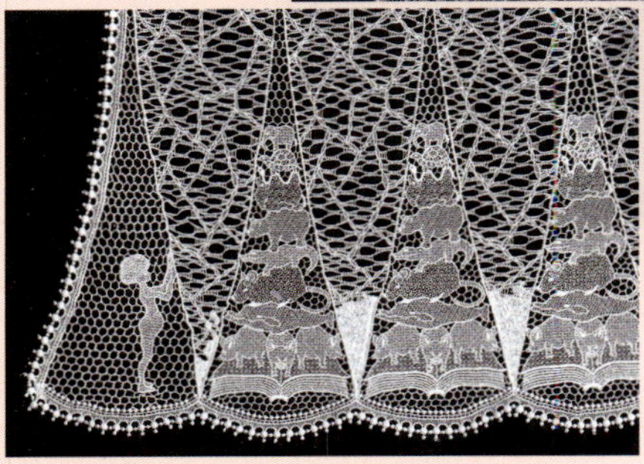

2006, collection #01 ***before run away from home*** (21_21 DESIGN SIGHT). "By imagining a teenage girl running away from home in distress, I made a world map out of lace. I hardened the lace by imagining this distressed girl's room, then made a globe that makes girls want to travel." The globe was praised as an art object and was in fact purchased by a private collector.

2007, collection #02 ***sleeping in the book bed***. "I made a large bed and a special pajama so you can have sweet dreams in a big book." (Yoshikazu Yamagata)

2007, collection #03 ***prince prince prince.*** "I often hear the word 'prince' mentioned around me. So I described my own interpretation of a prince on a white horse as an ideal man imagined by girls. The result was a prince who looks like *Pikachu*; he looks a bit funny but he's charming and he transcends gender in his yellow veil. I took many elements from *Pikachu*, comedies, politics, and other contemporary topics as sources for this collection" (Yoshikazu Yamagata). The show was run as a theatrical play alongside an exhibition at Puk Pupa Teatro in Yoyogi, Tokyo. The collection was also displayed at Arnhem Mode Biennale in The Netherlands in 2007.

photo:Shunichiro Miura

Collection #03

photo:Shunichiro Miura

Collection #02

photo:Shunichiro Miura

Collection #04

2009, collection #04 ***graduate fashion show—0point—*** (Claska). "There are a lot of meanings in the main 'graduate fashion show.' The core concept of it is 'to look at the basic point and have the courage for transition.' I think that the basic point of a fashion designer is his or her graduation work that forms the culmination of their school days, in other words their first collection. You can perceive the creativity as a quality of the designer when you see his or her graduation work. I introduced 20 styles in my collection under the theme of graduation works being the basic point of a designer. I went to various art and fashion schools to obtain waste materials of failed work, discarded things, and scrap paper for use in my collection. A collection made from materials other than fabrics is something you do at fashion school when you start out, which is again the basic point of clothing production" (Yoshikazu Yamagata). In addition, Yamagata set up "0 score in claska," an exhibition of original drawings for his illustrated book "I Scored a Zero," alongside the show. These were later also displayed as "graduate examination 0 exhibition in rocket" at Gallery Rocket in Jingumae, Tokyo.

2009, collection #05 ***the fashion show of the gods*** (Taito Designer's Village). "I tried to look at the 'basic point' of fashion history and that of creativity. I imagined what would happen if the first fashion show was carried out by the gods in front of creatures aeons ago... The gods are encased in the variety of modern fabrics; each of them takes one roll of fabric, wraps himself up and holds a cane that is made of bent cardboard. Then the latest fashion for the gods would be complete" (Yoshikazu Yamagata).

2010, collection #06 ***crime and punishment*** (Tabloid). "This collection describes the sensitive age of youth from childhood to adolescence. This is a time in which everyone experiences something bitter and something sweet. I tried to express

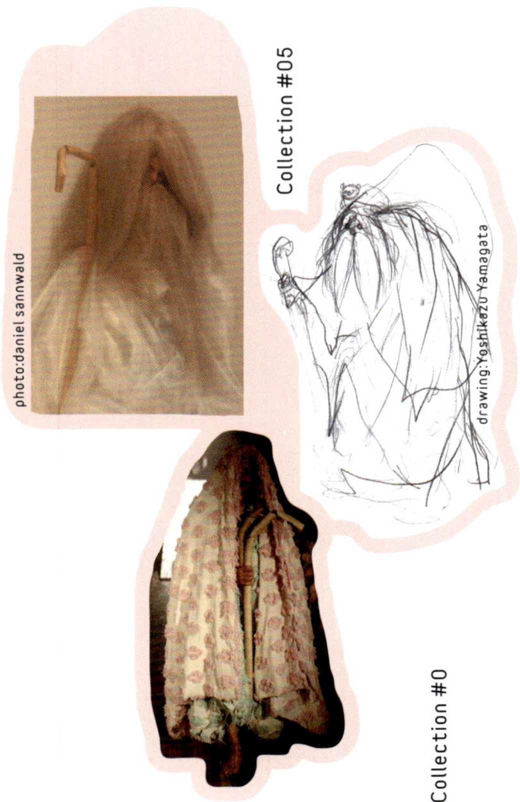

photo:daniel sannwald

drawing:Yoshikazu Yamagata

Collection #06

photo:kanako sasaki

Collection #0

this wavering feeling of youth through the eyes of a boy. Looking at the view of Japanese women, I have no doubt that Lolita culture is deeply rooted in our society. Different from Western culture's focus on maturity, we somehow carry an aesthetic feeling towards the mystique and the perpetuity of immaturity. Fashion blogs by girls are a worldwide phenomenon. So I tried to describe the paradoxical phenomenon of the maturity of fashion possessed by teenagers and youth who age without becoming mature in modern society – an immature girl who looks mature. From the freshest and most stylish girls' fashion to grandmothers' fashion, in other words the most mature girly fashion. Only boys of the same age can invade (or are allowed to invade?) the sacred girlhood with their own impurity and purity. Boys become interested in girls and behave mischievously toward them: they tuck up girls' skirts, peep into the girls' room, steal girls' underwear, and so on. This kind of mischief toward girls is described through the eyes of a boy. You will be punished if you commit sin" (Yoshikazu Yamagata).

2011, collection #0 ***2012 S/S by freemaison*** (VACANT). The show was meant to investigate forms of fashion that stand for more than mere consumption, an idea that came about after the earthquake on March 11th. The audience performed in their own styles in accordance with the dress code "forever fashion," walking on the runway while being protected by "the gods." No new items were presented. The photo above on the right is a 0written bill, a new item by writtenafterwards.

writtenafterwards

Designer's profile:
writtenafterwards / Yoshikazu Yamagata

Yoshikazu Yamagata was born in Tottori in 1980. He worked as an assistant for John Galliano while a student at Central St. Martins College of Art and Design, and won the international competition ITS#THREE, Italy, in three categories. He graduated top of his class from CSM and returned to Japan in 2005. He founded writtenafterwards with Kentaro Tamai (who went independent in 2009) in 2007. Since then, he has proposed the role of fashion as a medium to communicate in terms of culture, society, education and environment, and set up a private school in fashion design "Coconogacco."

Brand history:
writtenafterwards founded with Kentaro Tamai.

2006 Planned and participated in a joint exhibition at 21_21 DESIGN SIGHT.

2008 Tokyo Collection debut in AW08-09.
Designed masks for a Hedi Slimane photoshoot.

2009 Published his illustrated book "I scored a zero" and presented his fourth collection with the fashion show "Graduate fashion show 0point" at Claska Hotel.
Opening show at Arnhem Mode Biennale in The Netherlands.
Fifth collection "The Fashion Show of the Gods."

2010 Sixth collection "Crime and Punishment" presented in Tabloid.
Fifth collection presented as an installation in Sydney and Melbourne, Australia.

2011 Fashion show for the seventh collection "freemaison" held at VACANT.
The sixth fashion show presented in Vienna.

Feel and Think: A New Era of Tokyo Fashion

Texts and curation: Yoko Takagi, Hiroshi Narumi, Mariko Nishitani, Motoaki Hori

Cover design: Tetsuji Ban (BANG! Design, inc)

Book design: Tetsuji Ban+Masaya Hakiri (BANG! Design, inc)

Translation: Yuki Tamura, Maki Tamura, Chihiro Ishida

Proof reading: Anthony C. Erwin, Tom Mes

Publisher: Mitsumasa Katsumata
Ibunsha
Musashiya Bldg, 2-7 Kanda Jimbocho, Chiyoda-ku,
Tokyo 101-0051 Japan
tel: 03-6272-6536, fax:03-6272-6538
www.ibunsha.co.jp/

Picture credits © Ryuji Nakamura pp.25-27, ANREALAGE pp.28-43, h.NAOTO pp.44-59, keisuke kanda pp.60-75, matohu pp.76-91, minä perhonen pp.92-107, mintdesigns pp.108-123, SASQUATCHfabrix. pp.124-139, SOMARTA pp.140-155, THEATRE PRODUCTS pp.156-171, writtenafterwards pp.172-189

Original Japanese edition published in 2011 by Ibunsha Co., Ltd., Tokyo.
English translation rights arranged with Ibunsha Co., Ltd. through Japan UNI Agency, Inc., Tokyo

This book was published in conjunction with the exhibition *Feel and Think: A New Era of Tokyo Fashion*, held at Tokyo Opera City Art Gallery from 18 October to 25 December 2011.

Front cover: (from left to right) h.NAOTO, ANREALAGE, kaisuke kanda, mintdesigns, writtenafterwards, mina perhonen, THEATRE PRODUCTS, SASQUATCHfabrix., matohu, SOMARTA, detail see each page
Back cover: illustration by Tetsuji Ban (BANG! Design inc.)

Prestel Verlag
Neumarkter Strasse 28
81673 Munich
Tel. +49 (0)89 4136-0
Fax +49 (0)89 4136-2335
www.prestel.de

Prestel Publishing Ltd.
4 Bloomsbury Place
London WC1A 2QA
Tel. +44 (0)20 7323-5004
Fax +44 (0)20 7636-8004

Prestel Publishing
900 Broadway, Suite 603
New York, NY 10003
Tel. +1 (212) 995-2720
Fax +1 (212) 995-2733
www.prestel.com

Library of Congress Control Number: 2012934418
British Library Cataloguing-in-Publication Data: a catalogue record for this book is available from the British Library; Deutsche Nationalbibliothek holds a record of this publication in the Deutsche Nationalbibliografie; detailed bibliographical data can be found under: http://dnb.d-nb.de

Prestel books are available worldwide. Please contact your nearest bookseller or one of the above addresses for information concerning your local distributor.

Editorial direction: Martina Zwack
Copyediting by: Jane Michael
Production: Friederike Schirge
Art direction: Cilly Klotz
Printing and binding: APPL aprinta druck GmbH & Co. KG, Wemding
Printed in Germany

ISBN 978-3-7913-5190-2

Verlagsgruppe Random House FSC-DEU-0100
The FSC®-certified paper Profimatt has been supplied by Igepa, Germany